AIC 33 Course Guide

Claim Handling Principles and Practices

1st Edition

American Institute for Chartered Property Casualty Underwriters/Insurance Institute of America

720 Providence Road • Suite 100 • Malvern, PA 19355-3433

Table of Contents

 # Study Materials Available for AIC 33

Donna J. Popow, *Claim Handling Principles and Practices*, 1st ed., 2006, AICPCU/IIA.

AIC 33 *Course Guide*, 1st ed., 2006, AICPCU/IIA.

AIC 33 SMART Study Aids—Review Notes and Flash Cards, 1st ed.

Student Resources

Catalog A complete listing of our offerings can be found in *Succeed*, the Institutes' professional development catalog, including information about:

- Current programs and courses

- Current textbooks, course guides, and SMART Study Aids

- Program completion requirements

- Exam registration

To obtain a copy of the catalog, visit our Web site at www.aicpcu.org or contact Customer Support at (800) 644-2101.

How To Pass Institute Exams! This free handbook, printable from the Student Services Center on the Institutes' Web site at www.aicpcu.org, or available by calling Customer Support at (800) 644-2101, is designed to help you by:

- Giving you ideas on how to use textbooks and course guides as effective learning tools

- Providing steps for answering exam questions effectively

- Recommending exam-day strategies

Institutes Online Forums Do you wish you could talk with people around the country about course questions and share information with others who have similar professional interests? We host forums at our Web site, where you can do just that. To access our forums:

- Go to the Institutes' Web site at www.aicpcu.org

- Click on the "Log on. Learn." link

- Scroll down and click on "Forums"

- Read the instructions, and you're ready to go!

Educational Counseling Services To ensure that you take courses matching both your needs and your skills, you can obtain free counseling from the Institutes by:

- E-mailing your questions to edserv@cpcuiia.org

- Calling an Institutes' counselor directly at (610) 644-2100, ext. 7630 or ext. 7633

- Obtaining and completing a self-inventory form, available on our Web site at www.aicpcu.org or by contacting Customer Support at (800) 644-2101

Exam Registration Information As you proceed with your studies, be sure to arrange for your exam.

- Consult the registration booklet that accompanied this course guide for complete information regarding exam dates and fees worldwide. Plan to register with the Institutes well in advance of your exam.

- If your registration booklet does not include exam dates for the current year, you can obtain up-to-date exam information by visiting the Institutes' Web site at www.aicpcu.org, sending an e-mail to customersupport@cpcuiia.org, or calling the Institutes at (800) 644-2101.

How to Contact the Institutes For more information on any of these publications and services:

- Visit our Web site at www.aicpcu.org

- Telephone us at (800) 644-2101 or (610) 644-2100 outside the U.S.

- E-mail us at customersupport@cpcuiia.org

- Fax us at (610) 640-9576

- Write us at AICPCU/IIA, Customer Support, 720 Providence Road, Suite 100, Malvern, PA 19355-3433

Using This Course Guide

This course guide will help you learn the course content and pass the exam.

Each assignment in this course guide typically includes the following components:

Educational Objectives These are the most important study tools in the course guide. Because all of the questions on the exam are based on the Educational Objectives, the best way to study for the exam is to focus on these objectives.

Each educational objective typically begins with one of the following action words, which indicate the level of understanding required for the exam:

Analyze—Determine the nature and the relationship of the parts.

Apply—Put to use for a practical purpose.

Calculate—Determine numeric values by mathematical process.

Classify—Arrange or organize according to class or category.

Compare—Show similarities and differences.

Contrast—Show only differences.

Define—Give a clear, concise meaning.

Describe—Represent or give an account.

Evaluate—Determine the value or merit.

Explain—Relate the importance or application.

Identify or list—Name or make a list.

Illustrate—Give an example.

Justify—Show to be right or reasonable.

Paraphrase—Restate in your own words.

Summarize—Concisely state the main points.

Required Reading The items listed in this section indicate what portion of the study materials (the textbook chapter(s), course guide readings, or other assigned materials) correspond to the assignment.

Outline The outline lists the topics in the assignment. Read the outline before the required reading to become familiar with the assignment content and the relationships of topics.

Key Words and Phrases These words and phrases are fundamental to understanding the assignment and have a common meaning for those working in insurance. After completing the required reading, test your understanding of the assignment's key words and phrases by writing their definitions. For help, refer to the page numbers that appear in parentheses after each key word and phrase.

Review Questions The review questions test your understanding of what you have read. Review the educational objectives and required reading, then answer the questions to the best of your ability. When you are finished, check the answers at the end of the assignment to evaluate your comprehension.

Application Questions These questions continue to test your knowledge of the required reading by applying what you've studied to real-life situations. Again, check the suggested answers at the end of the assignment to review your progress.

Sample Exam The sample exam helps you test your knowledge of the material. Use the sample exam at the back of the course guide or on the SMART practice exam CD-ROM (if it accompanies this course guide) to become familiar with the test format.

More Study Aids

The Institutes also produce supplemental study tools, called SMART Study Aids, for many of their courses. When SMART Study Aids are available for a course, they are listed on both page iii of this course guide and on the first page of each assignment. SMART Study Aids include review notes and flash cards and are excellent tools to help you learn and retain the information contained in each assignment.

AIC Advisory Committee

The following individuals were instrumental in helping to analyze the audience for the AIC program and to design the revisions and updates of the study materials for AIC 33.

Elise M. Farnham, CPCU, ARM, AIM
Illumine Consulting

James A. Franz, CPCU, AIC, ARM
United Farm Family Mutual Ins. Co.
Farm Bureau Insurance

James Jones, CPCU, AIC, ARM
Katie School of Insurance & Financial Services
Illinois State University

Douglas J. Kent, Esq.
Marshall, Dennehey, Warner, Coleman & Goggin

William McCullough, CPCU, CLU, AIC
State Farm Insurance

Kevin M. Quinley, CPCU, ARM, AIC
Medmarc Insurance Group

James Sherlock, CPCU, CLU, ARM
ACE USA

Robert D. Stevens, Sr., CPCU, CLU, AIC
Crawford & Co.

William C. Stewart, Jr., CPCU, AIC, RPA
Claims Training Services

Christine A. Sullivan, CPCU, AIM
Allstate Insurance Company

Assignments

1. Risk and Insurance
2. Claim Handling Process
3. Investigation of Cause of Loss, Liability, and Damages
4. Insurance Fraud

Segment A is the first of two segments in the AIC 33 course.
These segments are designed to help structure your study.

Risk and Insurance

Direct Direct Your Learning

Assignment
1

Study Materials

Required Reading:

■ Claim Handling Principles and Practices—Chapter 1

Study Aids:

■ SMART Practice Exam CD-ROM
■ SMART Study Aids Review Notes and Flash Cards— Assignment 1

Educational Objectives

After learning the content of this assignment, you should be able to:

1. Explain how hazard risk differs from business risk and what risk management techniques can be used to manage risk.

2. Describe the parties to, benefits of, and costs of insurance.

3. Describe the claim department structure, types and functions of claim personnel, and claim personnel performance measures.

4. Describe each of the different insurance company functions and their purposes.

5. Summarize the following aspects of insurance regulation:

   • The three major federal statutes that regulate insurance and their significance

   • The role of the NAIC in insurance regulation

   • The purposes of insurance regulation

   • The activities of insurance regulators

   • The types of insurance regulation

6. Define or describe each of the Key Words and Phrases for this assignment.

Outline

■ **Risk**

A. Hazard Risk and Business Risk

B. Risk Management Techniques

   1. Risk Control

   2. Risk Financing

■ **Insurance**

A. Parties to the Insurance Contract

B. Benefits of Insurance

C. Costs of Insurance

■ **Claim Function**

A. Claim Department Structure

B. Claim Personnel

   1. Staff Claim Representatives

   2. Independent Adjusters

   3. Third-Party Administrators

   4. Producers

   5. Public Adjusters

C. Performance Measures

   1. Profitability Measures

   2. Quality Measures

■ **Other Insurance Company Functions**

A. Marketing and Sales

B. Underwriting

C. Loss Control

D. Reinsurance

E. Actuarial

F. Finance and Accounting

G. Information Technology (IT)

H. Miscellaneous Functions

■ **Insurance Regulation**

A. Evolution of Insurance Regulation

   1. McCarran-Ferguson Act

   2. Insurance Fraud Protection Act

   3. Gramm-Leach-Bliley Act of 1999

B. Role of National Association of Insurance Commissioners (NAIC)

C. Purposes of Insurance Regulation

   1. Protect Consumers

   2. Maintain Insurer Solvency

   3. Prevent Destructive Competition

D. Activities of Insurance Regulators

E. Types of Insurance Regulation

   1. Rate Regulation

   2. Solvency Regulation

   3. Insurance Policy Regulation

   4. Consumer Protection

■ **Summary**

Key Words and Phrases

Define or describe each of the words and phrases listed below.

Risk (p. 1.3)

Hazard risk (p. 1.5)

Business risk (p. 1.5)

Retention (p. 1.6)

Noninsurance transfer (p. 1.7)

Insurance (p. 1.7)

Insured (p. 1.7)

Law of large numbers (p. 1.7)

Principle of indemnity (p. 1.8)

Insurable interest (p. 1.8)

First-party claim (p. 1.8)

Third-party claim (p. 1.8)

Moral hazard (p. 1.11)

Morale hazard, or attitudinal hazard (p. 1.11)

Third-party administrator (p. 1.12)

Independent adjuster (p. 1.14)

Insurance agent (p. 1.15)

Insurance broker (p. 1.15)

Public adjuster (p. 1.15)

Incurred losses (p. 1.16)

Loss ratio (p. 1.16)

Loss reserves (p. 1.16)

Combined ratio (p. 1.16)

Reinsurer (p. 1.21)

Insurance guaranty funds (p. 1.31)

Unfair trade practices acts (p. 1.33)

Unfair claim practices acts (p. 1.35)

Bad faith (p. 1.35)

Review Questions

1. Explain the distinction between possibility and probability. (p. 1.4)

2. Explain the distinction between hazard risk and business risk, and give an example of each. (p. 1.5)

3. What are the two methods individuals and organizations can use to manage the risk of potential financial loss? (pp. 1.5–1.7)

4. Describe how an individual or organization might use each of the following risk management techniques: (pp. 1.6–1.7)

   a.   Avoidance

   b.   Loss prevention

   c.   Loss reduction

   d.   Separation

   e.   Duplication

f. Diversification

g. Retention

h. Noninsurance transfer

i. Insurance transfer

5. Define each of the following insurance concepts. (pp. 1.7–1.8)

a. Law of large numbers

b. Principle of indemnity

c. Insurable interest

6. Who are the parties to an insurance contract? (p. 1.8)

7. For each of the following items, indicate whether it is B–benefit of insurance, C–cost of insurance, or N–neither. (pp. 1.9–1.12)

    a.   Payment for losses

    b.   Support for credit

    c.   Portion of premium used to pay insurer's expenses

    d.   Peace of mind

    e.   Portion of premium used to pay losses

    f.   Loss control

    g.   Efficient use of resources

    h.   Moral hazards

    i.   Insurance pool of money to pay claims of anyone who suffered injury or property damage

    j.   Source of employment and tax revenue

    k.   Opportunity costs

    l.   Funds for loans and investments

    m.   Reduction of social burdens

    n.   Increased litigation

    o.   Satisfaction of legal and business requirements

8. Diagram the claim department structure you work in or are most familiar with, and explain each job function. (pp. 1.12–1.15)

9. Differentiate among the following claim personnel. (pp. 1.14–1.15)

   a. Staff claim representatives

   b. Independent adjusters

   c. Third-party administrators

   d. Producers

   e. Public adjusters

10. Describe the two types of performance measures used to measure claim personnel performance, and give an example of each. (pp. 1.15–1.19)

11. Describe each of the following functions within an insurance
    company. (pp. 1.19–1.23)

    a. Marketing and sales

    b. Underwriting

    c. Loss control

    d. Reinsurance

    e. Actuarial

    f. Finance and accounting

g.   Information technology

h.   Miscellaneous

12. Explain the significance of each of the following federal statutes
    in relation to insurance. (pp. 1.24–1.25)

    a.   McCarran-Ferguson Act

    b.   Insurance Fraud Protection Act

    c.   Gramm-Leach-Bliley Act of 1999

13. Who are the members of the NAIC, and what is the NAIC's role
    in insurance regulation? (p. 1.25)

14. What are the three purposes of insurance regulation?
    (pp. 1.26–1.27)

15. How does insurance regulation help protect consumers? (p. 1.26)

16. Describe three regulatory activities in which an insurance regulator
    typically is involved. (pp. 1.27–1.28)

17. States use four types of insurance regulation. Briefly describe each
    type. (pp. 1.28–1.35)

    a. Rate regulation

    b. Solvency surveillance

c. Insurance policy regulation

d. Consumer protection

Application Questions

1. Grocery Store is a chain of 200 large grocery stores throughout New England. Annually, Grocery Store receives 750 complaints regarding dents to customers' vehicles from grocery carts. The carts, left in parking lots by other customers, roll into vehicles, causing dents and scratches. The average damage to a vehicle is $250. What risk management techniques might Grocery Store use to control and finance this risk of loss?

2. It has been a tough week for ABC Retail Store. On Tuesday, saleswoman Sharon hurts her back lifting a box in the stockroom. On Thursday, ABC receives notice of a lawsuit filed by a customer who alleges that he slipped and fell because of a puddle of water in an aisle. ABC has insurance to cover these losses. Explain how ABC benefits from this insurance and what costs are associated with these benefits.

3. For each of the following items, indicate which claim personnel are most likely to perform the task.

   a. Handle claims, keep claim records, and perform statistical analyses for businesses that self-insure their risks

   b. Handle claims that involve investigating the loss scene; meeting with insureds, claimants, lawyers, and others; and inspecting damage for their employer, the insurer

   c. Often handle losses requiring an expert in highly specialized fields (such as aircraft accidents)

   d. Often the first party the insured calls when a loss occurs

   e. Handle claims for an insured on a case-by-case basis for a fee

f. Likely to work from the insurer's branch, regional, or home office

g. Often assist insurers in handling large numbers of claims quickly when weather-related disasters occur

h. Often associated with large independent adjusting firms

i. Might have draft authority to settle small claims quickly

j. Might work for a subsidiary company established by an insurer

k. Assist the insurer by reporting the loss and explaining to the insured how the claim will be handled

l. Often handle claims for an insurer in areas where there are few insureds

4. On January 2, 2006, the state of X begins auditing ABC Insurance Company's 2005 financial records and finds the following information for 2005:

- Incurred losses were $65 million.

- Loss adjustment expenses were $20 million.

- Written premium was $80 million.

- Underwriting and other related expenses were $20 million.

Using this information, calculate the following for ABC Insurance Company.

a. Loss ratio

b. Expense ratio

    c.   Combined ratio

5. ABC Insurance Company has had a terrible year. Their loss ratio is 110 percent. The senior vice president of claims has decided to implement an audit program to ensure compliance with best practices and to determine if there are claim handling trends that may be causing the high loss ratio. Pick three quantitative and three qualitative audit factors, and explain how they can help identify trends that require corrective action.

6. After a series of hurricanes hits a southern state, the insurers doing business in that state implement sharp increases in rates and strict underwriting guidelines that result in cancellations of many homeowners' policies. How are the policyholders protected from excessive rates and unreasonable underwriting guidelines?

Answers to Assignment 1 Questions

NOTE: These answers are provided to give students a basic understanding of acceptable types of responses. They often are not the only valid answers and are not intended to provide an exhaustive response to the questions.

Review Questions

1. Possibility means that something could happen. Probability is the mathematical likelihood that an event will occur in the long run. Probability is measurable; possibility is not.

2. Hazard risk is the risk from accidental loss, including the possibility of loss or no loss. The risk of a fire to a home is a hazard risk. Business risk is the risk that is inherent in the operation of a particular organization, including the possibility of loss, no loss, or gain. The introduction of a new product creates a business risk for an organization because the new product may cause the company to lose money, break even, or make a profit.

3. Individuals and organizations can control risk (risk control) by taking steps to avoid loss, prevent loss, or mitigate loss; or they can finance the risk (risk financing) by having funds available to pay for a loss or by transferring the possibility of financial loss to others.

4. There are various answers to this question.
   a. Avoidance—A person might avoid the risk of dying in a plane crash by avoiding airline travel.
   b. Loss prevention—A business can minimize the number of auto accidents it has by having fewer cars on the road, thus reducing the frequency or chance of loss.
   c. Loss reduction—An individual can reduce the severity of an auto accident by wearing a seat-belt.
   d. Separation—A manufacturer may store inventory in several locations rather than in one, so that all inventory would not be subject to a single loss occurrence.
   e. Duplication—An electric generating plant may have several generators working, while maintaining a spare generator off-line that could be used if another generator fails.
   f. Diversification—An organization might diversify its geographic exposure by having business locations throughout the United States rather than in one centralized location.
   g. Retention—A driver can select a large deductible on his auto policy, thereby retaining that portion of a loss.
   h. Noninsurance transfer—The owner of a building can state in the lease agreement that the renter will be responsible for certain types of losses.
   i. Insurance transfer—A business owner can buy insurance to cover risk of loss to the building that houses the business and for the property owned by and used in the business.

5. a. Law of large numbers—a mathematical principle that states that when the number of similar, independent exposure units increases, the relative accuracy of predictions about future outcomes based on those exposure units increases.
   b. Principle of indemnity—states that no insured should profit from an insured loss. An insured should be compensated for the amount of a loss, but not more.
   c. Insurable interest—an exposure to financial loss that a party must have to purchase a legally binding insurance contract.

6. The parties to an insurance contract are the insured (first party) and the insurer (second party).

7. a.–B, b.–B, c.–C, d.–B, e.–N, f.–B, g.–B, h.–C, i.–C or N, j.–B, k.–C, l.–B, m.–B, n.–C, o.–B

8. Answers to this question will vary. However, the diagram should include a senior claim officer and at least one claim office. Within the claim office there would probably be a claim manager, claim supervisors, and claim representatives.

9. a. Staff claim representatives are insurer employees who handle most claims.

    b. Independent adjusters offer their claim handling services to insurers for a fee.

    c. Third-party administrators are organizations that employ their own personnel to handle the claims for other organizations, such as self-insureds.

    d. Producers are those who sell insurance and are often authorized by insurers to handle claims up to a specific dollar threshold.

    e. Public adjusters are adjusters hired by insureds to assist in the presentation of insureds' claims to insurers.

10. The two types of performance measures are profitability measures and quality measures. Loss ratio and combined ratio are examples of profitability measures. Best practices, claim audits, and customer satisfaction are examples of quality measures.

11. The functions within an insurance company are as follows:

    a. Marketing and sales—This function brings the business to the insurer. Marketing is usually the broader function of actually delivering products and services to the customer, whereas the sales function is usually to contact the customer and bring the insurance application to the insurer.

    b. Underwriting—This function receives the application for insurance and determines if the application meets insurer guidelines. Underwriting is involved in risk selection, pricing, and determination of coverage terms and conditions.

    c. Loss control—This function inspects businesses that apply for insurance and suggests ways to prevent losses and reduce the severity of losses that might occur.

    d. Reinsurance—This function establishes reinsurance programs within the insurer and negotiates the terms of those programs with reinsurers. This function also establishes guidelines for reinsurance procedures.

    e. Actuarial—This function performs all the mathematical calculations underlying insurance operations. This function calculates rates, develops rating plans, and estimates loss reserves. This function can also assist in corporate planning.

    f. Finance and accounting—This function invests the premiums received from policyholders until they are needed to pay losses. This function also prepares financial statements for regulators and can also be responsible for the insurer's day-to-day cash operations.

    g. Information technology—This function provides the technological infrastructure that supports all the insurer's internal and external communications. This function collects and stores data for use by the insurer, its customers, and regulators.

    h. Miscellaneous—These functions can include premium audit, human resources, training and development, and legal services.

12. a. The McCarran-Ferguson Act clarifies the federal government's power to assume insurance regulatory functions in the absence of state regulation. It states that insurers are exempt from federal antitrust laws, if the states maintain their own regulatory system.

b.   The Insurance Fraud Protection Act is part of a federal anti-crime bill that protects consumers and insureds against insurer insolvencies resulting from fraud. The act also prohibits insurers, reinsurers, producers, and others from employing anyone who has been convicted of a felony involving breach of trust or dishonesty.

c.   Gramm-Leach-Bliley Act states that each segment of the financial services industry is regulated separately. States continue to have primary regulatory authority for all insurance activities. The act also addresses privacy concerns through a provision requiring banks to disclose to customers their information-sharing policies and practices.

13. The NAIC is made up of regulators from the fifty states and the District of Columbia, Puerto Rico, and Guam. These members meet to discuss insurance industry problems and issues in insurance regulation. While it has no direct regulatory authority, the NAIC drafts model laws and regulations that are consequently adopted by states.

14. The three purposes of insurance regulation are to protect consumers, maintain insurer solvency, and prevent destructive competition.

15. Insurance regulation helps protect consumers by providing a mechanism for review insurance policy forms to determine whether they are fair contracts, for responding to complaints about insurer's behavior, for ensuring that insurance is readily available, and for providing consumer information on insurance matters.

16. An insurance regulator can be involved in any of the following activities:

- Approving policy forms
- Holding rate hearings and reviewing rate filings
- Licensing new insurers
- Licensing producers, adjusters, and claim representatives
- Investigating policyholder complaints
- Rehabilitating or liquidating insolvent insurers
- Issuing cease-and-desist orders
- Conducting periodic audits of insurers
- Evaluating solvency information
- Performing market conduct examinations
- Publishing consumer information

17. Answers may vary.

a.   Rate regulation:

- Ensures that rates are adequate to pay losses but not excessive or unfairly discriminatory
- Ensures that rates charged to individual insureds or groups of insureds reflect the exposure to loss

b.   Solvency surveillance:

- Identifies insurers in financial trouble and places insurers with potential problems on a watch list for closely scrutiny.
- Provides rules governing how funds are to be liquidated and claims are to be paid if an insurer becomes insolvent
- Provides rules for the creation of insurance guaranty funds to help cover the unpaid claims of certain types of insolvent insurers

c.   Insurance policy regulation
  • Ensures that policies are clear, fair, and readable
  • May prescribe specific policy language
  • Implements directives from the legislature relating to insurance policies through formal regulations, informal circulars, and precedents set during the policy application approval process

d.   Consumer protection:
  • Requires licensing for some employees and representatives of insurers who transact business with the public
  • Might require insurers to file policy forms for approval to ensure that the language is fair, clear, and readable
  • Includes complaint bureaus and laws that address unfair trade and claim practices

Application Questions

1.   Grocery Store is probably unable to avoid such losses because customers need carts. Despite its best efforts, Grocery Store will be unable to prevent all such losses. Grocery Store can reduce the frequency and severity of the losses by providing customers with carts that have bumpers on them. It can also provide convenient, safe areas for customers to return their carts. Grocery Store can retain this risk of loss by setting aside funds to pay for these losses. It can also purchase insurance that will pay for all or part of these losses.

2.   ABC benefits by having these losses covered by insurance. ABC's owners and managers have peace of mind from knowing that losses such as these are taken care of. Because ABC does not have to maintain a reserve of money to pay for these losses, its has more money to use to expand its business interests. Additionally, ABC must have the insurance to comply with the legal and business requirements of its state. ABC's cost of insurance includes the premiums paid and any lost opportunities resulting from the use of available funds to pay for insurance rather than to expand the business. ABC may have a morale hazard if store personnel knew about the puddle in the aisle and did not clean it up.

3.   a.   Third-party administrator
     b.   Staff claim representative
     c.   Independent adjuster
     d.   Producer
     e.   Public adjuster
     f.   Staff claim representative
     g.   Independent adjuster
     h.   Independent adjuster or third-party administrator
     i.   Producer
     j.   Third-party administrator
     k.   Producer
     l.   Independent adjuster

4. a. Loss ratio $= \dfrac{\text{Incurred losses} + \text{Loss adjustment expenses}}{\text{Earned premium}} \times 100\%$

$$= \dfrac{65\ \text{million} + 20\ \text{million}}{80\ \text{million}} \times 100$$

$$= 1.0625 \times 100$$

$$= 106.25\%.$$

   b. Expense ratio $= \dfrac{\text{Expenses}}{\text{Written premium}} \times 100\%$

$$= \dfrac{20\ \text{million}}{80\ \text{million}} \times 100$$

$$= 0.25 \times 100$$

$$= 25\%.$$

   c. Combined ratio = Loss ratio + Expense ratio

$$= 106.25\% + 25\%$$

$$= 131.25\%.$$

5. Answers to this question may vary.

   Three quantitative audit factors are (1) number of files reopened each month, (2) percentage of recovery from subrogation, and (3) percentage of claims entering litigation. If the number of files reopened each month is higher than the established best practice, it may be that the claim representatives in this company are closing files prematurely. If the percentage of recovery from subrogation is very low, it may be that the claim representatives are not doing an adequate investigation for potentially responsible third parties or that they are not vigorously pursuing subrogation when opportunities arise. If a high percentage of claims are entering litigation, it may be that the claim representatives are ignoring or mishandling claims.

   Three qualitative audit factors are (1) litigation cost management, (2) correct coverage evaluation, and (3) thorough investigations. If litigation costs are extremely high, it may be that too many claims are going into litigation. It may also be that claim representatives are not adequately monitoring litigation and minimizing expenses. Incorrect coverage evaluations lead to unnecessary or incorrect claim payments. Lack of thorough investigations could lead to incorrect coverage evaluations and missed subrogation opportunities.

6. Each state has an insurance department that ensures that rates are not excessive and that underwriting guidelines are not unfairly discriminatory. The insurance department also has a consumer complaint department to address each policyholder's concerns individually.

study tips

If you are not sure that you have the current edition of the textbook(s), course guide, or registration booklet for the exam you plan to take, please contact the Institutes (see page iv).

Claim Handling Process

Direct Direct Your Learning

Educational Objectives

After learning the content of this assignment, you should be able to:

1. Describe the physical construction of insurance policies and the function of each of the insurance policy components.

2. Describe the framework for coverage analysis and the information obtained by following it.

3. Describe the activities in the claim handling process, including the following:

    • Acknowledging and assigning the claim

    • Identifying the policy

    • Contacting the insured or the insured's representative

    • Investigating and documenting the claim

    • Concluding the claim

4. Given a claim, determine coverage for a loss using the framework for coverage analysis and the activities in the claim handling process.

5. Define or describe each of the Key Words and Phrases for this assignment.

Study Materials

Required Reading:

■ Claim Handling Principles and Practices—Chapter 2

■ "Homeowners 3—Special Form," Course Guide Reading 2-1

■ "Personal Auto Policy," Course Guide Reading 2-2

Study Aids:

■ SMART Practice Exam CD-ROM

■ SMART Study Aids Review Notes and Flash Cards—Assignment 2

Outline

- **Insurance Policy Structure**
  - A. Physical Construction
  - B. Policy Components and Their Functions
    1. Declarations
    2. Definitions
    3. Insuring Agreements
    4. Exclusions
    5. Conditions
    6. Miscellaneous Provisions
    7. Endorsements

- **Framework for Coverage Analysis**
  - A. Is the Person Involved Covered?
  - B. Did the Loss Occur During the Policy Period?
  - C. Is the Cause of Loss Covered?
  - D. Is the Damaged Property Covered?
  - E. Is the Type of Loss Covered?
  - F. Are the Amounts of Loss or Damages Covered?
  - G. Is the Location of the Loss Covered?
  - H. Do Any Exclusions Apply?
  - I. Does Other Insurance Apply?

- **Claim Handling Process**
  - A. Acknowledging and Assigning the Claim
  - B. Identifying the Policy
    1. Reserves
    2. Causes of Reserve Errors
  - C. Contacting the Insured or the Insured's Representative
    1. Good Faith
    2. Waiver and Estoppel
  - D. Investigating and Documenting the Claim
    1. Claimant Investigation
    2. Insured/Witness Investigation
    3. Accident Scene Investigation
    4. Property Damage Investigation
    5. Medical Investigation
    6. Prior Claim Investigation
    7. Subrogation Investigation and Recovery
    8. File Review
    9. File Documentation
    10. File Reports
  - E. Determining the Cause of Loss and the Loss Amount
  - F. Concluding the Claim
    1. Payments
    2. Claim Denial
    3. Alternative Dispute Resolution
    4. Litigation
    5. Closing Reports

- **Applying the Framework for Coverage Analysis and the Claim Handling Process**

- **Summary**

- **Homeowners 3—Special Form (Course Guide Reading 2-1)**

- **Personal Auto Policy (Course Guide Reading 2-2)**

Reading 2-1

HOMEOWNERS 3 – SPECIAL FORM

AGREEMENT

We will provide the insurance described in this policy in return for the premium and compliance with all applicable provisions of this policy.

DEFINITIONS

A. In this policy, "you" and "your" refer to the "named insured" shown in the Declarations and the spouse if a resident of the same household. "We", "us" and "our" refer to the Company providing this insurance.

B. In addition, certain words and phrases are defined as follows:

1. "Aircraft Liability", "Hovercraft Liability", "Motor Vehicle Liability" and "Watercraft Liability", subject to the provisions in **b.** below, mean the following:

a. Liability for "bodily injury" or "property damage" arising out of the:

(1) Ownership of such vehicle or craft by an "insured";

(2) Maintenance, occupancy, operation, use, loading or unloading of such vehicle or craft by any person;

(3) Entrustment of such vehicle or craft by an "insured" to any person;

(4) Failure to supervise or negligent supervision of any person involving such vehicle or craft by an "insured"; or

(5) Vicarious liability, whether or not imposed by law, for the actions of a child or minor involving such vehicle or craft.

b. For the purpose of this definition:

(1) Aircraft means any contrivance used or designed for flight except model or hobby aircraft not used or designed to carry people or cargo;

(2) Hovercraft means a self-propelled motorized ground effect vehicle and includes, but is not limited to, flarecraft and air cushion vehicles;

(3) Watercraft means a craft principally designed to be propelled on or in water by wind, engine power or electric motor; and

(4) Motor vehicle means a "motor vehicle" as defined in **7.** below.

2. "Bodily injury" means bodily harm, sickness or disease, including required care, loss of services and death that results.

3. "Business" means:

a. A trade, profession or occupation engaged in on a full-time, part-time or occasional basis; or

b. Any other activity engaged in for money or other compensation, except the following:

(1) One or more activities, not described in **(2)** through **(4)** below, for which no "insured" receives more than $2,000 in total compensation for the 12 months before the beginning of the policy period;

(2) Volunteer activities for which no money is received other than payment for expenses incurred to perform the activity;

(3) Providing home day care services for which no compensation is received, other than the mutual exchange of such services; or

(4) The rendering of home day care services to a relative of an "insured".

4. "Employee" means an employee of an "insured", or an employee leased to an "insured" by a labor leasing firm under an agreement between an "insured" and the labor leasing firm, whose duties are other than those performed by a "residence employee".

5. "Insured" means:

a. You and residents of your household who are:

(1) Your relatives; or

(2) Other persons under the age of 21 and in the care of any person named above;

b. A student enrolled in school full time, as defined by the school, who was a resident of your household before moving out to attend school, provided the student is under the age of:

(1) 24 and your relative; or

(2) 21 and in your care or the care of a person described in **a.(1)** above; or

© ISO Properties, Inc., 2000

c. Under Section **II**:

(1) With respect to animals or watercraft to which this policy applies, any person or organization legally responsible for these animals or watercraft which are owned by you or any person included in **a.** or **b.** above. "Insured" does not mean a person or organization using or having custody of these animals or watercraft in the course of any "business" or without consent of the owner; or

(2) With respect to a "motor vehicle" to which this policy applies:

(a) Persons while engaged in your employ or that of any person included in **a.** or **b.** above; or

(b) Other persons using the vehicle on an "insured location" with your consent.

Under both Sections **I** and **II**, when the word an immediately precedes the word "insured", the words an "insured" together mean one or more "insureds".

6. "Insured location" means:

a. The "residence premises";

b. The part of other premises, other structures and grounds used by you as a residence; and

(1) Which is shown in the Declarations; or

(2) Which is acquired by you during the policy period for your use as a residence;

c. Any premises used by you in connection with a premises described in **a.** and **b.** above;

d. Any part of a premises:

(1) Not owned by an "insured"; and

(2) Where an "insured" is temporarily residing;

e. Vacant land, other than farm land, owned by or rented to an "insured";

f. Land owned by or rented to an "insured" on which a one, two, three or four family dwelling is being built as a residence for an "insured";

g. Individual or family cemetery plots or burial vaults of an "insured"; or

h. Any part of a premises occasionally rented to an "insured" for other than "business" use.

7. "Motor vehicle" means:

a. A self-propelled land or amphibious vehicle; or

b. Any trailer or semitrailer which is being carried on, towed by or hitched for towing by a vehicle described in **a.** above.

8. "Occurrence" means an accident, including continuous or repeated exposure to substantially the same general harmful conditions, which results, during the policy period, in:

a. "Bodily injury"; or

b. "Property damage".

9. "Property damage" means physical injury to, destruction of, or loss of use of tangible property.

10. "Residence employee" means:

a. An employee of an "insured", or an employee leased to an "insured" by a labor leasing firm, under an agreement between an "insured" and the labor leasing firm, whose duties are related to the maintenance or use of the "residence premises", including household or domestic services; or

b. One who performs similar duties elsewhere not related to the "business" of an "insured".

A "residence employee" does not include a temporary employee who is furnished to an "insured" to substitute for a permanent "residence employee" on leave or to meet seasonal or short-term workload conditions.

11. "Residence premises" means:

a. The one family dwelling where you reside;

b. The two, three or four family dwelling where you reside in at least one of the family units; or

c. That part of any other building where you reside;

and which is shown as the "residence premises" in the Declarations.

"Residence premises" also includes other structures and grounds at that location.

                   HO 00 03 05 01

DEDUCTIBLE

Unless otherwise noted in this policy, the following deductible provision applies:

Subject to the policy limits that apply, we will pay only that part of the total of all loss payable under Section I that exceeds the deductible amount shown in the Declarations.

SECTION I – PROPERTY COVERAGES

A. Coverage A – Dwelling

1. We cover:

   a. The dwelling on the "residence premises" shown in the Declarations, including structures attached to the dwelling; and

   b. Materials and supplies located on or next to the "residence premises" used to construct, alter or repair the dwelling or other structures on the "residence premises".

2. We do not cover land, including land on which the dwelling is located.

B. Coverage B – Other Structures

1. We cover other structures on the "residence premises" set apart from the dwelling by clear space. This includes structures connected to the dwelling by only a fence, utility line, or similar connection.

2. We do not cover:

   a. Land, including land on which the other structures are located;

   b. Other structures rented or held for rental to any person not a tenant of the dwelling, unless used solely as a private garage;

   c. Other structures from which any "business" is conducted; or

   d. Other structures used to store "business" property. However, we do cover a structure that contains "business" property solely owned by an "insured" or a tenant of the dwelling provided that "business" property does not include gaseous or liquid fuel, other than fuel in a permanently installed fuel tank of a vehicle or craft parked or stored in the structure.

3. The limit of liability for this coverage will not be more than 10% of the limit of liability that applies to Coverage A. Use of this coverage does not reduce the Coverage A limit of liability.

C. Coverage C – Personal Property

1. **Covered Property**

   We cover personal property owned or used by an "insured" while it is anywhere in the world. After a loss and at your request, we will cover personal property owned by:

   a. Others while the property is on the part of the "residence premises" occupied by an "insured"; or

   b. A guest or a "residence employee", while the property is in any residence occupied by an "insured".

2. **Limit For Property At Other Residences**

   Our limit of liability for personal property usually located at an "insured's" residence, other than the "residence premises", is 10% of the limit of liability for Coverage C, or $1,000, whichever is greater. However, this limitation does not apply to personal property:

   a. Moved from the "residence premises" because it is being repaired, renovated or rebuilt and is not fit to live in or store property in; or

   b. In a newly acquired principal residence for 30 days from the time you begin to move the property there.

3. **Special Limits Of Liability**

   The special limit for each category shown below is the total limit for each loss for all property in that category. These special limits do not increase the Coverage C limit of liability.

   a. $200 on money, bank notes, bullion, gold other than goldware, silver other than silverware, platinum other than platinumware, coins, medals, scrip, stored value cards and smart cards.

   b. $1,500 on securities, accounts, deeds, evidences of debt, letters of credit, notes other than bank notes, manuscripts, personal records, passports, tickets and stamps. This dollar limit applies to these categories regardless of the medium (such as paper or computer software) on which the material exists.

   This limit includes the cost to research, replace or restore the information from the lost or damaged material.

c. $1,500 on watercraft of all types, including their trailers, furnishings, equipment and outboard engines or motors.

d. $1,500 on trailers or semitrailers not used with watercraft of all types.

e. $1,500 for loss by theft of jewelry, watches, furs, precious and semiprecious stones.

f. $2,500 for loss by theft of firearms and related equipment.

g. $2,500 for loss by theft of silverware, silver-plated ware, goldware, gold-plated ware, platinumware, platinum-plated ware and pewterware. This includes flatware, hollow-ware, tea sets, trays and trophies made of or including silver, gold or pewter.

h. $2,500 on property, on the "residence premises", used primarily for "business" purposes.

i. $500 on property, away from the "residence premises", used primarily for "business" purposes. However, this limit does not apply to loss to electronic apparatus and other property described in Categories **j.** and **k.** below.

j. $1,500 on electronic apparatus and accessories, while in or upon a "motor vehicle", but only if the apparatus is equipped to be operated by power from the "motor vehicle's" electrical system while still capable of being operated by other power sources.

Accessories include antennas, tapes, wires, records, discs or other media that can be used with any apparatus described in this Category **j.**

k. $1,500 on electronic apparatus and accessories used primarily for "business" while away from the "residence premises" and not in or upon a "motor vehicle". The apparatus must be equipped to be operated by power from the "motor vehicle's" electrical system while still capable of being operated by other power sources.

Accessories include antennas, tapes, wires, records, discs or other media that can be used with any apparatus described in this Category **k.**

4. **Property Not Covered**

We do not cover:

a. Articles separately described and specifically insured, regardless of the limit for which they are insured, in this or other insurance;

b. Animals, birds or fish;

c. "Motor vehicles".

(1) This includes:

(a) Their accessories, equipment and parts; or

(b) Electronic apparatus and accessories designed to be operated solely by power from the electrical system of the "motor vehicle". Accessories include antennas, tapes, wires, records, discs or other media that can be used with any apparatus described above.

The exclusion of property described in **(a)** and **(b)** above applies only while such property is in or upon the "motor vehicle".

(2) We do cover "motor vehicles" not required to be registered for use on public roads or property which are:

(a) Used solely to service an "insured's" residence; or

(b) Designed to assist the handicapped;

d. Aircraft meaning any contrivance used or designed for flight including any parts whether or not attached to the aircraft.

We do cover model or hobby aircraft not used or designed to carry people or cargo;

e. Hovercraft and parts. Hovercraft means a self-propelled motorized ground effect vehicle and includes, but is not limited to, flarecraft and air cushion vehicles;

f. Property of roomers, boarders and other tenants, except property of roomers and boarders related to an "insured";

g. Property in an apartment regularly rented or held for rental to others by an "insured", except as provided in **E.10.** Landlord's Furnishings under Section **I** – Property Coverages;

h. Property rented or held for rental to others off the "residence premises";

i. "Business" data, including such data stored in:

(1) Books of account, drawings or other paper records; or

(2) Computers and related equipment.

We do cover the cost of blank recording or storage media, and of prerecorded computer programs available on the retail market;

© ISO Properties, Inc., 2000 **HO 00 03 05 01**

j. Credit cards, electronic fund transfer cards or access devices used solely for deposit, withdrawal or transfer of funds except as provided in **E.6.** Credit Card, Electronic Fund Transfer Card Or Access Device, Forgery And Counterfeit Money under Section **I** – Property Coverages; or

k. Water or steam.

D. Coverage D – Loss Of Use

The limit of liability for Coverage **D** is the total limit for the coverages in **1.** Additional Living Expense, **2.** Fair Rental Value and **3.** Civil Authority Prohibits Use below.

1. Additional Living Expense

If a loss covered under Section **I** makes that part of the "residence premises" where you reside not fit to live in, we cover any necessary increase in living expenses incurred by you so that your household can maintain its normal standard of living.

Payment will be for the shortest time required to repair or replace the damage or, if you permanently relocate, the shortest time required for your household to settle elsewhere.

2. Fair Rental Value

If a loss covered under Section **I** makes that part of the "residence premises" rented to others or held for rental by you not fit to live in, we cover the fair rental value of such premises less any expenses that do not continue while it is not fit to live in.

Payment will be for the shortest time required to repair or replace such premises.

3. Civil Authority Prohibits Use

If a civil authority prohibits you from use of the "residence premises" as a result of direct damage to neighboring premises by a Peril Insured Against, we cover the loss as provided in **1.** Additional Living Expense and **2.** Fair Rental Value above for no more than two weeks.

4. Loss Or Expense Not Covered

We do not cover loss or expense due to cancellation of a lease or agreement.

The periods of time under **1.** Additional Living Expense, **2.** Fair Rental Value and **3.** Civil Authority Prohibits Use above are not limited by expiration of this policy.

E. Additional Coverages

1. Debris Removal

a. We will pay your reasonable expense for the removal of:

(1) Debris of covered property if a Peril Insured Against that applies to the damaged property causes the loss; or

(2) Ash, dust or particles from a volcanic eruption that has caused direct loss to a building or property contained in a building.

This expense is included in the limit of liability that applies to the damaged property. If the amount to be paid for the actual damage to the property plus the debris removal expense is more than the limit of liability for the damaged property, an additional 5% of that limit of liability is available for debris removal expense.

b. Fallen Trees

(1) If circumstances of a loss meet those specified in (2) below, we will pay your reasonable expense, up to $1000, for the removal from the "residence premises" of:

(a) Your tree(s) felled by the peril of Windstorm Or Hail or Weight Of Ice, Snow Or Sleet; or

(b) A neighbor's tree(s) felled by a Peril Insured Against under Coverage **C.**

The $1000 limit is the most we will pay in any one loss regardless of the number of fallen trees. No more than $500 of this limit will be paid for the removal of any one tree.

This coverage is additional insurance.

(2) Tree removal coverage as described in b.(1) above applies only if:

(a) The tree damages a structure covered under this policy;

(b) Windstorm or Hail or Weight of Ice, Snow or Sleet causes damage to a structure covered under this policy and the Pennsylvania Governor declares the area in which the "residence premises" is located to be a disaster area as a result of such weather conditions; or

© ISO Properties, Inc., 2000

(c) The tree does not damage a structure covered under the policy, but:

(i) Blocks a driveway on the "residence premises" which prevents a "motor vehicle", that is registered for use on public roads or property, from entering or leaving the "residence premises"; or

(ii) Blocks a ramp or other fixture designed to assist a handicapped person to enter or leave the dwelling building

2. Reasonable Repairs

a. We will pay the reasonable cost incurred by you for the necessary measures taken solely to protect covered property that is damaged by a Peril Insured Against from further damage.

b. If the measures taken involve repair to other damaged property, we will only pay if that property is covered under this policy and the damage is caused by a Peril Insured Against. This coverage does not:

(1) Increase the limit of liability that applies to the covered property; or

(2) Relieve you of your duties, in case of a loss to covered property, described in **B.4.** under Section **I** – Conditions.

3. Trees, Shrubs And Other Plants

We cover trees, shrubs, plants or lawns, on the "residence premises", for loss caused by the following Perils Insured Against:

a. Fire or Lightning;

b. Explosion;

c. Riot or Civil Commotion;

d. Aircraft;

e. Vehicles not owned or operated by a resident of the "residence premises";

f. Vandalism or Malicious Mischief; or

g. Theft.

We will pay up to 5% of the limit of liability that applies to the dwelling for all trees, shrubs, plants or lawns. No more than $500 of this limit will be paid for any one tree, shrub or plant. We do not cover property grown for "business" purposes.

This coverage is additional insurance.

4. Fire Department Service Charge

We will pay up to $500 for your liability assumed by contract or agreement for fire department charges incurred when the fire department is called to save or protect covered property from a Peril Insured Against. We do not cover fire department service charges if the property is located within the limits of the city, municipality or protection district furnishing the fire department response.

This coverage is additional insurance. No deductible applies to this coverage.

5. Property Removed

We insure covered property against direct loss from any cause while being removed from a premises endangered by a Peril Insured Against and for no more than 30 days while removed.

This coverage does not change the limit of liability that applies to the property being removed.

6. Credit Card, Electronic Fund Transfer Card Or Access Device, Forgery And Counterfeit Money

a. We will pay up to $500 for:

(1) The legal obligation of an "insured" to pay because of the theft or unauthorized use of credit cards issued to or registered in an "insured's" name;

(2) Loss resulting from theft or unauthorized use of an electronic fund transfer card or access device used for deposit, withdrawal or transfer of funds, issued to or registered in an "insured's" name;

(3) Loss to an "insured" caused by forgery or alteration of any check or negotiable instrument; and

(4) Loss to an "insured" through acceptance in good faith of counterfeit United States or Canadian paper currency.

All loss resulting from a series of acts committed by any one person or in which any one person is concerned or implicated is considered to be one loss.

This coverage is additional insurance. No deductible applies to this coverage.

b. We do not cover:

(1) Use of a credit card, electronic fund transfer card or access device:

(a) By a resident of your household;

(b) By a person who has been entrusted with either type of card or access device; or

(c) If an "insured" has not complied with all terms and conditions under which the cards are issued or the devices accessed; or

(2) Loss arising out of "business" use or dishonesty of an "insured".

c. If the coverage in **a.** above applies, the following defense provisions also apply:

(1) We may investigate and settle any claim or suit that we decide is appropriate. Our duty to defend a claim or suit ends when the amount we pay for the loss equals our limit of liability.

(2) If a suit is brought against an "insured" for liability under **a.(1)** or **(2)** above, we will provide a defense at our expense by counsel of our choice.

(3) We have the option to defend at our expense an "insured" or an "insured's" bank against any suit for the enforcement of payment under **a.(3)** above.

7. Loss Assessment

a. We will pay up to $1,000 for your share of loss assessment charged during the policy period against you, as owner or tenant of the "residence premises", by a corporation or association of property owners. The assessment must be made as a result of direct loss to property, owned by all members collectively, of the type that would be covered by this policy if owned by you, caused by a Peril Insured Against under Coverage **A,** other than:

(1) Earthquake; or

(2) Land shock waves or tremors before, during or after a volcanic eruption.

The limit of $1,000 is the most we will pay with respect to any one loss, regardless of the number of assessments. We will only apply one deductible, per unit, to the total amount of any one loss to the property described above, regardless of the number of assessments.

b. We do not cover assessments charged against you or a corporation or association of property owners by any governmental body.

c. Paragraph **P.** Policy Period under Section **I** – Conditions does not apply to this coverage.

This coverage is additional insurance.

8. Collapse

a. With respect to this Additional Coverage:

(1) Collapse means an abrupt falling down or caving in of a building or any part of a building with the result that the building or part of the building cannot be occupied for its current intended purpose.

(2) A building or any part of a building that is in danger of falling down or caving in is not considered to be in a state of collapse.

(3) A part of a building that is standing is not considered to be in a state of collapse even if it has separated from another part of the building.

(4) A building or any part of a building that is standing is not considered to be in a state of collapse even if it shows evidence of cracking, bulging, sagging, bending, leaning, settling, shrinkage or expansion.

b. We insure for direct physical loss to covered property involving collapse of a building or any part of a building if the collapse was caused by one or more of the following:

(1) The Perils Insured Against named under Coverage **C**;

(2) Decay that is hidden from view, unless the presence of such decay is known to an "insured" prior to collapse;

(3) Insect or vermin damage that is hidden from view, unless the presence of such damage is known to an "insured" prior to collapse;

(4) Weight of contents, equipment, animals or people;

(5) Weight of rain which collects on a roof; or

(6) Use of defective material or methods in construction, remodeling or renovation if the collapse occurs during the course of the construction, remodeling or renovation.

c. Loss to an awning, fence, patio, deck, pavement, swimming pool, underground pipe, flue, drain, cesspool, septic tank, foundation, retaining wall, bulkhead, pier, wharf or dock is not included under **b.(2)** through **(6)** above, unless the loss is a direct result of the collapse of a building or any part of a building.

d. This coverage does not increase the limit of liability that applies to the damaged covered property.

9. Glass Or Safety Glazing Material

a. We cover:

(1) The breakage of glass or safety glazing material which is part of a covered building, storm door or storm window;

(2) The breakage of glass or safety glazing material which is part of a covered building, storm door or storm window when caused directly by earth movement; and

(3) The direct physical loss to covered property caused solely by the pieces, fragments or splinters of broken glass or safety glazing material which is part of a building, storm door or storm window.

b. This coverage does not include loss:

(1) To covered property which results because the glass or safety glazing material has been broken, except as provided in **a.(3)** above; or

(2) On the "residence premises" if the dwelling has been vacant for more than 60 consecutive days immediately before the loss, except when the breakage results directly from earth movement as provided in **a.(2)** above. A dwelling being constructed is not considered vacant.

c. This coverage does not increase the limit of liability that applies to the damaged property.

10. Landlord's Furnishings

We will pay up to $2,500 for your appliances, carpeting and other household furnishings, in each apartment on the "residence premises" regularly rented or held for rental to others by an "insured", for loss caused by a Peril Insured Against in Coverage **C,** other than Theft.

This limit is the most we will pay in any one loss regardless of the number of appliances, carpeting or other household furnishings involved in the loss.

This coverage does not increase the limit of liability applying to the damaged property.

11. Ordinance Or Law

a. You may use up to 10% of the limit of liability that applies to Coverage **A** for the increased costs you incur due to the enforcement of any ordinance or law which requires or regulates:

(1) The construction, demolition, remodeling, renovation or repair of that part of a covered building or other structure damaged by a Peril Insured Against;

(2) The demolition and reconstruction of the undamaged part of a covered building or other structure, when that building or other structure must be totally demolished because of damage by a Peril Insured Against to another part of that covered building or other structure; or

(3) The remodeling, removal or replacement of the portion of the undamaged part of a covered building or other structure necessary to complete the remodeling, repair or replacement of that part of the covered building or other structure damaged by a Peril Insured Against.

b. You may use all or part of this ordinance or law coverage to pay for the increased costs you incur to remove debris resulting from the construction, demolition, remodeling, renovation, repair or replacement of property as stated in **a.** above.

c. We do not cover:

(1) The loss in value to any covered building or other structure due to the requirements of any ordinance or law; or

(2) The costs to comply with any ordinance or law which requires any "insured" or others to test for, monitor, clean up, remove, contain, treat, detoxify or neutralize, or in any way respond to, or assess the effects of, pollutants in or on any covered building or other structure.

Pollutants means any solid, liquid, gaseous or thermal irritant or contaminant, including smoke, vapor, soot, fumes, acids, alkalis, chemicals and waste. Waste includes materials to be recycled, reconditioned or reclaimed.

This coverage is additional insurance.

12. Grave Markers

We will pay up to $5,000 for grave markers, including mausoleums, on or away from the "residence premises" for loss caused by a Peril Insured Against under Coverage **C**.

This coverage does not increase the limits of liability that apply to the damaged covered property.

SECTION I – PERILS INSURED AGAINST

A. Coverage A – Dwelling And Coverage B – Other Structures

1. We insure against risk of direct physical loss to property described in Coverages **A** and **B**.

2. We do not insure, however, for loss:

   a. Excluded under Section **I** – Exclusions;

   b. Involving collapse, except as provided in **E.8.** Collapse under Section **I** – Property Coverages; or

   c. Caused by:

      (1) Freezing of a plumbing, heating, air conditioning or automatic fire protective sprinkler system or of a household appliance, or by discharge, leakage or overflow from within the system or appliance caused by freezing. This provision does not apply if you have used reasonable care to:

         (a) Maintain heat in the building; or

         (b) Shut off the water supply and drain all systems and appliances of water.

      However, if the building is protected by an automatic fire protective sprinkler system, you must use reasonable care to continue the water supply and maintain heat in the building for coverage to apply.

      For purposes of this provision a plumbing system or household appliance does not include a sump, sump pump or related equipment or a roof drain, gutter, downspout or similar fixtures or equipment;

      (2) Freezing, thawing, pressure or weight of water or ice, whether driven by wind or not, to a:

         (a) Fence, pavement, patio or swimming pool;

         (b) Footing, foundation, bulkhead, wall, or any other structure or device that supports all or part of a building, or other structure;

         (c) Retaining wall or bulkhead that does not support all or part of a building or other structure; or

         (d) Pier, wharf or dock;

      (3) Theft in or to a dwelling under construction, or of materials and supplies for use in the construction until the dwelling is finished and occupied;

      (4) Vandalism and malicious mischief, and any ensuing loss caused by any intentional and wrongful act committed in the course of the vandalism or malicious mischief, if the dwelling has been vacant for more than 60 consecutive days immediately before the loss. A dwelling being constructed is not considered vacant;

      (5) Mold, fungus or wet rot. However, we do insure for loss caused by mold, fungus or wet rot that is hidden within the walls or ceilings or beneath the floors or above the ceilings of a structure if such loss results from the accidental discharge or overflow of water or steam from within:

         (a) A plumbing, heating, air conditioning or automatic fire protective sprinkler system, or a household appliance, on the "residence premises"; or

         (b) A storm drain, or water, steam or sewer pipes, off the "residence premises".

      For purposes of this provision, a plumbing system or household appliance does not include a sump, sump pump or related equipment or a roof drain, gutter, downspout or similar fixtures or equipment; or

      (6) Any of the following:

         (a) Wear and tear, marring, deterioration;

(b) Mechanical breakdown, latent defect, inherent vice, or any quality in property that causes it to damage or destroy itself;

(c) Smog, rust or other corrosion, or dry rot;

(d) Smoke from agricultural smudging or industrial operations;

(e) Discharge, dispersal, seepage, migration, release or escape of pollutants unless the discharge, dispersal, seepage, migration, release or escape is itself caused by a Peril Insured Against named under Coverage **C**.

Pollutants means any solid, liquid, gaseous or thermal irritant or contaminant, including smoke, vapor, soot, fumes, acids, alkalis, chemicals and waste. Waste includes materials to be recycled, reconditioned or reclaimed;

(f) Settling, shrinking, bulging or expansion, including resultant cracking, of bulkheads, pavements, patios, footings, foundations, walls, floors, roofs or ceilings;

(g) Birds, vermin, rodents, or insects; or

(h) Animals owned or kept by an "insured".

Exception To c.(6)

Unless the loss is otherwise excluded, we cover loss to property covered under Coverage **A** or **B** resulting from an accidental discharge or overflow of water or steam from within a:

(i) Storm drain, or water, steam or sewer pipe, off the "residence premises"; or

(ii) Plumbing, heating, air conditioning or automatic fire protective sprinkler system or household appliance on the "residence premises". This includes the cost to tear out and replace any part of a building, or other structure, on the "residence premises", but only when necessary to repair the system or appliance. However, such tear out and replacement coverage only applies to other structures if the water or steam causes actual damage to a building on the "residence premises".

We do not cover loss to the system or appliance from which this water or steam escaped.

For purposes of this provision, a plumbing system or household appliance does not include a sump, sump pump or related equipment or a roof drain, gutter, down spout or similar fixtures or equipment.

Section **I** – Exclusion **A.3.** Water Damage, Paragraphs **a.** and **c.** that apply to surface water and water below the surface of the ground do not apply to loss by water covered under **c.(5)** and **(6)** above.

Under **2.b.** and **c.** above, any ensuing loss to property described in Coverages **A** and **B** not precluded by any other provision in this policy is covered.

B. Coverage C – Personal Property

We insure for direct physical loss to the property described in Coverage **C** caused by any of the following perils unless the loss is excluded in Section **I** – Exclusions.

1. Fire Or Lightning

2. Windstorm Or Hail

This peril includes loss to watercraft of all types and their trailers, furnishings, equipment, and outboard engines or motors, only while inside a fully enclosed building.

This peril does not include loss to the property contained in a building caused by rain, snow, sleet, sand or dust unless the direct force of wind or hail damages the building causing an opening in a roof or wall and the rain, snow, sleet, sand or dust enters through this opening.

3. Explosion

4. Riot Or Civil Commotion

5. Aircraft

This peril includes self-propelled missiles and spacecraft.

6. Vehicles

7. Smoke

This peril means sudden and accidental damage from smoke, including the emission or puffback of smoke, soot, fumes or vapors from a boiler, furnace or related equipment.

This peril does not include loss caused by smoke from agricultural smudging or industrial operations.

 HO 00 03 05 01

8. **Vandalism Or Malicious Mischief**

9. **Theft**

   a. This peril includes attempted theft and loss of property from a known place when it is likely that the property has been stolen.

   b. This peril does not include loss caused by theft:

      (1) Committed by an "insured";

      (2) In or to a dwelling under construction, or of materials and supplies for use in the construction until the dwelling is finished and occupied;

      (3) From that part of a "residence premises" rented by an "insured" to someone other than another "insured"; or

      (4) That occurs off the "residence premises" of:

         (a) Trailers, semitrailers and campers;

         (b) Watercraft of all types, and their furnishings, equipment and outboard engines or motors; or

         (c) Property while at any other residence owned by, rented to, or occupied by an "insured", except while an "insured" is temporarily living there. Property of an "insured" who is a student is covered while at the residence the student occupies to attend school as long as the student has been there at any time during the 60 days immediately before the loss.

10. **Falling Objects**

   This peril does not include loss to property contained in a building unless the roof or an outside wall of the building is first damaged by a falling object. Damage to the falling object itself is not included.

11. **Weight Of Ice, Snow Or Sleet**

   This peril means weight of ice, snow or sleet which causes damage to property contained in a building.

12. **Accidental Discharge Or Overflow Of Water Or Steam**

   a. This peril means accidental discharge or overflow of water or steam from within a plumbing, heating, air conditioning or automatic fire protective sprinkler system or from within a household appliance.

   b. This peril does not include loss:

      (1) To the system or appliance from which the water or steam escaped;

      (2) Caused by or resulting from freezing except as provided in Peril Insured Against **14.** Freezing;

      (3) On the "residence premises" caused by accidental discharge or overflow which occurs off the "residence premises"; or

      (4) Caused by mold, fungus or wet rot unless hidden within the walls or ceilings or beneath the floors or above the ceilings of a structure.

   c. In this peril, a plumbing system or household appliance does not include a sump, sump pump or related equipment or a roof drain, gutter, downspout or similar fixtures or equipment.

   d. Section I – Exclusion **A.3.** Water Damage, Paragraphs **a.** and **c.** that apply to surface water and water below the surface of the ground do not apply to loss by water covered under this peril.

13. **Sudden And Accidental Tearing Apart, Cracking, Burning Or Bulging**

   This peril means sudden and accidental tearing apart, cracking, burning or bulging of a steam or hot water heating system, an air conditioning or automatic fire protective sprinkler system, or an appliance for heating water.

   We do not cover loss caused by or resulting from freezing under this peril.

14. **Freezing**

   a. This peril means freezing of a plumbing, heating, air conditioning or automatic fire protective sprinkler system or of a household appliance but only if you have used reasonable care to:

      (1) Maintain heat in the building; or

      (2) Shut off the water supply and drain all systems and appliances of water.

      However, if the building is protected by an automatic fire protective sprinkler system, you must use reasonable care to continue the water supply and maintain heat in the building for coverage to apply.

   b. In this peril, a plumbing system or household appliance does not include a sump, sump pump or related equipment or a roof drain, gutter, downspout or similar fixtures or equipment.

15. Sudden And Accidental Damage From Artificially Generated Electrical Current

This peril does not include loss to tubes, transistors, electronic components or circuitry that are a part of appliances, fixtures, computers, home entertainment units or other types of electronic apparatus.

16. Volcanic Eruption

This peril does not include loss caused by earthquake, land shock waves or tremors.

SECTION I – EXCLUSIONS

A. We do not insure for loss caused directly or indirectly by any of the following. Such loss is excluded regardless of any other cause or event contributing concurrently or in any sequence to the loss. These exclusions apply whether or not the loss event results in widespread damage or affects a substantial area.

1. Ordinance Or Law

Ordinance Or Law means any ordinance or law:

a. Requiring or regulating the construction, demolition, remodeling, renovation or repair of property, including removal of any resulting debris. This Exclusion **A.1.a.** does not apply to the amount of coverage that may be provided for in **E.11.** Ordinance Or Law under Section **I** – Property Coverages;

b. The requirements of which result in a loss in value to property; or

c. Requiring any "insured" or others to test for, monitor, clean up, remove, contain, treat, detoxify or neutralize, or in any way respond to, or assess the effects of, pollutants.

Pollutants means any solid, liquid, gaseous or thermal irritant or contaminant, including smoke, vapor, soot, fumes, acids, alkalis, chemicals and waste. Waste includes materials to be recycled, reconditioned or reclaimed.

This Exclusion **A.1.** applies whether or not the property has been physically damaged.

2. Earth Movement

Earth Movement means:

a. Earthquake, including land shock waves or tremors before, during or after a volcanic eruption;

b. Landslide, mudslide or mudflow;

c. Subsidence or sinkhole; or

d. Any other earth movement including earth sinking, rising or shifting;

caused by or resulting from human or animal forces or any act of nature unless direct loss by fire or explosion ensues and then we will pay only for the ensuing loss.

This Exclusion **A.2.** does not apply to loss by theft.

3. Water Damage

Water Damage means:

a. Flood, surface water, waves, tidal water, overflow of a body of water, or spray from any of these, whether or not driven by wind;

b. Water or water-borne material which backs up through sewers or drains or which overflows or is discharged from a sump, sump pump or related equipment; or

c. Water or water-borne material below the surface of the ground, including water which exerts pressure on or seeps or leaks through a building, sidewalk, driveway, foundation, swimming pool or other structure;

caused by or resulting from human or animal forces or any act of nature.

Direct loss by fire, explosion or theft resulting from water damage is covered.

4. Power Failure

Power Failure means the failure of power or other utility service if the failure takes place off the "residence premises". But if the failure results in a loss, from a Peril Insured Against on the "residence premises", we will pay for the loss caused by that peril.

5. Neglect

Neglect means neglect of an "insured" to use all reasonable means to save and preserve property at and after the time of a loss.

6. War

War includes the following and any consequence of any of the following:

a. Undeclared war, civil war, insurrection, rebellion or revolution;

b. Warlike act by a military force or military personnel; or

c. Destruction, seizure or use for a military purpose.

Discharge of a nuclear weapon will be deemed a warlike act even if accidental.

7. Nuclear Hazard

This Exclusion **A.7.** pertains to Nuclear Hazard to the extent set forth in **M.** Nuclear Hazard Clause under Section **I** – Conditions.

8. Intentional Loss

Intentional Loss means any loss arising out of any act an "insured" commits or conspires to commit with the intent to cause a loss.

In the event of such loss, no "insured" is entitled to coverage, even "insureds" who did not commit or conspire to commit the act causing the loss.

9. Governmental Action

Governmental Action means the destruction, confiscation or seizure of property described in Coverage **A, B** or **C** by order of any governmental or public authority.

This exclusion does not apply to such acts ordered by any governmental or public authority that are taken at the time of a fire to prevent its spread, if the loss caused by fire would be covered under this policy.

B. We do not insure for loss to property described in Coverages **A** and **B** caused by any of the following. However, any ensuing loss to property described in Coverages **A** and **B** not precluded by any other provision in this policy is covered.

1. Weather conditions. However, this exclusion only applies if weather conditions contribute in any way with a cause or event excluded in **A.** above to produce the loss.

2. Acts or decisions, including the failure to act or decide, of any person, group, organization or governmental body.

3. Faulty, inadequate or defective:

a. Planning, zoning, development, surveying, siting;

b. Design, specifications, workmanship, repair, construction, renovation, remodeling, grading, compaction;

c. Materials used in repair, construction, renovation or remodeling; or

d. Maintenance;

of part or all of any property whether on or off the "residence premises".

SECTION I – CONDITIONS

A. Insurable Interest And Limit Of Liability

Even if more than one person has an insurable interest in the property covered, we will not be liable in any one loss:

1. To an "insured" for more than the amount of such "insured's" interest at the time of loss; or

2. For more than the applicable limit of liability.

B. Duties After Loss

In case of a loss to covered property, we have no duty to provide coverage under this policy if the failure to comply with the following duties is prejudicial to us. These duties must be performed either by you, an "insured" seeking coverage, or a representative of either:

1. Give prompt notice to us or our agent;

2. Notify the police in case of loss by theft;

3. Notify the credit card or electronic fund transfer card or access device company in case of loss as provided for in **E.6.** Credit Card, Electronic Fund Transfer Card Or Access Device, Forgery And Counterfeit Money under Section **I** – Property Coverages;

4. Protect the property from further damage. If repairs to the property are required, you must:

a. Make reasonable and necessary repairs to protect the property; and

b. Keep an accurate record of repair expenses;

5. Cooperate with us in the investigation of a claim;

6. Prepare an inventory of damaged personal property showing the quantity, description, actual cash value and amount of loss. Attach all bills, receipts and related documents that justify the figures in the inventory;

7. As often as we reasonably require:

a. Show the damaged property;

b. Provide us with records and documents we request and permit us to make copies; and

c. Submit to examination under oath, while not in the presence of another "insured", and sign the same;

8. Send to us, within 60 days after our request, your signed, sworn proof of loss which sets forth, to the best of your knowledge and belief:

   a. The time and cause of loss;

   b. The interests of all "insureds" and all others in the property involved and all liens on the property;

   c. Other insurance which may cover the loss;

   d. Changes in title or occupancy of the property during the term of the policy;

   e. Specifications of damaged buildings and detailed repair estimates;

   f. The inventory of damaged personal property described in **6.** above;

   g. Receipts for additional living expenses incurred and records that support the fair rental value loss; and

   h. Evidence or affidavit that supports a claim under **E.6.** Credit Card, Electronic Fund Transfer Card Or Access Device, Forgery And Counterfeit Money under Section **I** – Property Coverages, stating the amount and cause of loss.

C. Loss Settlement

In this Condition **C.**, the terms "cost to repair or replace" and "replacement cost" do not include the increased costs incurred to comply with the enforcement of any ordinance or law, except to the extent that coverage for these increased costs is provided in **E.11.** Ordinance Or Law under Section **I** – Property Coverages. Covered property losses are settled as follows:

1. Property of the following types:

   a. Personal property;

   b. Awnings, carpeting, household appliances, outdoor antennas and outdoor equipment, whether or not attached to buildings;

   c. Structures that are not buildings; and

   d. Grave markers, including mausoleums;

   at actual cash value at the time of loss but not more than the amount required to repair or replace.

2. Buildings covered under Coverage **A** or **B** at replacement cost without deduction for depreciation, subject to the following:

   a. If, at the time of loss, the amount of insurance in this policy on the damaged building is 80% or more of the full replacement cost of the building immediately before the loss, we will pay the cost to repair or replace, after application of any deductible and without deduction for depreciation, but not more than the least of the following amounts:

      (1) The limit of liability under this policy that applies to the building;

      (2) The replacement cost of that part of the building damaged with material of like kind and quality and for like use; or

      (3) The necessary amount actually spent to repair or replace the damaged building.

      If the building is rebuilt at a new premises, the cost described in **(2)** above is limited to the cost which would have been incurred if the building had been built at the original premises.

   b. If, at the time of loss, the amount of insurance in this policy on the damaged building is less than 80% of the full replacement cost of the building immediately before the loss, we will pay the greater of the following amounts, but not more than the limit of liability under this policy that applies to the building:

      (1) The actual cash value of that part of the building damaged; or

      (2) That proportion of the cost to repair or replace, after application of any deductible and without deduction for depreciation, that part of the building damaged, which the total amount of insurance in this policy on the damaged building bears to 80% of the replacement cost of the building.

   c. To determine the amount of insurance required to equal 80% of the full replacement cost of the building immediately before the loss, do not include the value of:

      (1) Excavations, footings, foundations, piers, or any other structures or devices that support all or part of the building, which are below the undersurface of the lowest basement floor;

(2) Those supports described in **(1)** above which are below the surface of the ground inside the foundation walls, if there is no basement; and

(3) Underground flues, pipes, wiring and drains.

d. We will pay no more than the actual cash value of the damage until actual repair or replacement is complete. Once actual repair or replacement is complete, we will settle the loss as noted in **2.a.** and **b.** above.

However, if the cost to repair or replace the damage is both:

(1) Less than 5% of the amount of insurance in this policy on the building; and

(2) Less than $2,500;

we will settle the loss as noted in **2.a.** and **b.** above whether or not actual repair or replacement is complete.

e. You may disregard the replacement cost loss settlement provisions and make claim under this policy for loss to buildings on an actual cash value basis. You may then make claim for any additional liability according to the provisions of this Condition **C.** Loss Settlement, provided you notify us of your intent to do so within 180 days after the date of loss.

D. Loss To A Pair Or Set

In case of loss to a pair or set we may elect to:

1. Repair or replace any part to restore the pair or set to its value before the loss; or

2. Pay the difference between actual cash value of the property before and after the loss.

E. Appraisal

If you and we fail to agree on the amount of loss, either may demand an appraisal of the loss. In this event, each party will choose a competent and impartial appraiser within 20 days after receiving a written request from the other. The two appraisers will choose an umpire. If they cannot agree upon an umpire within 15 days, you or we may request that the choice be made by a judge of a court of record in the state where the "residence premises" is located. The appraisers will separately set the amount of loss. If the appraisers submit a written report of an agreement to us, the amount agreed upon will be the amount of loss. If they fail to agree, they will submit their differences to the umpire. A decision agreed to by any two will set the amount of loss.

Each party will:

1. Pay its own appraiser; and

2. Bear the other expenses of the appraisal and umpire equally.

F. Other Insurance And Service Agreement

If a loss covered by this policy is also covered by:

1. Other insurance, we will pay only the proportion of the loss that the limit of liability that applies under this policy bears to the total amount of insurance covering the loss; or

2. A service agreement, this insurance is excess over any amounts payable under any such agreement. Service agreement means a service plan, property restoration plan, home warranty or other similar service warranty agreement, even if it is characterized as insurance.

G. Suit Against Us

No action can be brought against us unless there has been full compliance with all of the terms under Section I of this policy and the action is started within two years after the date of loss.

H. Our Option

We may repair or replace any part of the damaged property with material or property of like kind and quality if we give you written notice of our intention to do so within 15 working days after we receive your signed, sworn proof of loss.

I. Loss Payment

We will adjust all losses with you. We will pay you unless some other person is named in the policy or is legally entitled to receive payment. Loss will be payable 60 days after we receive your proof of loss and:

1. Reach an agreement with you;

2. There is an entry of a final judgment; or

3. There is a filing of an appraisal award with us.

J. Abandonment Of Property

We need not accept any property abandoned by an "insured".

K. Mortgage Clause

1. If a mortgagee is named in this policy, any loss payable under Coverage **A** or **B** will be paid to the mortgagee and you, as interests appear. If more than one mortgagee is named, the order of payment will be the same as the order of precedence of the mortgages.

2. If we deny your claim, that denial will not apply to a valid claim of the mortgagee, if the mortgagee:

a. Notifies us of any change in ownership, occupancy or substantial change in risk of which the mortgagee is aware;

b. Pays any premium due under this policy on demand if you have neglected to pay the premium; and

c. Submits a signed, sworn statement of loss within 60 days after receiving notice from us of your failure to do so. Paragraphs **E.** Appraisal, **G.** Suit Against Us and **I.** Loss Payment under Section **I** – Conditions also apply to the mortgagee.

3. If we decide to cancel or not to renew this policy, the mortgagee will be notified at least 10 days before the date cancellation or nonrenewal takes effect.

4. If we pay the mortgagee for any loss and deny payment to you:

a. We are subrogated to all the rights of the mortgagee granted under the mortgage on the property; or

b. At our option, we may pay to the mortgagee the whole principal on the mortgage plus any accrued interest. In this event, we will receive a full assignment and transfer of the mortgage and all securities held as collateral to the mortgage debt.

5. Subrogation will not impair the right of the mortgagee to recover the full amount of the mortgagee's claim.

L. No Benefit To Bailee

We will not recognize any assignment or grant any coverage that benefits a person or organization holding, storing or moving property for a fee regardless of any other provision of this policy.

M. Nuclear Hazard Clause

1. "Nuclear Hazard" means any nuclear reaction, radiation, or radioactive contamination, all whether controlled or uncontrolled or however caused, or any consequence of any of these.

2. Loss caused by the nuclear hazard will not be considered loss caused by fire, explosion, or smoke, whether these perils are specifically named in or otherwise included within the Perils Insured Against.

3. This policy does not apply under Section **I** to loss caused directly or indirectly by nuclear hazard, except that direct loss by fire resulting from the nuclear hazard is covered.

N. Recovered Property

If you or we recover any property for which we have made payment under this policy, you or we will notify the other of the recovery. At your option, the property will be returned to or retained by you or it will become our property. If the recovered property is returned to or retained by you, the loss payment will be adjusted based on the amount you received for the recovered property.

O. Volcanic Eruption Period

One or more volcanic eruptions that occur within a 72 hour period will be considered as one volcanic eruption.

P. Policy Period

This policy applies only to loss which occurs during the policy period.

Q. Concealment Or Fraud

We provide coverage to no "insureds" under this policy if, whether before or after a loss, an "insured" has:

1. Intentionally concealed or misrepresented any material fact or circumstance;

2. Engaged in fraudulent conduct; or

3. Made false statements;

relating to this insurance.

R. Loss Payable Clause

If the Declarations show a loss payee for certain listed insured personal property, the definition of "insured" is changed to include that loss payee with respect to that property.

If we decide to cancel or not renew this policy, that loss payee will be notified in writing.

SECTION II – LIABILITY COVERAGES

A. Coverage E – Personal Liability

If a claim is made or a suit is brought against an "insured" for damages because of "bodily injury" or "property damage" caused by an "occurrence" to which this coverage applies, we will:

1. Pay up to our limit of liability for the damages for which an "insured" is legally liable; and

2. Provide a defense at our expense by counsel of our choice, even if the suit is groundless, false or fraudulent. We may investigate and settle any claim or suit that we decide is appropriate. Our duty to settle or defend ends when our limit of liability for the "occurrence" has been exhausted by payment of a judgment or settlement.

B. Coverage F – Medical Payments To Others

We will pay the necessary medical expenses that are incurred or medically ascertained within three years from the date of an accident causing "bodily injury". Medical expenses means reasonable charges for medical, surgical, x-ray, dental, ambulance, hospital, professional nursing and prosthetic devices. Medical expenses do not include expenses for funeral services. This coverage does not apply to you or regular residents of your household except "residence employees". As to others, this coverage applies only:

1. To a person on the "insured location" with the permission of an "insured"; or

2. To a person off the "insured location", if the "bodily injury":

   a. Arises out of a condition on the "insured location" or the ways immediately adjoining;

   b. Is caused by the activities of an "insured";

   c. Is caused by a "residence employee" in the course of the "residence employee's" employment by an "insured"; or

   d. Is caused by an animal owned by or in the care of an "insured".

SECTION II – EXCLUSIONS

A. "Motor Vehicle Liability"

1. Coverages **E** and **F** do not apply to any "motor vehicle liability" if, at the time and place of an "occurrence", the involved "motor vehicle":

   a. Is registered for use on public roads or property;

   b. Is not registered for use on public roads or property, but such registration is required by a law, or regulation issued by a government agency, for it to be used at the place of the "occurrence"; or

   c. Is being:

      (1) Operated in, or practicing for, any prearranged or organized race, speed contest or other competition;

      (2) Rented to others;

      (3) Used to carry persons or cargo for a charge; or

      (4) Used for any "business" purpose except for a motorized golf cart while on a golfing facility.

2. If Exclusion **A.1.** does not apply, there is still no coverage for "motor vehicle liability" unless the "motor vehicle" is:

   a. In dead storage on an "insured location";

   b. Used solely to service an "insured's" residence;

   c. Designed to assist the handicapped and, at the time of an "occurrence", it is:

      (1) Being used to assist a handicapped person; or

      (2) Parked on an "insured location";

   d. Designed for recreational use off public roads and:

      (1) Not owned by an "insured"; or

      (2) Owned by an "insured" provided the "occurrence" takes place on an "insured location" as defined in Definitions **B.6.a., b., d., e.** or **h.**; or

   e. A motorized golf cart that is owned by an "insured", designed to carry up to 4 persons, not built or modified after manufacture to exceed a speed of 25 miles per hour on level ground and, at the time of an "occurrence", is within the legal boundaries of:

      (1) A golfing facility and is parked or stored there, or being used by an "insured" to:

         (a) Play the game of golf or for other recreational or leisure activity allowed by the facility;

         (b) Travel to or from an area where "motor vehicles" or golf carts are parked or stored; or

         (c) Cross public roads at designated points to access other parts of the golfing facility; or

      (2) A private residential community, including its public roads upon which a motorized golf cart can legally travel, which is subject to the authority of a property owners association and contains an "insured's" residence.

B. "Watercraft Liability"

1. Coverages **E** and **F** do not apply to any "watercraft liability" if, at the time of an "occurrence", the involved watercraft is being:

   a. Operated in, or practicing for, any prearranged or organized race, speed contest or other competition. This exclusion does not apply to a sailing vessel or a predicted log cruise;

b. Rented to others;

c. Used to carry persons or cargo for a charge; or

d. Used for any "business" purpose.

2. If Exclusion **B.1.** does not apply, there is still no coverage for "watercraft liability" unless, at the time of the "occurrence", the watercraft:

a. Is stored;

b. Is a sailing vessel, with or without auxiliary power, that is:

(1) Less than 26 feet in overall length; or

(2) 26 feet or more in overall length and not owned by or rented to an "insured"; or

c. Is not a sailing vessel and is powered by:

(1) An inboard or inboard-outdrive engine or motor, including those that power a water jet pump, of:

(a) 50 horsepower or less and not owned by an "insured"; or

(b) More than 50 horsepower and not owned by or rented to an "insured"; or

(2) One or more outboard engines or motors with:

(a) 25 total horsepower or less;

(b) More than 25 horsepower if the outboard engine or motor is not owned by an "insured";

(c) More than 25 horsepower if the outboard engine or motor is owned by an "insured" who acquired it during the policy period; or

(d) More than 25 horsepower if the outboard engine or motor is owned by an "insured" who acquired it before the policy period, but only if:

(i) You declare them at policy inception; or

(ii) Your intent to insure them is reported to us in writing within 45 days after you acquire them.

The coverages in **(c)** and **(d)** above apply for the policy period.

Horsepower means the maximum power rating assigned to the engine or motor by the manufacturer.

C. "Aircraft Liability"

This policy does not cover "aircraft liability".

D. "Hovercraft Liability"

This policy does not cover "hovercraft liability".

E. Coverage E – Personal Liability And Coverage F – Medical Payments To Others

Coverages **E** and **F** do not apply to the following:

1. Expected Or Intended Injury

"Bodily injury" or "property damage" which is expected or intended by an "insured" even if the resulting "bodily injury" or "property damage":

a. Is of a different kind, quality or degree than initially expected or intended; or

b. Is sustained by a different person, entity, real or personal property, than initially expected or intended.

However, this Exclusion **E.1.** does not apply to "bodily injury" resulting from the use of reasonable force by an "insured" to protect persons or property;

2. "Business"

a. "Bodily injury" or "property damage" arising out of or in connection with a "business" conducted from an "insured location" or engaged in by an "insured", whether or not the "business" is owned or operated by an "insured" or employs an "insured".

This Exclusion **E.2.** applies but is not limited to an act or omission, regardless of its nature or circumstance, involving a service or duty rendered, promised, owed, or implied to be provided because of the nature of the "business".

b. This Exclusion **E.2.** does not apply to:

(1) The rental or holding for rental of an "insured location";

(a) On an occasional basis if used only as a residence;

(b) In part for use only as a residence, unless a single family unit is intended for use by the occupying family to lodge more than two roomers or boarders; or

(c) In part, as an office, school, studio or private garage; and

(2) An "insured" under the age of 21 years involved in a part-time or occasional, self-employed "business" with no employees;

3. **Professional Services**

"Bodily injury" or "property damage" arising out of the rendering of or failure to render professional services;

4. **"Insured's" Premises Not An "Insured Location"**

"Bodily injury" or "property damage" arising out of a premises:

a. Owned by an "insured";

b. Rented to an "insured"; or

c. Rented to others by an "insured";

that is not an "insured location";

5. **War**

"Bodily injury" or "property damage" caused directly or indirectly by war, including the following and any consequence of any of the following:

a. Undeclared war, civil war, insurrection, rebellion or revolution;

b. Warlike act by a military force or military personnel; or

c. Destruction, seizure or use for a military purpose.

Discharge of a nuclear weapon will be deemed a warlike act even if accidental;

6. **Communicable Disease**

"Bodily injury" or "property damage" which arises out of the transmission of a communicable disease by an "insured";

7. **Sexual Molestation, Corporal Punishment Or Physical Or Mental Abuse**

"Bodily injury" or "property damage" arising out of sexual molestation, corporal punishment or physical or mental abuse; or

8. **Controlled Substance**

"Bodily injury" or "property damage" arising out of the use, sale, manufacture, delivery, transfer or possession by any person of a Controlled Substance as defined by the Federal Food and Drug Law at 21 U.S.C.A. Sections 811 and 812. Controlled Substances include but are not limited to cocaine, LSD, marijuana and all narcotic drugs. However, this exclusion does not apply to the legitimate use of prescription drugs by a person following the orders of a licensed physician.

Exclusions **A.** "Motor Vehicle Liability", **B.** "Watercraft Liability", **C.** "Aircraft Liability", **D.** "Hovercraft Liability" and **E.4.** "Insured's" Premises Not An "Insured Location" do not apply to "bodily injury" to a "residence employee" arising out of and in the course of the "residence employee's" employment by an "insured".

F. **Coverage E – Personal Liability**

Coverage **E** does not apply to:

1. Liability:

a. For any loss assessment charged against you as a member of an association, corporation or community of property owners, except as provided in **D.** Loss Assessment under Section **II** – Additional Coverages;

b. Under any contract or agreement entered into by an "insured". However, this exclusion does not apply to written contracts:

(1) That directly relate to the ownership, maintenance or use of an "insured location"; or

(2) Where the liability of others is assumed by you prior to an "occurrence";

unless excluded in **a.** above or elsewhere in this policy;

2. "Property damage" to property owned by an "insured". This includes costs or expenses incurred by an "insured" or others to repair, replace, enhance, restore or maintain such property to prevent injury to a person or damage to property of others, whether on or away from an "insured location";

3. "Property damage" to property rented to, occupied or used by or in the care of an "insured". This exclusion does not apply to "property damage" caused by fire, smoke or explosion;

4. "Bodily injury" to any person eligible to receive any benefits voluntarily provided or required to be provided by an "insured" under any:

a. Workers' compensation law;

b. Non-occupational disability law; or

c. Occupational disease law;

5. "Bodily injury" or "property damage" for which an "insured" under this policy:

a. Is also an insured under a nuclear energy liability policy issued by the:

(1) Nuclear Energy Liability Insurance Association;

(2) Mutual Atomic Energy Liability Underwriters;

(3) Nuclear Insurance Association of Canada;

or any of their successors; or

b. Would be an insured under such a policy but for the exhaustion of its limit of liability; or

6. "Bodily injury" to you or an "insured" as defined under Definitions **5.a.** or **b.**

This exclusion also applies to any claim made or suit brought against you or an "insured":

a. To repay; or

b. Share damages with;

another person who may be obligated to pay damages because of "bodily injury" to an "insured".

G. Coverage F – Medical Payments To Others

Coverage **F** does not apply to "bodily injury":

1. To a "residence employee" if the "bodily injury":

a. Occurs off the "insured location"; and

b. Does not arise out of or in the course of the "residence employee's" employment by an "insured";

2. To any person eligible to receive benefits voluntarily provided or required to be provided under any:

a. Workers' compensation law;

b. Non-occupational disability law; or

c. Occupational disease law;

3. From any:

a. Nuclear reaction;

b. Nuclear radiation; or

c. Radioactive contamination;

all whether controlled or uncontrolled or however caused; or

d. Any consequence of any of these; or

4. To any person, other than a "residence employee" of an "insured", regularly residing on any part of the "insured location".

SECTION II – ADDITIONAL COVERAGES

We cover the following in addition to the limits of liability:

A. Claim Expenses

We pay:

1. Expenses we incur and costs taxed against an "insured" in any suit we defend;

2. Premiums on bonds required in a suit we defend, but not for bond amounts more than the Coverage **E** limit of liability. We need not apply for or furnish any bond;

3. Reasonable expenses incurred by an "insured" at our request, including actual loss of earnings (but not loss of other income) up to $250 per day, for assisting us in the investigation or defense of a claim or suit; and

4. Interest on the entire judgment which accrues after entry of the judgment and before we pay or tender, or deposit in court that part of the judgment which does not exceed the limit of liability that applies.

5. Prejudgment interest awarded against an "insured" on that part of the judgment we pay. Any prejudgment interest awarded against an "insured" is subject to the applicable Pennsylvania Rules of Civil Procedure.

B. First Aid Expenses

We will pay expenses for first aid to others incurred by an "insured" for "bodily injury" covered under this policy. We will not pay for first aid to an "insured".

C. Damage To Property Of Others

1. We will pay, at replacement cost, up to $1,000 per "occurrence" for "property damage" to property of others caused by an "insured".

2. We will not pay for "property damage":

a. To the extent of any amount recoverable under Section **I**;

b. Caused intentionally by an "insured" who is 13 years of age or older;

c. To property owned by an "insured";

d. To property owned by or rented to a tenant of an "insured" or a resident in your household; or

e. Arising out of:

(1) A "business" engaged in by an "insured";

(2) Any act or omission in connection with a premises owned, rented or controlled by an "insured", other than the "insured location"; or

(3) The ownership, maintenance, occupancy, operation, use, loading or unloading of aircraft, hovercraft, watercraft or "motor vehicles".

This exclusion **e.(3)** does not apply to a "motor vehicle" that:

(a) Is designed for recreational use off public roads;

(b) Is not owned by an "insured"; and

(c) At the time of the "occurrence", is not required by law, or regulation issued by a government agency, to have been registered for it to be used on public roads or property.

D. Loss Assessment

1. We will pay up to $1,000 for your share of loss assessment charged against you, as owner or tenant of the "residence premises", during the policy period by a corporation or association of property owners, when the assessment is made as a result of:

   a. "Bodily injury" or "property damage" not excluded from coverage under Section II – Exclusions; or

   b. Liability for an act of a director, officer or trustee in the capacity as a director, officer or trustee, provided such person:

      (1) Is elected by the members of a corporation or association of property owners; and

      (2) Serves without deriving any income from the exercise of duties which are solely on behalf of a corporation or association of property owners.

2. Paragraph I. Policy Period under Section II – Conditions does not apply to this Loss Assessment Coverage.

3. Regardless of the number of assessments, the limit of $1,000 is the most we will pay for loss arising out of:

   a. One accident, including continuous or repeated exposure to substantially the same general harmful condition; or

   b. A covered act of a director, officer or trustee. An act involving more than one director, officer or trustee is considered to be a single act.

4. We do not cover assessments charged against you or a corporation or association of property owners by any governmental body.

SECTION II – CONDITIONS

A. Limit Of Liability

Our total liability under Coverage **E** for all damages resulting from any one "occurrence" will not be more than the Coverage **E** limit of liability shown in the Declarations. This limit is the same regardless of the number of "insureds", claims made or persons injured. All "bodily injury" and "property damage" resulting from any one accident or from continuous or repeated exposure to substantially the same general harmful conditions shall be considered to be the result of one "occurrence".

Our total liability under Coverage **F** for all medical expense payable for "bodily injury" to one person as the result of one accident will not be more than the Coverage **F** limit of liability shown in the Declarations.

B. Severability Of Insurance

This insurance applies separately to each "insured". This condition will not increase our limit of liability for any one "occurrence".

C. Duties After "Occurrence"

In case of an "occurrence", you or another "insured" will perform the following duties that apply. We have no duty to provide coverage under this policy if your failure to comply with the following duties is prejudicial to us. You will help us by seeing that these duties are performed:

1. Give written notice to us or our agent as soon as is practical, which sets forth:

   a. The identity of the policy and the "named insured" shown in the Declarations;

   b. Reasonably available information on the time, place and circumstances of the "occurrence"; and

   c. Names and addresses of any claimants and witnesses;

2. Cooperate with us in the investigation, settlement or defense of any claim or suit;

3. Promptly forward to us every notice, demand, summons or other process relating to the "occurrence";

4. At our request, help us:

   a. To make settlement;

   b. To enforce any right of contribution or indemnity against any person or organization who may be liable to an "insured";

   c. With the conduct of suits and attend hearings and trials; and

   d. To secure and give evidence and obtain the attendance of witnesses;

5. With respect to **C.** Damage To Property Of Others under Section **II** – Additional Coverages, submit to us within 60 days after the loss, a sworn statement of loss and show the damaged property, if in an "insured's" control;

6. No "insured" shall, except at such "insured's" own cost, voluntarily make payment, assume obligation or incur expense other than for first aid to others at the time of the "bodily injury".

D. Duties Of An Injured Person – Coverage F – Medical Payments To Others

1. The injured person or someone acting for the injured person will:

   a. Give us written proof of claim, under oath if required, as soon as is practical; and

   b. Authorize us to obtain copies of medical reports and records.

2. The injured person will submit to a physical exam by a doctor of our choice when and as often as we reasonably require.

E. Payment Of Claim – Coverage F – Medical Payments To Others

Payment under this coverage is not an admission of liability by an "insured" or us.

F. Suit Against Us

1. No action can be brought against us unless there has been full compliance with all of the terms under this Section **II.**

2. No one will have the right to join us as a party to any action against an "insured".

3. Also, no action with respect to Coverage **E** can be brought against us until the obligation of such "insured" has been determined by final judgment or agreement signed by us.

G. Bankruptcy Of An "Insured"

Bankruptcy or insolvency of an "insured" will not relieve us of our obligations under this policy.

H. Other Insurance

This insurance is excess over other valid and collectible insurance except insurance written specifically to cover as excess over the limits of liability that apply in this policy.

I. Policy Period

This policy applies only to "bodily injury" or "property damage" which occurs during the policy period.

J. Concealment Or Fraud

We do not provide coverage to an "insured" who, whether before or after a loss, has:

1. Intentionally concealed or misrepresented any material fact or circumstance;

2. Engaged in fraudulent conduct; or

3. Made false statements;

relating to this insurance.

SECTIONS I AND II – CONDITIONS

A. Liberalization Clause

If we make a change which broadens coverage under this edition of our policy without additional premium charge, that change will automatically apply to your insurance as of the date we implement the change in your state, provided that this implementation date falls within 60 days prior to or during the policy period stated in the Declarations.

This Liberalization Clause does not apply to changes implemented with a general program revision that includes both broadenings and restrictions in coverage, whether that general program revision is implemented through introduction of:

1. A subsequent edition of this policy; or

2. An amendatory endorsement.

B. Waiver Or Change Of Policy Provisions

A waiver or change of a provision of this policy must be in writing by us to be valid. Our request for an appraisal or examination will not waive any of our rights.

C. Cancellation

1. You may cancel this policy at any time by returning it to us or by letting us know in writing of the date cancellation is to take effect.

HO 00 03 05 01

2. We may cancel this policy only for the reasons stated below by notifying the "insured" named in the Declarations in writing of the date cancellation takes effect. This cancellation notice may be delivered to or mailed to the "insured" named in the Declarations at the mailing address shown in the policy or at a forwarding address. Proof of mailing will be sufficient proof of notice.

   a. When this policy has been in effect for less than 60 days and is not a renewal with us, we may cancel for any reason by notifying the "insured" named in the Declarations at least 30 days before the cancellation takes effect.

   b. When this policy has been in effect for 60 days or more, or at any time if it is a renewal with us, we may cancel only for one or more of the following reasons by notifying the "insured" named in the Declarations at least 30 days prior to the proposed cancellation date:

      (1) This policy was obtained through material misrepresentation, fraudulent statements, omissions or concealment of fact material to the acceptance of the risk or to the hazard assumed by us;

      (2) There has been a substantial change or increase in hazard in the risk assumed by us subsequent to the date the policy was issued;

      (3) There is a substantial increase in hazard insured against by reason of willful or negligent acts or omissions by the "insured";

      (4) The "insured" has failed to pay the premium by the due date, whether payable to us or to our agent or under any finance or credit plan; or

      (5) For any other reason approved by the Pennsylvania Insurance Commissioner.

      This provision shall not apply if the named "insured" has demonstrated by some overt action to us or to our agent that the "insured" wishes the policy to be cancelled.

      Delivery of such written notice by us to the "insured" named in the Declarations at the mailing address shown in the policy or at a forwarding address shall be equivalent to mailing.

3. When this policy is canceled, the premium for the period from the date of cancellation to the expiration date will be refunded pro rata.

4. If the return premium is not refunded with the notice of cancellation or when this policy is returned to us, we will refund it within a reasonable time after the date cancellation takes effect.

D. Nonrenewal

We will not fail to renew this policy except for one of the reasons referred to in **C.** Cancellation above. We may refuse to renew for one of the listed reasons by mailing to the "insured" named in the Declarations at the mailing address shown in the policy or at a forwarding address, written notice at least 30 days prior to the expiration date of this policy.

This provision does not apply if:

   1. We have indicated our willingness to renew and the "insured" has failed to pay the premium by the due date; or

   2. The named "insured" has indicated to us or our agent that the "insured" does not wish the policy to be renewed.

Delivery of such written notice by us to the "insured" named in the Declarations at the mailing address shown in the policy or at a forwarding address shall be equivalent to mailing.

E. Assignment

Assignment of this policy will not be valid unless we give our written consent.

F. Subrogation

An "insured" may waive in writing before a loss all rights of recovery against any person. If not waived, we may require an assignment of rights of recovery for a loss to the extent that payment is made by us.

If an assignment is sought, an "insured" must sign and deliver all related papers and cooperate with us.

Subrogation does not apply to Coverage **F** or Paragraph **C.** Damage To Property Of Others under Section **II** – Additional Coverages.

G. Death

If any person named in the Declarations or the spouse, if a resident of the same household, dies, the following apply:

   1. We insure the legal representative of the deceased but only with respect to the premises and property of the deceased covered under the policy at the time of death; and

2. Insurance under this policy will continue as provided in **a.** or **b.** below, whichever is later:

   a. For 180 days after your death regardless of the policy period shown in the Declarations, unless your premises and property, covered under the policy at the time of your death, is sold prior to that date; or

   b. Until the end of the policy period shown in the Declarations, unless your premises and property, covered under the policy at the time of your death, is sold prior to that date.

   Coverage during the period of time after your death is subject to all the provisions of this policy including payment of any premium due for the policy period shown in the Declarations and any extension of that period;

3. "Insured" includes:

   a. An insured who is a member of your household at the time of your death, but only while a resident of the "residence premises"; and

   b. With respect to your property, the person having proper temporary custody of the property until appointment and qualification of a legal representative.

HO 00 03 05 01

Reading 2-2

PERSONAL AUTO POLICY

AGREEMENT

In return for payment of the premium and subject to all the terms of this policy, we agree with you as follows:

DEFINITIONS

A. Throughout this policy, "you" and "your" refer to:

1. The "named insured" shown in the Declarations; and

2. The spouse if a resident of the same household.

If the spouse ceases to be a resident of the same household during the policy period or prior to the inception of this policy, the spouse will be considered "you" and "your" under this policy but only until the earlier of:

1. The end of 90 days following the spouse's change of residency;

2. The effective date of another policy listing the spouse as a named insured; or

3. The end of the policy period.

B. "We", "us" and "our" refer to the Company providing this insurance.

C. For purposes of this policy, a private passenger type auto, pickup or van shall be deemed to be owned by a person if leased:

1. Under a written agreement to that person; and

2. For a continuous period of at least 6 months.

Other words and phrases are defined. They are in quotation marks when used.

D. "Bodily injury" means bodily harm, sickness or disease, including death that results.

E. "Business" includes trade, profession or occupation.

F. "Family member" means a person related to you by blood, marriage or adoption who is a resident of your household. This includes a ward or foster child.

G. "Occupying" means in, upon, getting in, on, out or off.

H. "Property damage" means physical injury to, destruction of or loss of use of tangible property.

I. "Trailer" means a vehicle designed to be pulled by a:

1. Private passenger auto; or

2. Pickup or van.

It also means a farm wagon or farm implement while towed by a vehicle listed in 1. or 2. above.

J. "Your covered auto" means:

1. Any vehicle shown in the Declarations.

2. A "newly acquired auto".

3. Any "trailer" you own.

4. Any auto or "trailer" you do not own while used as a temporary substitute for any other vehicle described in this definition which is out of normal use because of its:

a. Breakdown;

b. Repair;

c. Servicing;

d. Loss; or

e. Destruction.

This Provision (J.4.) does not apply to Coverage For Damage To Your Auto.

K. "Newly acquired auto":

1. "Newly acquired auto" means any of the following types of vehicles you become the owner of during the policy period:

a. A private passenger auto; or

b. A pickup or van, for which no other insurance policy provides coverage, that:

(1) Has a Gross Vehicle Weight of less than 10,000 lbs.; and

(2) Is not used for the delivery or transportation of goods and materials unless such use is:

(a) Incidental to your "business" of installing, maintaining or repairing furnishings or equipment; or

(b) For farming or ranching.

2. Coverage for a "newly acquired auto" is provided as described below. If you ask us to insure a "newly acquired auto" after a specified time period described below has elapsed, any coverage we provide for a "newly acquired auto" will begin at the time you request the coverage.

a. For any coverage provided in this policy except Coverage For Damage To Your Auto, a "newly acquired auto" will have the broadest coverage we now provide for any vehicle shown in the Declarations. Coverage begins on the date you become the owner. However, for this coverage to apply to a "newly acquired auto" which is in addition to any vehicle shown in the Declarations, you must ask us to insure it within 14 days after you become the owner.

Copyright, Insurance Services Office, Inc., 1997

If a "newly acquired auto" replaces a vehicle shown in the Declarations, coverage is provided for this vehicle without your having to ask us to insure it.

b. Collision Coverage for a "newly acquired auto" begins on the date you become the owner. However, for this coverage to apply, you must ask us to insure it within:

(1) 14 days after you become the owner if the Declarations indicate that Collision Coverage applies to at least one auto. In this case, the "newly acquired auto" will have the broadest coverage we now provide for any auto shown in the Declarations.

(2) Four days after you become the owner if the Declarations do not indicate that Collision Coverage applies to at least one auto. If you comply with the 4 day requirement and a loss occurred before you asked us to insure the "newly acquired auto", a Collision deductible of $500 will apply.

c. Other Than Collision Coverage for a "newly acquired auto" begins on the date you become the owner. However, for this coverage to apply, you must ask us to insure it within:

(1) 14 days after you become the owner if the Declarations indicate that Other Than Collision Coverage applies to at least one auto. In this case, the "newly acquired auto" will have the broadest coverage we now provide for any auto shown in the Declarations.

(2) Four days after you become the owner if the Declarations do not indicate that Other Than Collision Coverage applies to at least one auto. If you comply with the 4 day requirement and a loss occurred before you asked us to insure the "newly acquired auto", an Other Than Collision deductible of $500 will apply.

PART A – LIABILITY COVERAGE

INSURING AGREEMENT

A. We will pay damages for "bodily injury" or "property damage" for which any "insured" becomes legally responsible because of an auto accident. Damages include prejudgment interest awarded against the "insured". We will settle or defend, as we consider appropriate, any claim or suit asking for these damages. In addition to our limit of liability, we will pay all defense costs we incur. Our duty to settle or defend ends when our limit of liability for this coverage has been exhausted by payment of judgments or settlements. We have no duty to defend any suit or settle any claim for "bodily injury" or "property damage" not covered under this policy.

B. "Insured" as used in this Part means:

1. You or any "family member" for the ownership, maintenance or use of any auto or "trailer".

2. Any person using "your covered auto".

3. For "your covered auto", any person or organization but only with respect to legal responsibility for acts or omissions of a person for whom coverage is afforded under this Part.

4. For any auto or "trailer", other than "your covered auto", any other person or organization but only with respect to legal responsibility for acts or omissions of you or any "family member" for whom coverage is afforded under this Part. This Provision (B.4.) applies only if the person or organization does not own or hire the auto or "trailer".

SUPPLEMENTARY PAYMENTS

In addition to our limit of liability, we will pay on behalf of an "insured":

1. Up to $250 for the cost of bail bonds required because of an accident, including related traffic law violations. The accident must result in "bodily injury" or "property damage" covered under this policy.

2. Premiums on appeal bonds and bonds to release attachments in any suit we defend.

3. Interest accruing after a judgment is entered in any suit we defend. Our duty to pay interest ends when we offer to pay that part of the judgment which does not exceed our limit of liability for this coverage.

4. Up to $200 a day for loss of earnings, but not other income, because of attendance at hearings or trials at our request.

5. Other reasonable expenses incurred at our request.

EXCLUSIONS

A. We do not provide Liability Coverage for any "insured":

1. Who intentionally causes "bodily injury" or "property damage".

2. For "property damage" to property owned or being transported by that "insured".

3. For "property damage" to property:
   a. Rented to;
   b. Used by; or
   c. In the care of;

   that "insured".

   This Exclusion (A.3.) does not apply to "property damage" to a residence or private garage.

4. For "bodily injury" to an employee of that "insured" during the course of employment. This Exclusion (A.4.) does not apply to "bodily injury" to a domestic employee unless workers' compensation benefits are required or available for that domestic employee.

5. For that "insured's" liability arising out of the ownership or operation of a vehicle while it is being used as a public or livery conveyance. This Exclusion (A.5.) does not apply to a share-the-expense car pool.

6. While employed or otherwise engaged in the "business" of:
   a. Selling;
   b. Repairing;
   c. Servicing;
   d. Storing; or
   e. Parking;

   vehicles designed for use mainly on public highways. This includes road testing and delivery. This Exclusion (A.6.) does not apply to the ownership, maintenance or use of "your covered auto" by:
   a. You;
   b. Any "family member"; or
   c. Any partner, agent or employee of you or any "family member".

7. Maintaining or using any vehicle while that "insured" is employed or otherwise engaged in any "business" (other than farming or ranching) not described in Exclusion A.6.

   This Exclusion (A.7.) does not apply to the maintenance or use of a:
   a. Private passenger auto;
   b. Pickup or van; or
   c. "Trailer" used with a vehicle described in a. or b. above.

8. Using a vehicle without a reasonable belief that that "insured" is entitled to do so. This Exclusion (A.8.) does not apply to a "family member" using "your covered auto" which is owned by you.

9. For "bodily injury" or "property damage" for which that "insured":
   a. Is an insured under a nuclear energy liability policy; or
   b. Would be an insured under a nuclear energy liability policy but for its termination upon exhaustion of its limit of liability.

   A nuclear energy liability policy is a policy issued by any of the following or their successors:
   a. Nuclear Energy Liability Insurance Association;
   b. Mutual Atomic Energy Liability Underwriters; or
   c. Nuclear Insurance Association of Canada.

B. We do not provide Liability Coverage for the ownership, maintenance or use of:

1. Any vehicle which:
   a. Has fewer than four wheels; or
   b. Is designed mainly for use off public roads.

   This Exclusion (B.1.) does not apply:
   a. While such vehicle is being used by an "insured" in a medical emergency;
   b. To any "trailer"; or
   c. To any non-owned golf cart.

2. Any vehicle, other than "your covered auto", which is:
   a. Owned by you; or
   b. Furnished or available for your regular use.

3. Any vehicle, other than "your covered auto", which is:
   a. Owned by any "family member"; or
   b. Furnished or available for the regular use of any "family member".

   However, this Exclusion (B.3.) does not apply to you while you are maintaining or "occupying" any vehicle which is:
   a. Owned by a "family member"; or
   b. Furnished or available for the regular use of a "family member".

4. Any vehicle, located inside a facility designed for racing, for the purpose of:
   a. Competing in; or
   b. Practicing or preparing for;

   any prearranged or organized racing or speed contest.

LIMIT OF LIABILITY

A. The limit of liability shown in the Declarations for each person for Bodily Injury Liability is our maximum limit of liability for all damages, including damages for care, loss of services or death, arising out of "bodily injury" sustained by any one person in any one auto accident. Subject to this limit for each person, the limit of liability shown in the Declarations for each accident for Bodily Injury Liability is our maximum limit of liability for all damages for "bodily injury" resulting from any one auto accident.

The limit of liability shown in the Declarations for each accident for Property Damage Liability is our maximum limit of liability for all "property damage" resulting from any one auto accident.

This is the most we will pay regardless of the number of:

  1. "Insureds";

  2. Claims made;

  3. Vehicles or premiums shown in the Declarations; or

  4. Vehicles involved in the auto accident.

B. No one will be entitled to receive duplicate payments for the same elements of loss under this coverage and:

  1. Part **B** or Part **C** of this policy; or

  2. Any Underinsured Motorists Coverage provided by this policy.

OUT OF STATE COVERAGE

If an auto accident to which this policy applies occurs in any state or province other than the one in which "your covered auto" is principally garaged, we will interpret your policy for that accident as follows:

A. If the state or province has:

  1. A financial responsibility or similar law specifying limits of liability for "bodily injury" or "property damage" higher than the limit shown in the Declarations, your policy will provide the higher specified limit.

  2. A compulsory insurance or similar law requiring a nonresident to maintain insurance whenever the nonresident uses a vehicle in that state or province, your policy will provide at least the required minimum amounts and types of coverage.

B. No one will be entitled to duplicate payments for the same elements of loss.

FINANCIAL RESPONSIBILITY

When this policy is certified as future proof of financial responsibility, this policy shall comply with the law to the extent required.

OTHER INSURANCE

If there is other applicable liability insurance we will pay only our share of the loss. Our share is the proportion that our limit of liability bears to the total of all applicable limits. However, any insurance we provide for a vehicle you do not own shall be excess over any other collectible insurance.

PART B – MEDICAL PAYMENTS COVERAGE

INSURING AGREEMENT

A. We will pay reasonable expenses incurred for necessary medical and funeral services because of "bodily injury":

  1. Caused by accident; and

  2. Sustained by an "insured".

We will pay only those expenses incurred for services rendered within 3 years from the date of the accident.

B. "Insured" as used in this Part means:

  1. You or any "family member":

    a. While "occupying"; or

    b. As a pedestrian when struck by;

    a motor vehicle designed for use mainly on public roads or a trailer of any type.

  2. Any other person while "occupying" "your covered auto".

EXCLUSIONS

We do not provide Medical Payments Coverage for any "insured" for "bodily injury":

  1. Sustained while "occupying" any motorized vehicle having fewer than four wheels.

  2. Sustained while "occupying" "your covered auto" when it is being used as a public or livery conveyance. This Exclusion (**2.**) does not apply to a share-the-expense car pool.

  3. Sustained while "occupying" any vehicle located for use as a residence or premises.

  4. Occurring during the course of employment if workers' compensation benefits are required or available for the "bodily injury".

  5. Sustained while "occupying", or when struck by, any vehicle (other than "your covered auto") which is:

    a. Owned by you; or

    b. Furnished or available for your regular use.

  6. Sustained while "occupying", or when struck by, any vehicle (other than "your covered auto") which is:

    a. Owned by any "family member"; or

    b. Furnished or available for the regular use of any "family member".

    However, this Exclusion (**6.**) does not apply to you.

7. Sustained while "occupying" a vehicle without a reasonable belief that that "insured" is entitled to do so. This Exclusion **(7.)** does not apply to a "family member" using "your covered auto" which is owned by you.

8. Sustained while "occupying" a vehicle when it is being used in the "business" of an "insured". This Exclusion **(8.)** does not apply to "bodily injury" sustained while "occupying" a:

   a. Private passenger auto;

   b. Pickup or van that you own; or

   c. "Trailer" used with a vehicle described in **a.** or **b.** above.

9. Caused by or as a consequence of:

   a. Discharge of a nuclear weapon (even if accidental);

   b. War (declared or undeclared);

   c. Civil war;

   d. Insurrection; or

   e. Rebellion or revolution.

10. From or as a consequence of the following, whether controlled or uncontrolled or however caused:

    a. Nuclear reaction;

    b. Radiation; or

    c. Radioactive contamination.

11. Sustained while "occupying" any vehicle located inside a facility designed for racing, for the purpose of:

    a. Competing in; or

    b. Practicing or preparing for;

    any prearranged or organized racing or speed contest.

LIMIT OF LIABILITY

A. The limit of liability shown in the Declarations for this coverage is our maximum limit of liability for each person injured in any one accident. This is the most we will pay regardless of the number of:

1. "Insureds";

2. Claims made;

3. Vehicles or premiums shown in the Declarations; or

4. Vehicles involved in the accident.

B. No one will be entitled to receive duplicate payments for the same elements of loss under this coverage and:

1. Part **A** or Part **C** of this policy; or

2. Any Underinsured Motorists Coverage provided by this policy.

OTHER INSURANCE

If there is other applicable auto medical payments insurance we will pay only our share of the loss. Our share is the proportion that our limit of liability bears to the total of all applicable limits. However, any insurance we provide with respect to a vehicle you do not own shall be excess over any other collectible auto insurance providing payments for medical or funeral expenses.

PART C – UNINSURED MOTORISTS COVERAGE

INSURING AGREEMENT

A. We will pay compensatory damages which an "insured" is legally entitled to recover from the owner or operator of an "uninsured motor vehicle" because of "bodily injury":

1. Sustained by an "insured"; and

2. Caused by an accident.

The owner's or operator's liability for these damages must arise out of the ownership, maintenance or use of the "uninsured motor vehicle".

Any judgment for damages arising out of a suit brought without our written consent is not binding on us.

B. "Insured" as used in this Part means:

1. You or any "family member".

2. Any other person "occupying" "your covered auto".

3. Any person for damages that person is entitled to recover because of "bodily injury" to which this coverage applies sustained by a person described in **1.** or **2.** above.

C. "Uninsured motor vehicle" means a land motor vehicle or trailer of any type:

1. To which no bodily injury liability bond or policy applies at the time of the accident.

2. To which a bodily injury liability bond or policy applies at the time of the accident. In this case its limit for bodily injury liability must be less than the minimum limit for bodily injury liability specified by the financial responsibility law of the state in which "your covered auto" is principally garaged.

---

3. Which is a hit-and-run vehicle whose operator or owner cannot be identified and which hits:

   a. You or any "family member";

   b. A vehicle which you or any "family member" are "occupying"; or

   c. "Your covered auto".

4. To which a bodily injury liability bond or policy applies at the time of the accident but the bonding or insuring company:

   a. Denies coverage; or

   b. Is or becomes insolvent.

However, "uninsured motor vehicle" does not include any vehicle or equipment:

1. Owned by or furnished or available for the regular use of you or any "family member".

2. Owned or operated by a self-insurer under any applicable motor vehicle law, except a self-insurer which is or becomes insolvent.

3. Owned by any governmental unit or agency.

4. Operated on rails or crawler treads.

5. Designed mainly for use off public roads while not on public roads.

6. While located for use as a residence or premises.

EXCLUSIONS

A. We do not provide Uninsured Motorists Coverage for "bodily injury" sustained:

1. By an "insured" while "occupying", or when struck by, any motor vehicle owned by that "insured" which is not insured for this coverage under this policy. This includes a trailer of any type used with that vehicle.

2. By any "family member" while "occupying", or when struck by, any motor vehicle you own which is insured for this coverage on a primary basis under any other policy.

B. We do not provide Uninsured Motorists Coverage for "bodily injury" sustained by any "insured":

1. If that "insured" or the legal representative settles the "bodily injury" claim without our consent.

2. While "occupying" "your covered auto" when it is being used as a public or livery conveyance. This Exclusion (B.2.) does not apply to a share-the-expense car pool.

3. Using a vehicle without a reasonable belief that that "insured" is entitled to do so. This Exclusion (B.3.) does not apply to a "family member" using "your covered auto" which is owned by you.

C. This coverage shall not apply directly or indirectly to benefit any insurer or self-insurer under any of the following or similar law:

1. Workers' compensation law; or

2. Disability benefits law.

D. We do not provide Uninsured Motorists Coverage for punitive or exemplary damages.

LIMIT OF LIABILITY

A. The limit of liability shown in the Declarations for each person for Uninsured Motorists Coverage is our maximum limit of liability for all damages, including damages for care, loss of services or death, arising out of "bodily injury" sustained by any one person in any one accident. Subject to this limit for each person, the limit of liability shown in the Declarations for each accident for Uninsured Motorists Coverage is our maximum limit of liability for all damages for "bodily injury" resulting from any one accident.

This is the most we will pay regardless of the number of:

1. "Insureds";

2. Claims made;

3. Vehicles or premiums shown in the Declarations; or

4. Vehicles involved in the accident.

B. No one will be entitled to receive duplicate payments for the same elements of loss under this coverage and:

1. Part A. or Part B. of this policy; or

2. Any Underinsured Motorists Coverage provided by this policy.

C. We will not make a duplicate payment under this coverage for any element of loss for which payment has been made by or on behalf of persons or organizations who may be legally responsible.

D. We will not pay for any element of loss if a person is entitled to receive payment for the same element of loss under any of the following or similar law:

1. Workers' compensation law; or

2. Disability benefits law.

OTHER INSURANCE

If there is other applicable insurance available under one or more policies or provisions of coverage that is similar to the insurance provided under this Part of the policy:

1. Any recovery for damages under all such policies or provisions of coverage may equal but not exceed the highest applicable limit for any one vehicle under any insurance providing coverage on either a primary or excess basis.

2. Any insurance we provide with respect to a vehicle you do not own shall be excess over any collectible insurance providing such coverage on a primary basis.

3. If the coverage under this policy is provided:

   a. On a primary basis, we will pay only our share of the loss that must be paid under insurance providing coverage on a primary basis. Our share is the proportion that our limit of liability bears to the total of all applicable limits of liability for coverage provided on a primary basis.

   b. On an excess basis, we will pay only our share of the loss that must be paid under insurance providing coverage on an excess basis. Our share is the proportion that our limit of liability bears to the total of all applicable limits of liability for coverage provided on an excess basis.

ARBITRATION

A. If we and an "insured" do not agree:

   1. Whether that "insured" is legally entitled to recover damages; or

   2. As to the amount of damages which are recoverable by that "insured";

   from the owner or operator of an "uninsured motor vehicle", then the matter may be arbitrated. However, disputes concerning coverage under this Part may not be arbitrated.

Both parties must agree to arbitration. If so agreed, each party will select an arbitrator. The two arbitrators will select a third. If they cannot agree within 30 days, either may request that selection be made by a judge of a court having jurisdiction.

B. Each party will:

   1. Pay the expenses it incurs; and

   2. Bear the expenses of the third arbitrator equally.

C. Unless both parties agree otherwise, arbitration will take place in the county in which the "insured" lives. Local rules of law as to procedure and evidence will apply. A decision agreed to by two of the arbitrators will be binding as to:

   1. Whether the "insured" is legally entitled to recover damages; and

   2. The amount of damages. This applies only if the amount does not exceed the minimum limit for bodily injury liability specified by the financial responsibility law of the state in which "your covered auto" is principally garaged. If the amount exceeds that limit, either party may demand the right to a trial. This demand must be made within 60 days of the arbitrators' decision. If this demand is not made, the amount of damages agreed to by the arbitrators will be binding.

PART D – COVERAGE FOR DAMAGE TO YOUR AUTO

INSURING AGREEMENT

A. We will pay for direct and accidental loss to "your covered auto" or any "non-owned auto", including their equipment, minus any applicable deductible shown in the Declarations. If loss to more than one "your covered auto" or "non-owned auto" results from the same "collision", only the highest applicable deductible will apply. We will pay for loss to "your covered auto" caused by:

   1. Other than "collision" only if the Declarations indicate that Other Than Collision Coverage is provided for that auto.

   2. "Collision" only if the Declarations indicate that Collision Coverage is provided for that auto.

   If there is a loss to a "non-owned auto", we will provide the broadest coverage applicable to any "your covered auto" shown in the Declarations.

B. "Collision" means the upset of "your covered auto" or a "non-owned auto" or their impact with another vehicle or object.

   Loss caused by the following is considered other than "collision":

   1. Missiles or falling objects;

   2. Fire;

   3. Theft or larceny;

   4. Explosion or earthquake;

   5. Windstorm;

   6. Hail, water or flood;

   7. Malicious mischief or vandalism;

   8. Riot or civil commotion;

   9. Contact with bird or animal; or

   10. Breakage of glass.

   If breakage of glass is caused by a "collision", you may elect to have it considered a loss caused by "collision".

C. "Non-owned auto" means:

   1. Any private passenger auto, pickup, van or "trailer" not owned by or furnished or available for the regular use of you or any "family member" while in the custody of or being operated by you or any "family member"; or

   2. Any auto or "trailer" you do not own while used as a temporary substitute for "your covered auto" which is out of normal use because of its:

      a. Breakdown;

      b. Repair;

      c. Servicing;

      d. Loss; or

      e. Destruction.

TRANSPORTATION EXPENSES

A. In addition, we will pay, without application of a deductible, up to a maximum of $600 for:

1. Temporary transportation expenses not exceeding $20 per day incurred by you in the event of a loss to "your covered auto". We will pay for such expenses if the loss is caused by:

   a. Other than "collision" only if the Declarations indicate that Other Than Collision Coverage is provided for that auto.

   b. "Collision" only if the Declarations indicate that Collision Coverage is provided for that auto.

2. Expenses for which you become legally responsible in the event of loss to a "non-owned auto". We will pay for such expenses if the loss is caused by:

   a. Other than "collision" only if the Declarations indicate that Other Than Collision Coverage is provided for any "your covered auto".

   b. "Collision" only if the Declarations indicate that Collision Coverage is provided for any "your covered auto".

   However, the most we will pay for any expenses for loss of use is $20 per day.

B. If the loss is caused by:

1. A total theft of "your covered auto" or a "non-owned auto", we will pay only expenses incurred during the period:

   a. Beginning 48 hours after the theft; and

   b. Ending when "your covered auto" or the "non-owned auto" is returned to use or we pay for its loss.

2. Other than theft of a "your covered auto" or a "non-owned auto", we will pay only expenses beginning when the auto is withdrawn from use for more than 24 hours.

C. Our payment will be limited to that period of time reasonably required to repair or replace the "your covered auto" or the "non-owned auto".

EXCLUSIONS

We will not pay for:

1. Loss to "your covered auto" or any "non-owned auto" which occurs while it is being used as a public or livery conveyance. This Exclusion (1.) does not apply to a share-the-expense car pool.

2. Damage due and confined to:

   a. Wear and tear;

   b. Freezing;

   c. Mechanical or electrical breakdown or failure; or

   d. Road damage to tires.

This Exclusion (2.) does not apply if the damage results from the total theft of "your covered auto" or any "non-owned auto".

3. Loss due to or as a consequence of:

   a. Radioactive contamination;

   b. Discharge of any nuclear weapon (even if accidental);

   c. War (declared or undeclared);

   d. Civil war;

   e. Insurrection; or

   f. Rebellion or revolution.

4. Loss to any electronic equipment designed for the reproduction of sound and any accessories used with such equipment. This includes but is not limited to:

   a. Radios and stereos;

   b. Tape decks; or

   c. Compact disc players.

This Exclusion (4.) does not apply to equipment designed solely for the reproduction of sound and accessories used with such equipment, provided:

   a. The equipment is permanently installed in "your covered auto" or any "non-owned auto"; or

   b. The equipment is:

   (1) Removable from a housing unit which is permanently installed in the auto;

   (2) Designed to be solely operated by use of the power from the auto's electrical system; and

   (3) In or upon "your covered auto" or any "non-owned auto" at the time of loss.

5. Loss to any electronic equipment that receives or transmits audio, visual or data signals and any accessories used with such equipment. This includes but is not limited to:

   a. Citizens band radios;

   b. Telephones;

   c. Two-way mobile radios;

   d. Scanning monitor receivers;

   e. Television monitor receivers;

   f. Video cassette recorders;

   g. Audio cassette recorders; or

   h. Personal computers.

This Exclusion (5.) does not apply to:

   a. Any electronic equipment that is necessary for the normal operation of the auto or the monitoring of the auto's operating systems; or

 PP 00 01 06 98

b. A permanently installed telephone designed to be operated by use of the power from the auto's electrical system and any accessories used with the telephone.

6. Loss to tapes, records, discs or other media used with equipment described in Exclusions **4.** and **5.**

7. A total loss to "your covered auto" or any "non-owned auto" due to destruction or confiscation by governmental or civil authorities.

   This Exclusion **(7.)** does not apply to the interests of Loss Payees in "your covered auto".

8. Loss to:

   a. A "trailer", camper body, or motor home, which is not shown in the Declarations; or

   b. Facilities or equipment used with such "trailer", camper body or motor home. Facilities or equipment include but are not limited to:

      (1) Cooking, dining, plumbing or refrigeration facilities;

      (2) Awnings or cabanas; or

      (3) Any other facilities or equipment used with a "trailer", camper body, or motor home.

   This Exclusion **(8.)** does not apply to a:

   a. "Trailer", and its facilities or equipment, which you do not own; or

   b. "Trailer", camper body, or the facilities or equipment in or attached to the "trailer" or camper body, which you:

      (1) Acquire during the policy period; and

      (2) Ask us to insure within 14 days after you become the owner.

9. Loss to any "non-owned auto" when used by you or any "family member" without a reasonable belief that you or that "family member" are entitled to do so.

10. Loss to equipment designed or used for the detection or location of radar or laser.

11. Loss to any custom furnishings or equipment in or upon any pickup or van. Custom furnishings or equipment include but are not limited to:

    a. Special carpeting or insulation;

    b. Furniture or bars;

    c. Height-extending roofs; or

    d. Custom murals, paintings or other decals or graphics.

       This Exclusion **(11.)** does not apply to a cap, cover or bedliner in or upon any "your covered auto" which is a pickup.

12. Loss to any "non-owned auto" being maintained or used by any person while employed or otherwise engaged in the "business" of:

    a. Selling;

    b. Repairing;

    c. Servicing;

    d. Storing; or

    e. Parking;

    vehicles designed for use on public highways. This includes road testing and delivery.

13. Loss to "your covered auto" or any "non-owned auto", located inside a facility designed for racing, for the purpose of:

    a. Competing in; or

    b. Practicing or preparing for;

    any prearranged or organized racing or speed contest.

14. Loss to, or loss of use of, a "non-owned auto" rented by:

    a. You; or

    b. Any "family member";

    if a rental vehicle company is precluded from recovering such loss or loss of use, from you or that "family member", pursuant to the provisions of any applicable rental agreement or state law.

LIMIT OF LIABILITY

A. Our limit of liability for loss will be the lesser of the:

   1. Actual cash value of the stolen or damaged property; or

   2. Amount necessary to repair or replace the property with other property of like kind and quality.

   However, the most we will pay for loss to:

   1. Any "non-owned auto" which is a trailer is $500.

   2. Equipment designed solely for the reproduction of sound, including any accessories used with such equipment, which is installed in locations not used by the auto manufacturer for installation of such equipment or accessories, is $1,000.

B. An adjustment for depreciation and physical condition will be made in determining actual cash value in the event of a total loss.

C. If a repair or replacement results in better than like kind or quality, we will not pay for the amount of the betterment.

PAYMENT OF LOSS

We may pay for loss in money or repair or replace the damaged or stolen property. We may, at our expense, return any stolen property to:

1. You; or

2. The address shown in this policy.

If we return stolen property we will pay for any damage resulting from the theft. We may keep all or part of the property at an agreed or appraised value.

If we pay for loss in money, our payment will include the applicable sales tax for the damaged or stolen property.

NO BENEFIT TO BAILEE

This insurance shall not directly or indirectly benefit any carrier or other bailee for hire.

OTHER SOURCES OF RECOVERY

If other sources of recovery also cover the loss, we will pay only our share of the loss. Our share is the proportion that our limit of liability bears to the total of all applicable limits. However, any insurance we provide with respect to a "non-owned auto" shall be excess over any other collectible source of recovery including, but not limited to:

1. Any coverage provided by the owner of the "non-owned auto";

2. Any other applicable physical damage insurance;

3. Any other source of recovery applicable to the loss.

APPRAISAL

A. If we and you do not agree on the amount of loss, either may demand an appraisal of the loss. In this event, each party will select a competent appraiser. The two appraisers will select an umpire. The appraisers will state separately the actual cash value and the amount of loss. If they fail to agree, they will submit their differences to the umpire. A decision agreed to by any two will be binding. Each party will:

1. Pay its chosen appraiser; and

2. Bear the expenses of the appraisal and umpire equally.

B. We do not waive any of our rights under this policy by agreeing to an appraisal.

PART E – DUTIES AFTER AN ACCIDENT OR LOSS

We have no duty to provide coverage under this policy unless there has been full compliance with the following duties:

A. We must be notified promptly of how, when and where the accident or loss happened. Notice should also include the names and addresses of any injured persons and of any witnesses.

B. A person seeking any coverage must:

1. Cooperate with us in the investigation, settlement or defense of any claim or suit.

2. Promptly send us copies of any notices or legal papers received in connection with the accident or loss.

3. Submit, as often as we reasonably require:

   a. To physical exams by physicians we select. We will pay for these exams.

   b. To examination under oath and subscribe the same.

4. Authorize us to obtain:

   a. Medical reports; and

   b. Other pertinent records.

5. Submit a proof of loss when required by us.

C. A person seeking Uninsured Motorists Coverage must also:

1. Promptly notify the police if a hit-and-run driver is involved.

2. Promptly send us copies of the legal papers if a suit is brought.

D. A person seeking Coverage For Damage To Your Auto must also:

1. Take reasonable steps after loss to protect "your covered auto" or any "non-owned auto" and their equipment from further loss. We will pay reasonable expenses incurred to do this.

2. Promptly notify the police if "your covered auto" or any "non-owned auto" is stolen.

3. Permit us to inspect and appraise the damaged property before its repair or disposal.

Copyright, Insurance Services Office, Inc., 1997   **PP 00 01 06 98**

PART F – GENERAL PROVISIONS

BANKRUPTCY

Bankruptcy or insolvency of the "insured" shall not relieve us of any obligations under this policy.

CHANGES

A. This policy contains all the agreements between you and us. Its terms may not be changed or waived except by endorsement issued by us.

B. If there is a change to the information used to develop the policy premium, we may adjust your premium. Changes during the policy term that may result in a premium increase or decrease include, but are not limited to, changes in:

1. The number, type or use classification of insured vehicles;

2. Operators using insured vehicles;

3. The place of principal garaging of insured vehicles;

4. Coverage, deductible or limits.

If a change resulting from **A.** or **B.** requires a premium adjustment, we will make the premium adjustment in accordance with our manual rules.

C. If we make a change which broadens coverage under this edition of your policy without additional premium charge, that change will automatically apply to your policy as of the date we implement the change in your state. This Paragraph **(C.)** does not apply to changes implemented with a general program revision that includes both broadenings and restrictions in coverage, whether that general program revision is implemented through introduction of:

1. A subsequent edition of your policy; or

2. An Amendatory Endorsement.

FRAUD

We do not provide coverage for any "insured" who has made fraudulent statements or engaged in fraudulent conduct in connection with any accident or loss for which coverage is sought under this policy.

LEGAL ACTION AGAINST US

A. No legal action may be brought against us until there has been full compliance with all the terms of this policy. In addition, under Part **A,** no legal action may be brought against us until:

1. We agree in writing that the "insured" has an obligation to pay; or

2. The amount of that obligation has been finally determined by judgment after trial.

B. No person or organization has any right under this policy to bring us into any action to determine the liability of an "insured".

OUR RIGHT TO RECOVER PAYMENT

A. If we make a payment under this policy and the person to or for whom payment was made has a right to recover damages from another we shall be subrogated to that right. That person shall do:

1. Whatever is necessary to enable us to exercise our rights; and

2. Nothing after loss to prejudice them.

However, our rights in this Paragraph **(A.)** do not apply under Part **D,** against any person using "your covered auto" with a reasonable belief that that person is entitled to do so.

B. If we make a payment under this policy and the person to or for whom payment is made recovers damages from another, that person shall:

1. Hold in trust for us the proceeds of the recovery; and

2. Reimburse us to the extent of our payment.

POLICY PERIOD AND TERRITORY

A. This policy applies only to accidents and losses which occur:

1. During the policy period as shown in the Declarations; and

2. Within the policy territory.

B. The policy territory is:

1. The United States of America, its territories or possessions;

2. Puerto Rico; or

3. Canada.

This policy also applies to loss to, or accidents involving, "your covered auto" while being transported between their ports.

TERMINATION

A. Cancellation

This policy may be cancelled during the policy period as follows:

1. The named insured shown in the Declarations may cancel by:

   a. Returning this policy to us; or

   b. Giving us advance written notice of the date cancellation is to take effect.

2. We may cancel by mailing to the named insured shown in the Declarations at the address shown in this policy:

   a. At least 10 days notice:

      (1) If cancellation is for nonpayment of premium; or

(2) If notice is mailed during the first 60 days this policy is in effect and this is not a renewal or continuation policy; or

b. At least 20 days notice in all other cases.

3. After this policy is in effect for 60 days, or if this is a renewal or continuation policy, we will cancel only:

a. For nonpayment of premium; or

b. If your driver's license or that of:

(1) Any driver who lives with you; or

(2) Any driver who customarily uses "your covered auto";

has been suspended or revoked. This must have occurred:

(1) During the policy period; or

(2) Since the last anniversary of the original effective date if the policy period is other than 1 year; or

c. If the policy was obtained through material misrepresentation.

B. Nonrenewal

If we decide not to renew or continue this policy, we will mail notice to the named insured shown in the Declarations at the address shown in this policy. Notice will be mailed at least 20 days before the end of the policy period. Subject to this notice requirement, if the policy period is:

1. Less than 6 months, we will have the right not to renew or continue this policy every 6 months, beginning 6 months after its original effective date.

2. 6 months or longer, but less than one year, we will have the right not to renew or continue this policy at the end of the policy period.

3. 1 year or longer, we will have the right not to renew or continue this policy at each anniversary of its original effective date.

C. Automatic Termination

If we offer to renew or continue and you or your representative do not accept, this policy will automatically terminate at the end of the current policy period. Failure to pay the required renewal or continuation premium when due shall mean that you have not accepted our offer.

If you obtain other insurance on "your covered auto", any similar insurance provided by this policy will terminate as to that auto on the effective date of the other insurance.

D. Other Termination Provisions

1. We may deliver any notice instead of mailing it. Proof of mailing of any notice shall be sufficient proof of notice.

2. If this policy is cancelled, you may be entitled to a premium refund. If so, we will send you the refund. The premium refund, if any, will be computed according to our manuals. However, making or offering to make the refund is not a condition of cancellation.

3. The effective date of cancellation stated in the notice shall become the end of the policy period.

TRANSFER OF YOUR INTEREST IN THIS POLICY

A. Your rights and duties under this policy may not be assigned without our written consent. However, if a named insured shown in the Declarations dies, coverage will be provided for:

1. The surviving spouse if resident in the same household at the time of death. Coverage applies to the spouse as if a named insured shown in the Declarations; and

2. The legal representative of the deceased person as if a named insured shown in the Declarations. This applies only with respect to the representative's legal responsibility to maintain or use "your covered auto".

B. Coverage will only be provided until the end of the policy period.

TWO OR MORE AUTO POLICIES

If this policy and any other auto insurance policy issued to you by us apply to the same accident, the maximum limit of our liability under all the policies shall not exceed the highest applicable limit of liability under any one policy.

PP 00 01 06 98

Key Words and Phrases

Define or describe each of the words and phrases listed below.

Manuscript policies (p. 2.6)

Insuring agreement (p. 2.8)

Policy condition (p. 2.10)

Specified causes of loss coverage (p. 2.15)

Special form coverage (p. 2.15)

Direct loss (p. 2.17)

Indirect loss (p. 2.17)

Compensatory damages (p. 2.18)

Special damages (p. 2.18)

General damages (p. 2.18)

Punitive damages (p. 2.18)

Reserve (p. 2.23)

Individual case method (p. 2.23)

Roundtable method (p. 2.25)

Average value method (p. 2.25)

Formula method (p. 2.25)

Expert system method (p. 2.26)

Loss ratio method (p. 2.26)

Waiver (p. 2.30)

Estoppel (p. 2.31)

Nonwaiver agreement (p. 2.32)

Reservation of rights letter (p. 2.32)

Subrogation (p. 2.35)

Alternative dispute resolution (ADR) (p. 2.44)

Mediation (p. 2.44)

Arbitration (p. 2.45)

Appraisal provision (p. 2.45)

Mini-trial (p. 2.45)

Summary jury trial (p. 2.46)

Review Questions

1. Policies can be classified in several ways. Distinguish the following types of policy classifications. (pp. 2.4–2.6)

   a. Self-contained and modular

   b. Package and monoline

   c. Preprinted and manuscript

2. Describe the purpose of the following categories of policy provisions, and give an example of the coverage details that might be found under each. (pp. 2.7–2.12)

   a. Declarations

   b. Definitions

c. Insuring agreement

d. Exclusions

e. Conditions

f. Miscellaneous provisions

g. Endorsements

3. Why is it important for a claim representative to follow a
   systematic framework for coverage analysis? (pp. 2.12–2.13)

4. What questions should a claim representative ask when performing a coverage analysis? (p. 2.13)

5. The claim handling process is initiated when the insured reports a loss to the producer or the insurer. Describe the methods and formats used to convey loss information. (p. 2.21)

6. What is the purpose of acknowledging the receipt of an insured's claim? (p. 2.22)

7. Describe the six common methods of setting case reserves. (pp. 2.23–2.26)

8. Reserve adequacy and accuracy are important to an insurer's solvency and ability to write new business. What are some causes of reserving errors and reserve inaccuracy? (pp. 2.27–2.28)

9. What is the purpose of the initial contact with the insured or the insured's representative? (pp. 2.28–2.29)

10. Give an example of the following: (pp. 2.30–2.31)

   a. Waiver

   b. Estoppel

11. What are the purposes of a nonwaiver agreement and a reservation of rights letter? (pp. 2.31–2.32)

12. Identify and describe three of the common types of claim investigations. (pp. 2.34–2.36)

13. Why should a claim representative check state and federal databases before issuing a claim payment? (p. 2.43)

14. Generally, what information should a denial letter contain?
    (pp. 2.43–2.44)

15. Describe the following methods of alternative dispute resolution
    (ADR). (pp. 2.44–2.46)

    a. Mediation

    b. Arbitration

    c. Appraisal

    d. Mini-trial

    e. Summary jury trial

Application Questions

1. John is a telecommuter who works in his basement office and uses his personal computer to perform his work and correspond with his employer. The computer's central processing unit sits on the floor in his office and is damaged when the clothes washer overflows. John reports the water damage claim to his homeowners insurer. The claim is assigned to Tom, who must determine whether the damage is covered by the homeowners policy. What sections of the policy should Tom review to determine whether the loss is covered?

2. Sally owns a 2003 Toyota Camry and has her car insurance with WEV Insurance Company. Her car is vandalized one evening while it is parked on the street in front of her house. Upon discovering the damage, Sally calls her producer and reports the loss. Within twenty-four hours, Sally has been contacted by Jim, the claim representative assigned to her claim.

   In his initial phone conversation with Sally, Jim tells her that she can arrange to have the car repaired at her local body shop and that she can rent a car because she has rental reimbursement coverage. In speaking with Sally about the vandalism, Jim begins to suspect that Sally may have hired someone to vandalize the car.

   After investigating the claim, Jim denies the claim because he believes that Sally hired someone to vandalize the car for her.

   a. What methods may have been used in assigning this loss to Jim?

   b. What reserving methods might Jim use with this claim?

c.   What steps would Jim have taken to learn that Sally has rental reimbursement coverage?

d.   Assume that Jim did not confirm that Sally had rental reimbursement coverage and Sally rented a car relying on Jim's statements. Would Jim be able to deny payment of the rental car bill?

e.   What methods might Jim use to ensure that he can investigate the claim without impairing his ability to later deny the claim if his suspicions are proven correct?

f.   What types of investigation might Jim perform for this claim?

g.   What options does Sally have to dispute Jim's decision to deny her claim?

Answers to Assignment 2 Questions

NOTE: These answers are provided to give students a basic understanding of acceptable types of responses. They often are not the only valid answers and are not intended to provide an exhaustive response to the questions.

Review Questions

1. a. A self-contained policy is a single document containing all agreements between the applicant and the insurer. Self-contained policies are appropriate for loss exposures that are similar among insureds, such as private passenger auto policies. In contrast, a modular policy is a mix-and-match set of components that can be assembled to meet an insured's unique combination of needs. An advantage of the modular policy is that a single policy can include several types of insurance, whereas a self-contained policy requires a separate policy for each coverage.

   b. Package policies contain carefully designed and coordinated provisions in the various component forms that minimize the possibility of coverage gaps or overlaps. Terminology, definitions, and language of the components are consistent, and fewer forms are required than if a series of self-contained policies were used to provide the same coverage. A monoline policy is a combination of documents forming a complete policy for a particular type of coverage or line of business. A monoline policy would be used when the insured needs only one particular type of insurance.

   c. Preprinted policies are those that are assembled from one or more preprinted forms and endorsements. A manuscript policy is a one-of-a-kind policy written to meet a unique coverage need.

2. a. Declarations—this document contains basic information about the insured taken from the insurance application, a description of the coverage provided under the policy, and information about what is unique to the policy.

   b. Definitions—this section contains definitions of terms used throughout the policy or form. The purpose of the definitions section is to establish a common understanding of what the terms in the policy mean.

   c. Insuring agreement—in this section of the policy, the insurer states that it will make a loss payment or provide a service under described circumstances.

   d. Exclusions—these policy provisions state what the insurer does not intend to cover. Exclusions clarify the coverages granted by the insurer in the insuring agreement.

   e. Conditions—these policy provisions qualify an otherwise enforceable promise made in the policy. If either party fails to fulfill the required conditions, the other party is released from its obligations under the policy.

   f. Miscellaneous provisions—these provisions are found throughout the policy and usually describe the relationship between the insurer and the insured or establish procedures for implementing policy conditions.

   g. Endorsements—endorsements are documents added to policies that add, delete, replace, or modify another policy provision. An endorsement takes precedence over any conflicting terms in the policy.

3. A systematic framework for coverage analysis can guide the claim representative to the parts of the policy that may provide or exclude coverage. It ensures that all the component parts are reviewed and reduces the incidence of erroneous coverage determinations.

4. When analyzing coverage, the claim representative should ask the following questions:
    - Is the person involved covered?
    - Did the loss occur during the policy period?
    - Is the cause of loss covered?
    - Is the damaged property covered?
    - Is the type of loss covered?
    - Are the amounts of loss or damages covered?
    - Is the location of the loss covered?
    - Do any exclusions apply?
    - Does other insurance apply?

5. Loss information can be conveyed by various methods and in various formats. Losses can be reported using a loss notice form such as those supplied by ACORD, which provide basic information about the loss and the insured. The forms are usually mailed, faxed, or electronically conveyed to the insurer. Additionally, losses reported over the phone are usually entered onto a loss notice form. Losses can also be reported in a letter or as part of a lawsuit. Claims reported using a letter or a lawsuit may not have all of the information a claim representative needs to begin investigation of the loss.

6. The purpose of the acknowledgment is to advise the insured that the claim has been received. It provides the name and contact information of the assigned claim representative and the claim number. Timely and accurate acknowledgements are also used to satisfy state regulatory requirements.

7. The six common methods of setting case reserves are as follows:
    - Individual case method—involves setting a reserve for each claim. The claim representative estimates the loss reserve based on the claim's circumstances and the claim representative's experience in similar claims. Because of the subjective nature of the evaluation, reserves can vary widely by claim representative.
    - Roundtable method—involves evaluation of the claim file by two or more claim personnel, each suggesting a reserve based on their evaluation. Ideally, the claim personnel should not initially know the reserves the others have set. After the evaluation and a discussion, a consensus reserve figure may be reached, or an average of all the figures may be calculated.
    - Average value method—used when there are small variations in loss size for a particular type of claim and when claims can be concluded quickly. The average values are usually based on data from past claims and adjusted to reflect current conditions. For some claims, the initial reserve is set based on the average value method, but claim representatives are required to modify the initial reserve within a set number of days to reflect each claim's circumstances.
    - Formula method—uses a mathematical formula to set reserves. For example, a formula might be based on the assumption that a certain ratio exists between the medical cost and the indemnity (or wage loss) in a workers' compensation claim. Based on an insurer's loss history with many similar claims, the indemnity reserve might be set at a certain percentage of the medical reserve. The formula method may also be used to set the additional living expense reserve under a homeowners' policy if the home is destroyed by fire. The reserve may be set as a certain percentage of the coverage limit. The formula is determined by the insurer and is automatically created for the claim representative, based on the facts of the claim.
    - Expert system method—uses a software application containing business rules to assist in estimating losses and loss adjustment expenses (LAE). The details of a particular claim are entered into the computer, and the program applies the appropriate rules to estimate the amount of the loss and the LAE. An expert system can provide greater consistency in

reserving than the individual case method. While similar in operation to the formula method, the expert system will include more subjective information, such as loss location or name of treating physician, in creating the reserve.

- Loss ratio method—used to establish aggregate reserves for all claims within a type of insurance. The actuarial department uses this method when other methods of establishing claim reserves are inadequate. For example, in medical malpractice insurance for physicians and surgeons, claims are often reported long after the expiration date of the policy that provided the coverage. To ensure that the insurer has adequate reserves for those claims, the actuarial department might project reserves using the loss ratio method.

8. Reserving errors can be caused in several ways. Initial reserves may be inaccurate because they are determined based on limited information. Reserve inaccuracy can be the result of the claim representative's poor planning, lack of expertise in estimating claim severity, or an unwillingness to reevaluate the facts. Claim representatives may underestimate the future settlement value of a claim if they are overconfident of their ability to conclude the claim for a lesser amount. Data process errors can occur during the entry of the reserve into the claim processing system.

9. A claim representative's initial contact with the insured serves several purposes. It can reassure the insured that the claim is being investigated. It provides the claim representative with the opportunity to explain the claim process and begin the claim investigation. It sets the tone for the claim and establishes expectations.

10. a. Waiver—a claim representative can waive a right contained in a policy condition or exclusion by telling an insured that a loss is covered before confirming that by checking the policy.

    b. Estoppel—a claim representative who tells an insured that damaged goods can be discarded before they are inspected would be estopped from later denying the claim on the grounds that the damaged goods were unavailable for inspection.

11. Nonwaiver agreements and reservation of rights letters both serve the following purposes:

- To advise the insured that any action taken by the insurer in investigating the cause of loss or in ascertaining the amount of loss is not intended to waive or invalidate any policy conditions.

- To clarify that the agreement's or the letter's intent is to permit a claim investigation and that neither the insured nor the insurer will thereby waive any respective rights or obligations.

12. Common types of claim investigations include the following:

    1. Claimant investigation—to learn the claimant's version of the incident that led to the claim; usually done by taking the claimant's statement to determine the value of the injury or damage, how the injury or damage was caused, and who was responsible.

    2. Insured/witness investigation—conducted by taking statements (either written or recorded) from the insured and witnesses. Information provided about the circumstances surrounding the loss could support or refute an insured's version of an incident, which can have an affect on the liability determination.

    3. Accident scene investigation—used in automobile, third-party liability, and workers' compensation claims; details such as tire tracks, curves in the roadway, and objects or conditions that might interfere with a driver's view or that might cause an accident (such as a pothole in the road) help the claim representative determine whether accounts of the accident are plausible or questionable. Claim representatives also consult weather or traffic reports in certain accident scene investigations to identify weather or traffic factors that may have contributed to the loss.

       (Descriptions of additional common types of claim investigations—property damage investigation, medical investigation, prior claim investigation, and subrogation investigation and recovery—can also be used to answer this question.)

13. Claim representatives must check various databases to ensure that the claim payment complies with federal and state laws. The Office of Foreign Asset Control, U.S. Department of the Treasury, requires all claim payors (insurers, self-insureds, and third-party administrators) to check the master list of potential terrorists and drug traffickers before making a claim payment. Claim payors may be prohibited from paying a claim to an individual or entity appearing on this list. Failure to comply with this requirement can result in substantial penalties to the payor. Many states have statutes that require a claim representative to check a database to determine if a claimant or beneficiary owes unpaid child support. If child support is owed, the claim representative must follow specific procedures when issuing the payment because the unpaid child support has priority.

14. Generally, a denial letter must state all the known reasons for the claim denial, quote specific policy language and cite the location of the language in the policy, and describe policy provisions in relation to the facts of the loss. An insured who disagrees with the denial should be invited to submit additional information that would give the insurer cause to reevaluate the claim.

15. a. Mediation is a give and take process managed by a mediator, a neutral outside person, often a retired judge or an expert in the field under dispute. The mediator might be appointed by the court or selected by the parties. Each party presents its case to the mediator, who leads the parties through in-depth settlement discussions. The mediator points out the weaknesses in each argument or in the evidence presented, proposes solutions, and helps the participants improve their relationship. The mediator assists the parties in reaching a mutually agreeable settlement.

    b. In arbitration, the two parties present their cases to an impartial third party, the arbitrator. The arbitrator acts as a judge, weighing the facts of the case and making a decision based on the evidence presented. The advantage of arbitration is that someone other than the insurer and the claimant decides the case. Under binding arbitration, which some states' laws require for arbitrated claim disputes, the parties must accept the arbitrator's decision. Under nonbinding arbitration, neither party is forced to accept the arbitrator's decision; however, the decision provides the "winner" with leverage for future negotiations.

    c. Appraisal is used to settle disputes between insurers and their insureds over the amount owed on a covered loss under property policies. It is not used to settle coverage disputes, only the amount of damages. Almost all property insurance policies contain an appraisal provision. For example, the HO-3 provides that the insurer or the insured can demand an appraisal if they disagree on the loss amount. Each party chooses an appraiser, and the two appraisers choose a third appraiser to act as an umpire. The appraisers can hear evidence that is typically excluded from trial. The two appraisers estimate the property damage separately. If their estimates match, the insurer pays the insured that amount. If the estimates are different, the umpire offers a binding decision on the loss amount.

    d. A mini-trial is an abbreviated version of a trial before a panel or an advisor, who poses questions and offers opinions on the outcome of a trial based on the evidence presented. Representatives (usually lawyers) of the two parties present the evidence. A mini-trial enables parties to test the validity of their positions and continue negotiations. The main advantage of mini-trials is that claimants and insurers can learn the likely outcome of their cases without having to contend with delays in the legal system.

    e. A summary jury trial is used when questions of coverage occur. It offers a forum for deciding the merits of cases for court proceedings and may assist in negotiations. A summary jury trial is staged much like a regular jury trial, except that only a few witnesses are used to present the case. Mock jurors are pulled from a pool of persons selected to serve as possible jurors in an actual court case. Evidence and witnesses' testimony may be presented in both oral and written format for the mock jurors. Lawyers summarize information for the sake of brevity. The mock jurors decide the case based on the limited, though representative, presentation of evidence.

Application Questions

1. Tom should review the following policy sections:
    *   Declarations page—confirms who the insured is.
    *   Definitions section—will describe any technical terms or words used in the policy.
    *   Insuring agreement—describes the broad circumstances under which payment or service is provided by the insurer.
    *   Exclusions—describe whether the computer used for business is covered and whether the water damage is a covered cause of loss.
    *   Conditions—describe the obligations of both the insured and the insurer.

2. a. The insurer may have assigned the case to Jim based on territory, type of claim, extent of damage, workload, or other criteria contained in the insurer's claim information system or based on the requirements of Jim's license.

    b. Jim could set an individual case reserve based on his expectation of what the insurer will pay. He could use the roundtable method and ask two or more claim representatives to evaluate the claim file, suggest a reserve, and reach a consensus reserve figure or average their suggested reserves. Jim might also set a reserve using the average value method, using data from past claims and adjusting the values to the current conditions. Jim could also use a mathematical formula to set the reserve, based on the insurer's loss history with similar types of claims, or an expert system, a software application containing business rules to assist in estimating losses and loss adjustment expenses. Finally, Jim may use the loss ratio method, using aggregate reserves for all claims within a type of insurance to establish a reserve.

    c. Jim would have identified Sally's policy and reviewed the details of her coverage. The declarations page of Sally's policy would have an entry showing rental reimbursement coverage was included with the policy.

    d. Jim would be estopped from denying the claim for rental reimbursement because he has told Sally that she had the coverage. Estoppel is a legal bar to asserting certain contractual conditions because of a party's pervious actions or words to the contrary.

    e. Jim may use a nonwaiver agreement or a reservation of rights letter to advise Sally that any action taken in investigating the loss is not intended to waive or invalidate any policy conditions and to clarify that neither Sally nor the insurer are waiving any respective rights or obligations.

    f. Jim may perform the following investigations in this claim:
        *   Claimant investigation—because this is a first-party claim, the claimant is Sally. Jim may take her statement to find out how the claim occurred.
        *   Insured/witness investigation—Jim may canvas the neighborhood to see if any neighbors saw the vandalism occur or if there were individuals in the neighborhood that evening that were not normally there.
        *   Accident scene investigation—Jim may go to the scene of the loss to see if it was possible for the vandalism to have occurred without anyone seeing it.
        *   Property damage investigation—Jim may inspect the vehicle himself or have an expert inspect the vehicle to confirm that vandalism is the cause of the loss.
        *   Medical investigation—Jim would not perform a medical investigation, because there were no bodily injuries associated with this claim.

- Prior claim investigation—Jim may check to see if Sally has had prior vandalism claims with this car or other cars. Checking prior claims ensures that the insurer will not pay for damage that may have already been paid for but that was not repaired.
- Subrogation investigation—Jim may conduct this investigation to see whether the individuals who vandalized Sally's car can be located and required to reimburse the insurer for the claim payment.

g. Sally can file a lawsuit to resolve the issue or she can use some form of alternative dispute resolution, such as mediation, arbitration, mini-trial, or summary jury trial. She could not use appraisal because the dispute is not over an amount owed on a covered loss.

Narrow the focus of what you need to learn. Remember, the Educational Objectives are the foundation of each of the Institutes' courses, and the exam is based on these Educational Objectives.

Investigation of Cause of Loss, Liability, and Damages

Direct

Direct Your Learning

Assignment

3

Study Materials

Required Reading:

- Claim Handling Principles and Practices
  - Chapter 3
- "Interview Techniques," Course Guide Reading 3-1

Study Aids:

- SMART Practice Exam CD-ROM
- SMART Study Aids Review Notes and Flash Cards— Assignment 3

Educational Objectives

After learning the content of this assignment, you should be able to:

1. Describe the three bases for legal liability.

2. Explain why and how each of the following general investigative tools is used in claim handling:
   - Loss notice forms
   - Policy information
   - Statements
   - Diagrams, photos, and videos
   - Experts
   - Records and reports
   - Industry databases
   - Internet
   - Other investigative tools

3. Explain how a claim representative investigates cause of loss, liability, and amount of damage in an auto physical damage claim.

4. Explain how a claim representative investigates cause of loss, liability, and amount of damage in a property damage claim other than auto.

5. Explain how a claim representative investigates cause of loss, liability, and amount of damages in a bodily injury liability claim.

6. Explain how a claim representative investigates compensability, liability, and benefits in a workers' compensation claim.

7. Define or describe each of the Key Words and Phrases for this assignment.

Outline

- **Bases for Legal Liability**
  - A. Liability Based on Tort
    1. Negligence
    2. Strict Liability
    3. Intentional Torts
  - B. Liability Based on Contract
  - C. Liability Based on Statute

- **General Investigative Tools**
  - A. Loss Notice Forms
    1. Automobile Loss Notice Form
    2. Property Loss Notice Form
    3. General Liability Notice of Occurrence Claim Form
    4. Workers Compensation Loss Notice Form
  - B. Policy Information
  - C. Statements
    1. Recorded Statements
    2. Written Statements
    3. Statement Content
    4. Types of Questions Used in Statements
    5. Consideration for Special Interviewees
  - D. Diagrams, Photos, and Videos
  - E. Experts
    1. Types of Experts
    2. Property Experts
    3. Bodily Injury Experts
  - F. Records and Reports
  - G. Industry Databases
  - H. Internet
  - I. Other Investigative Tools

- **Property Damage Claim Investigation**
  - A. Determining Cause of Loss—Auto Physical Damage
    1. Initial Contact and Statements
    2. Inspection
    3. Documentation
    4. Fire Claims
    5. Theft Claims
  - B. Determining Cause of Loss—Other Property Damage
    1. Initial Contact and Statements
    2. Inspection
    3. Documentation
    4. Contents Claims
    5. Loss of Income Claims
    6. Determining Liability
  - C. Determining Amount of Damage
    1. Auto Physical Damage
    2. All Other Property Damage

- **Bodily Injury Claim Investigation**
  - A. Determining Cause of Loss
    1. Initial Contact and Statements
    2. Documentation
    3. Using Experts
  - B. Determining Liability
  - C. Determining Amount of Damages
    1. Future Damages
    2. Punitive Damages
    3. Valuation of Special Damages
    4. Valuation of General Damages
    5. Methods for Determining the Value of a Bodily Injury Claim

- **Workers' Compensation Claim Investigation**
  - A. Determining Compensability
    1. Initial Contact and Statements
    2. Documentation
    3. Using Experts
  - B. Determining Liability
  - C. Determining Benefits

- **Summary**

- **Interview Techniques (Course Guide Reading 3-1)**

Reading 3-1

Interview Techniques

Plrb Conference
Anaheim, California
April 7–10, 2002

Written and compiled by
Bob Grandolfo and Norm Weisenfluh

We realize that the material covered in this handbook is directed at the Workers' Compensation Interview, which is what we initially designed it for, but the basic discussion on interviews is valid across all lines of business and the remainder may have some value as a guide to give you ideas on how to prepare standard question templates.

Introduction

Recorded Interviews vs. Written Interviews

The debate over which is better, a recorded interview or a handwritten statement, is one that causes much consternation. The type of interview you are going to conduct may dictate which you should use.

Pros:

In-Person Recorded Interview: For a lengthy, complex interview, a recorded interview may be best. This type of interview allows the interviewer to work from an interview outline and direct the questioning into different areas. An organized interviewer can accomplish a great deal and capture a lot of important facts in a short time frame. It allows the interviewer to focus on the interview and not worry about taking notes or having to ask the subject of the interview to repeat something missed in note taking.

Telephonic Recorded Interview: You can also take a recorded interview, telephonically, from a great distance from the person being interviewed. This saves time and expense of having to travel to a distant location to conduct an interview. In a simple, uncomplicated matter requiring an uncontested interview it may be the method of choice.

Handwritten Statement: For a short, uncomplicated matter, a handwritten statement may serve the purpose. A handwritten statement offers the signature and handwriting of the interviewee as proof positive these are the words of that person.

Cons:

In-Person Recorded Interview: The subject of the interview can refuse to allow a recorded interview, thus requiring the interviewer to take notes of the interview or have the interviewee prepare a handwritten statement or the interviewee to take notes.

Telephonic Recorded Interview: Again the subject of the interview can refuse to allow a recorded interview, thus requiring the interviewer to take notes of the interview, and since this is a telephonic interview a handwritten statement is not possible. You also lose an important component of an interview by conducting a telephonic interview, the ability to observe the interviewee's demeanor, motions and reactions (body language) to your questions.

Handwritten Statement: A lengthy, complex matter may require more of an effort than the interviewee is willing to give, to prepare a handwritten statement. It may result in the interviewee refusing to answer questions they do not feel are necessary and refusing to continue with the written statement, leaving the interviewee with a partial statement.

Recorded Interviews and the Law

Despite the interviewer's desire to record an interview, the interviewee may decline to allow the recording. As far as making a recorded record of a telephonic interview, again the interviewee has the option to refuse a recording. Federal law and laws in twelve states regarding the tape recording of a telephone conversation require only the permission of one of the participants to the conversation (one-party consent). Thirty-eight other states require the permission of both participants to the conversation be given before the conversation is recorded (all-party consent). Regardless of the law in the state in which you plan on conducting your interview, it is always safer to get the acknowledgement and consent of all parties before recording.

One approach is to explain to the interviewee that the purpose of the recording is for their protection as well as yours. The recording will not allow you to change anything they say and will be available at a later date should they dispute something attributed to them. You can also offer that the recording will be for your convenience to ensure you get your report correct and don't make a mistake in something they told you and will shorten the time it takes to complete the interview.

The same procedure applies to in-person and telephonic recorded interviews.

Interstate Phone Calls

In light of the differing state laws governing electronic recording of conversations between private parties, journalists are advised to err on the side of caution when recording or disclosing an interstate telephone call. The safest strategy is to assume that the stricter state law will apply.

For example, a reporter located in the District of Columbia who records a telephone conversation without the consent of a party located in Maryland would not violate District of Columbia law, but could be liable under Maryland law. A court located in the District of Columbia may apply Maryland law, depending on its "conflict of laws" rules. Therefore, an aggrieved party may choose to file suit in either jurisdiction, depending on which law is more favorable to the party's claim.

In one case, a New York trial court was asked to apply the Pennsylvania wiretap law—which requires consent of all parties—to a call placed by a prostitute in Pennsylvania to a man in New York. Unlike the Pennsylvania wiretap statute, the New York and federal statutes require the consent of only one party. The call was recorded with the woman's consent by reporters for The Globe, a national tabloid newspaper. The court ruled that the law of the state where the injury occurred, New York, should apply. (Krauss v. Globe International)

In another case involving Pennsylvania law, four employees of the Times Leader, a newspaper in Wilkes-Barre, were arrested after they printed a transcript of a telephone conversation between a columnist in Pennsylvania and a murder suspect living in Virginia that was recorded without the suspect's permission. The Virginia and federal statutes allow one party to record a conversation, while Pennsylvania, as discussed above, requires the consent of all parties. The man asked prosecutors to charge the journalists under the Pennsylvania law. The court eventually dismissed the charges against the newspaper staff—but on the unrelated ground that the suspect had no expectation of privacy during his telephone interview with the columnist. (Pennsylvania v. Duncan)

Federal law may apply when the conversation is between parties who are in different states, although it is unsettled whether a court will hold in a given case that federal law preempts state law. In Duncan, the newspaper argued that the federal law should preempt the state statutes, because the telephone call crossed state lines, placing it under federal jurisdiction. However, in that case, the court did not address the preemption issue. Moreover, as noted above, either state may choose to enforce its own laws.

Warning and Acknowledgement

Before you begin to record an interview ask for the permission of the person being interviewed. At the beginning of your recorded interview, state the date, time and location of the interview. Identify yourself, your position, and the name and position or relationship to the matter under investigation of everyone present. At that time, address the person being interviewed and ask them if they know you are recording the interview. Again, (this time on tape) ask for their permission to record the interview.

DO NOT misrepresent who you are, or the purpose of the telephone call/interview.

Should the interviewee have changed his/her mind about allowing a recorded interview and say that they do not want the interview recorded, turn the recorder off immediately in their presence.

For consistency, each time the tape recording is turned off prior to the conclusion of the interview, the date, time and purpose for the interruption should be stated on the recording and again when the recording is started again.

At the end of the interview, ask the interviewee again if he/she knew the interview was being recorded and if it was recorded with their permission. State that you are turning the tape off at the conclusion of the interview and state the date and time.

Using Checklists, Outlines or Prepared Question Lists for Interviews

Again there are two groups of thought regarding the use of checklists in the conduct of an interview. Some argue a checklist does not allow for a free exchange and inhibits both the interviewer and the person they are interviewing. Others argue that properly used checklists are the sign of an organized investigator and allow the investigator to conduct the interview in an organized manner while capturing everything the interview was intended for.

An area investigators have problems with when they start using checklists or prepared lists of questions to conduct an interview is they read the question and allow the answer and do not look for other question areas. Each question on a checklist or prepared list of questions has the potential to open another area of questioning based on the answer. The successful interviewer will follow the other lines of questions and then continue with the remainder of the checklist or prepared list of questions. This approach can lead to a lengthy interview but will also give the interviewer the opportunity to follow every possible lead.

Recorded Interview General

Preliminary Discussion

Call interviewee, introduce yourself, explain the purpose of your call and put interviewee at ease.

Request permission to record the conversation.

Ask that records, papers, driver's license, etc. be ready for reference.

Standard Introduction

There is standardized phraseology for the introduction, closing, and continuation of recorded statements and it is mandatory that this format be adhered to:

"This is (Your Name) calling on behalf on (Insured) interviewing (interviewee) by telephone on (Date) at (Time). Mr./Ms. (Interviewee) do you understand this is being recorded? Do I have your permission to record this interview?"

Interruptions

Once the recorded interview commences, do not stop the machine until the interview is over.

If interview is interrupted and the delay will be short, explain reason for delay and do not turn off recorder.

If the recording is going to exceed one tape, then prior to the end of the first tape the following should be inserted: "This is the end of tape No. 1, interview with (interviewee) on (Date) at (Time). This recording will be continued on tape No. 2. Do I have your permission to stop the tape?"

When resuming on tape No. 2 state, "This is (Your Name) interviewing (Interviewee). This is a continuation of tape No. 1 made on (Date). The time is ( ). Did we discuss the accident while the tape was being changed? Do you understand this is being recorded? Do I have your permission to continue recording? We will now resume."

Standard Conclusion

Once you have obtained everything you need in your statement, you should conclude with the following:

"Do you wish to add anything else? Have you understood the questions I have asked you? Do you understand Mr./Ms. (Interviewee), that this interview has been recorded? Did I have your permission to record? Have your answers been the truth to the best of your knowledge? This concludes the interview with Mr./Ms. (Interviewee) at (Time). With your permission I will turn off the recorder."

Recording Summary

While taking the recording or immediately after the completion of a recording, a written summary is to be made on the Recorded Interview Summary.

Identification and Filing of Recorded Statements

Record the statement on a recordable tape. Note: No more than one statement may be on the same tape.

Write the name of interviewee and the date of interview on the tape.

Write the claim number, dictator's name, date of recording and any other pertinent information you wish to retain on the tape folder.

Complete the Recorded Interview Summary as soon as possible after the interview and place it in the claim file.

Basic Workers' Compensation Interview—Claimant

Standard Introduction

Claimant Profile

1. Full name, spell last
2. Residence address, how long? Prior address?
3. Telephone number
4. S.S.#, driver's license #
5. Marital status, dependents, ages, maiden name
6. Spouse's work status and income
7. Birthdate and age
8. Height, weight, hair color

History of Employment With Insured

1. Name and address of employer, title and nature of current job
2. Rate of pay, hours and days per week (gross weekly income)
3. Any other remunerations (room, board, tips, etc.)
4. Concurrent employment/other income
5. Other jobs held at insured
6. Claim form received?
7. Full wages on DOI?

Past Employment (Chronological Order)

1. Name, address of employer
2. Length of employment, dates employed
3. Job title and nature of duties
4. Second job or business
5. "Are you working now?"
6. Off-hours activities (sports/hobbies)
7. Education
8. Other disability or insurance benefits
9. Description of accident
10. Date, time and exact place
11. Describe mechanics of accident (cover-weight lifted, etc.)
12. Describe symptom onset
13. To whom reported and when
14. LDW, dates of lost time
15. Return to work date
16. Witnesses—identify
17. Explore subrogation if applicable

Description of Injury

1. Detailed description of all injuries and symptoms
2. Rule out injuries to all other parts of the body.
3. Who authorized medical treatment?

4. Name, address and telephone of all attending physicians and hospitals where treatment was rendered

5. Physician's statement to claimant re: diagnosis treatment, prognosis

6. X-ray or lab results

7. Any prior injuries or claims? Obtain general medical history.

8. Determine if claimant is right or left handed.

9. Standard closing

Basic Workers' Compensation Interview—Employer

1. Standard introduction

2. Name of interviewee, position and home address

3. Nature of employer's business

4. Identify injured person.

5. Occupation, wages, how long employed?

6. By whom and where was he hired?

7. Description of accident

8. Was accident in course of employment?

9. Was employee performing regular duties?

10. Were any safety rules violated?

11. If so, was rule written, posted or orally given?

12. How was accident verified? Any witnesses? Names.

13. To whom was accident reported, when, by whom?

14. Nature of injuries

15. What medical care was given?

16. When did lost time commence?

17. Is employee continuing to receive regular salary? Did employee receive full wages on DOI?

18. Are there any light duty jobs available? List duties of light duty job and specify if salary changed.

19. Is modified or alternative work available?

20. Will employee be permitted to return to same job at same salary?

21. Any investigation by employer?

22. Any defective equipment, premises, etc. involved?

23. (Consider third-party possibilities.)

24. Standard conclusion

Basic Workers' Compensation Interview—Witness

1. Standard introduction

2. Name, age, address and phone number

3. Name of someone who would always know where to reach you

4. Occupation and capacity in insured's business

5. Any relation to claimant? How long known?

6. Actually witness accident? If not, how soon after did witness arrive at the scene

7. Describe in detail what was seen.

8. How close to claimant?

9. Cause of accident?

10. What was claimant's apparent injury?

11. Did claimant ever complain of prior injuries?

12. Do you know of any other witnesses?

13. Standard conclusion

Claimant Contact Guidelines

Whether or not a recorded statement is taken at the initial call, the following points should be covered and documented:

1. An explanation of benefits

2. How are they feeling?

3. Cover all aspects of how the injury occurred especially if you suspect [the possibility of subrogation]. Was it due to faulty equipment, another person or entity? Obtain as much detailed information as you can.

4. What is the nature and extent of injury, subjective and objective complaints?

5. Are they pleased with their current treatment? (If they aren't and you aren't, now is the time to prepare them for change or consults.)

6. Will surgery be a possibility?

7. When did the doctor tell them they could go back to work? Date? Do they agree?

8. When is the next doctor's appointment? Ask them to call you to let you know. Also, if they have any questions at any time, to call immediately.

9. Prior injury and prior employment history.

This initial contact is very important. Listen to what they have to say and how they express it. Do you detect any anger, problems, negative feelings towards the policyholder, doctor, injury, etc? The information will help in reserving the case and perhaps something can be done immediately to assist the claimant in his/her stressful situation. We are trying to establish rapport and a good foundation for future dealings. It's important to be diplomatic. Put yourself in their shoes. How would you like to be treated if you were the injured party?

Contact With the Treating Doctor

1. Patient history
2. Current history
3. Prior injuries or history of disabilities
4. Diagnosis (objective and subjective symptoms)
5. Causal relationship to history
6. Type of treatment to be rendered
7. Extent of disability to date
8. If fracture, determine type, extent and location.
9. Prognosis
10. Future treatment
11. Extent of future disability
12. Permanency or residuals
13. Bill
14. Amount and date of first treatment
15. Number of treatments, cost and type
16. X-rays
17. Total bill
18. Is all treatment for injury resulting from this accident?

AOE/COE Investigation

1. Full description of normal job duties
2. Full description of duties being performed at the time of the occurrence

3. At whose orders?
4. Under whose supervision?
5. Was the work required by employer's production of service or product?
6. Was there a need for employee to be at that location? Why?
7. What caused the occurrence:
   - Heart attack
   - Dizziness
   - Other
8. What was the result or injuries suffered?
9. Were job duties performed at more than one location? Where? Did they use same route between locations or did they deviate from that route?
10. Did employer supply transportation between locations? What type of transportation?
11. Did employer pay for travel time?
12. Did employer reimburse for travel expense?
13. Any stops between locations? Where? Why?
14. Was employee on overtime?
15. Did employee punch time card?
16. Was employee on call?
17. Was employee actually called to report?
18. Were they exposed to dealing with the public, i.e. policy, meter reader, home delivery, etc.?
19. Assault?
20. How well does the claimant know the suspect?
21. On-the-job contact—sports, drinking, fraternal clubs? Do you work together? In the same department?
22. Cause of dispute—production, tools
23. Location of assault.
24. During job duty hours?
25. How much time between end of shift and assault?
26. Parking lots—was parking lot owned by employer? Maintained by employer? Rented by employer or designated by employer?
27. Lunch or coffee breaks—were lunchroom or cooking facilities provided?
28. Were vending machines provided?

29. Usual to have lunch or coffee off the premises? Restaurant on premises?

30. Was supervisor there?

31. Was employee paid for the time away from premises?

32. Had employee punched out on time clock?

Independent Contractor— Employer Interview

1. Who hired the contractor?

2. Who obtained licenses, if required?

3. Who obtained or paid for any bonds required?

4. Any oral or written contract? Obtain copy.

5. Payroll—how paid, money withheld, expense account or per diem (room and board)?

6. Is contract for piecework? Hourly wage? Salary? Lump sum?

7. Who furnished the tools, materials, clothing, fuel, transportation, etc? Transportation allowance?

8. Who set work hours?

9. Who had right of inspection, supervision, direction of work assignments?

10. Does alleged contractor maintain and pay for separate offices or storage space, repair shop?

11. Business cards or other advertising to work for general public?

12. Who had right to fire?

13. Did subcontractor have right to hire or fire additional help?

14. Did they maintain separate payroll?

15. Do they have a separate retirement fund?

16. Are they working for others under contract at the same time? At other locations? Same type of work?

17. Is subcontractor incorporated?

18. Is subcontractor's work the same type as employer's? (inherent nature)

19. Does claimant report to same work location every day?

Independent Contractor or Employee Status Questionnaire

1. Name, address, telephone number, age, date of birth, social security number.

2. Marital status.

3. Any dependents—give names and address.

4. Date job commenced? Date scheduled to end? Or was it indefinite?

5. What is alleged employer's business? Is the work being done a part of the regular business of the alleged employer?

6. What kind of work was claimant to do? Give description of work.

7. Was there an arrangement for the performance of a certain piece or kind of work at a fixed price? Any oral or written contract? (Obtain copy.)

8. Is such work customarily performed by independent contractors?

9. Was the kind of work the claimant was doing a distinct calling? Did it have an independent nature from the alleged employer's business?

10. Does the claimant hold himself out to the public to be available for the same or similar work?

11. Does the claimant have a contractor's license?

12. Does claimant use stationery or a truck, which advertises his business or services?

13. Does claimant make his own social security payment and filing?

14. How is claimant's name listed in the telephone directory?

15. Is it listed in the classified section?

16. Did the claimant have the right to employ assistants with the right to supervise their activities?

17. Who paid the assistants? Who fixed their wage?

18. Who furnished necessary tools, supplies and materials? Describe the tools, supplies and materials.

19. Who controlled the progress of the work, not counting the final results?

20. Can the workman select his own time for doing the work?

21. How was worker paid—by time (week, day, etc.) or by the job?

22. Has the claimant done any work for the employer before? Was the relationship to cease when the job was finished?

23. Does the alleged employer have a right to terminate the contract at will or does it have to run to completion of the job?

24. Who has control of the premises where the work took place?

25. Does the alleged employer furnish the materials upon which the work is done and receive the output thereof?

26. Does the workman deal with no other person in respect to the output? Was there any supervision of the work?

27. Does the alleged employer have the right to prescribe and furnish the details of the kind and character of work to be done?

28. Anything he wished to add to this report?

Automobile Interview—Injured Worker/Driver

1. Standard introduction.

2. Full name, home and business address. Age, date of birth, marital status and dependents.

3. Wear glasses? Any other physical defects?

4. Occupation, employer, wages, how long employed?

5. Name and address of someone who will always know where to reach you.

6. Driving qualifications, license number.

7. Description of car. Type, year, identification number, color, registration number, speedometer reading.

8. Date, time and direction proceeding. Purpose for which car was being used. Permission (if not named insured).

9. Description of accident locality. Street condition—width, controls, lighting conditions.

10. Passengers' names, addresses and status.

11. Weather conditions (wipers working?).

12. Position of both cars when first seen. Distance to curbs, speed of both cars. Condition and use of brakes. Signals given, use of horn, lights. Attempts to avoid accident.

13. Position of cars before, during and after accident.

14. Name of other operator, address. Names and addresses of passengers in both cars.

15. Description of injuries. If any. Hospital? Doctor? Expenses? Other injury?

16. Skid marks on pavement.

17. Damage to property involved, include points of impact. Description of other car—make, type, year, color, identification number.

18. Witness names and address including police.

19. Report made to police or motor vehicle department.

20. Admission of liability at scene?

Automobile Interview—Witness

1. Standard introduction.

2. Full name, home and business address, occupation, age, date of birth, name of nearest relative.

3. Where was witness at time of accident?

4. Description of accident locality, street condition and construction. Widths, names of streets and directions, grade, visibility, traffic controls, traffic condition.

5. What caused witness to look?

6. Exactly what did witness see and hear? Position all parties involved, before, at time of and after accident.

7. Description of injury. If none, say so.

8. Description of property damage.

9. Know of any other witnesses? Names.

10. Did you know any of the parties involved in accident?

11. Standard conclusion.

Slip and Fall Claim

1. Who owns the property?
2. Floor surface—even, uneven, split level?
3. Type of floor material—tile, concrete, carpet, etc.?
4. Condition of floor—cracks, holes, rips, etc.?
5. Housekeeping—clean, dirty, boxes, etc.? When last mopped and waxed? Who did it? Brand of wax?
6. Foreign material—rocks, water, grease, ice, etc.
7. Stairs—how high was riser? How wide was tread? Handrail—type of construction, condition?
8. Shoes—sole construction, type of tread? Heel—type: high, wedge, flat, etc.? Condition and age of shoes. Who purchased or supplied shoes? Foreign material on shoes? Shoes approved for that work area (i.e., tennis shoes in cooler)?
9. Ladders or stools, and brand name.
10. Owner.
11. Where and when purchased?
12. Type of material or construction.
13. Condition—need repairs; had repairs been made?
14. On wood objects: Had they been painted? When? By whom?
15. Type of surface placed on.
16. Condition of surface.
17. Who placed the ladder or stool there? Was it locked or tied in position? By whom? How?
18. Ladder jacks and boards between ladder jacks—condition? Were they carrying or holding anything?
19. Using tools especially power tools—how did they fall? How far did they fall? How did they land, position? Did they land on anything—tools, materials, rocks, etc.?
20. Falls out of doors.
21. Weather conditions—rain, snow, ice, wind, etc.
22. Snow and ice falls—any cleaning, sanding, salt, etc.
23. Refreezing.

Product—Interview

1. Standard introduction.
2. Name, age, address, marital status, children.
3. Employer, type of work, position, wages. Only employer?
4. Exact date product purchased. By whom?
5. Name and address of seller.
6. Conversation at time of purchase.
7. What was asked for? For what purpose?
8. Any recommendations by sales clerk?
9. Did sales clerk describe function of product?
10. Description of product.
11. How was product stored, used or handled before accident?
12. When was product first used? How often? Anyone else ever use product? How did it function?
13. Was instruction read and followed?
14. Date, time and place of accident.
15. Describe accident in detail.
16. Any witnesses?
17. Describe injuries. (If food or drug, exactly what symptoms occurred and when? Continuing ill effects? List all items consumed for 24 hours prior to illness.)
18. Identify doctors, hospitals and type of treatment. Cost.
19. Any prior accidents, injuries, serious illnesses or allergies?
20. Are you losing time (and wages) from work?
21. Standard conclusion.

Claimant Questionnaire for Back Injuries

The Claimant

1. Name, address, telephone, how long at present address?
2. Social Security Number?
3. Age, date and place of birth, height and weight?
4. Wage, number of hours worked per week?

5. Dependency—marital status

6. Total—describe in detail

7. Partial

8. Previous industrial history

9. Employers past ten years?

10. Type of work done with each—duties on prior jobs?

11. Was work light or heavy?

12. If heavy—was it continuous or intermittent? Describe weights and other factors making the work heavy?

13. Employment record with insured.

14. How long employed with insured?

15. Job title—what work done for insured?

16. Does claimant consider work light or heavy—why?

17. What percent is heavy—how many minutes each hour?

18. Size of weights lifted and dimensions?

19. Amount of bending and/or twisting of the spine involved?

20. Off-hours activities

21. What did claimant do the two or three days preceding work incident? Heavy work at home?

22. Any sports or recreational activities?

23. Any other employment, other job, moonlighting?

The Occurrence

1. Date and hour if definite incident?

2. Did anything unusual happen?

3. What doing when symptoms first noticed? Complete description of the process.

4. Anything in hands at time of symptom onset?

5. Exact mechanism of incident—slip, fall, lift or blow?

6. Describe position of body and analysis of force applied.

7. Description of pain

8. What was noticed?

9. What kind of pain? Sharp? Dull? Severe? Describe.

10. Describe exact site of pain. Any other parts of body involved or hurt in any way? Rule out other parts of body.

11. Pinpoint trauma and limit it.

12. Was there a snap, click or tearing in back?

13. Was there leg pain? Immediate or delayed? Trace exact pain down the leg.

14. Was paresthesia present?

15. Was there inability to straighten up? Temporary paralysis of leg?

16. Description of activities after incident.

17. Immediately—did he quit at once or finish the day?

18. Activities since day of incident?

19. Any lost time—give dates?

20. If losing time—when can you return to work?

Witnesses

1. Name where can be located?

2. The conversation

3. Exactly what was said to fellow workers?

4. What did they say?

5. When reported to the insured? Foreman—or supervisor or nurse?

6. What reported to the insured?

Present Medical

1. Went to doctor and who engaged doctor?

2. Names and addresses of all doctors who examined or treated for this injury?

3. History given to Dr. and Dr.'s statement to claimant regarding condition. When did doctor say claimant could return to work?

4. Were x-rays or lab tests made? When? What were the results? Where?

5. If in hospital get name and address. How long in hospital?

Past Medical

1. Previous health record.

2. Have you ever had similar pain or feeling previously?

3. If so, when (exact date), how did it start, describe the pain or feeling, any medical attention? By whom?

4. Had it completely subsided? Symptom-free period, if any? How long? What caused it to recur?

5. When was last episode?

6. Continuous symptoms since then?

7. How do they compare with present symptoms?

8. Other previous injuries and operations?

9. Previous physical examinations, by whom and results?

10. Any previous back x-rays or lab test?

11. Family doctor's name and address? When did he last see him? Why?

12. Did you ever wear a back brace?

13. General health—colds, flu, rheumatic fever, stiffness pain in joints, swelling of joints, weight loss, fatigue, gout?

14. Any history of cancer?

15. Any local infections such as abscessed teeth, sinusitis, or prostatitis?

16. Are you now taking medication of any type? Describe.

17. Any injury or illness while in armed forces?

18. Seen any doctor in last ten years?

19. Previous claims

20. Kind, against whom, and amount received.

21. Name of carrier.

Third Party

1. Was any third party responsible for the incident, and if so, why?

2. If third party possibility, cover thoroughly.

Return to Work

1. Educational background?

2. Other skills or hobbies?

3. Will employer take claimant back? If so, what kind of favored work is available? Be specific as to job requirements.

Remarks

1. Anything claimant wishes to add?

Claimant Questionnaire for Dermatitis Claims

The Claimant

1. Name, address, telephone, social security number? How long at present address?

2. Age, date and place of birth, height and weight?

3. Wage, number of hours worked per week?

4. Marital status, dependents, ages?

5. Previous industrial history.

6. Employers past ten years?

7. Type of work done with each—describe duties.

8. Employment record with insured?

9. How long employed with insured?

10. Job title—what work done for insured?

11. Describe the materials handled and contacted and duration of time each handled?

12. Any protective clothing or devices of any kind?

13. Any special provisions for cleaning up after work?

14. Showers, soap, creams?

15. Any exposure in the employment environment that may be an irritant?

16. Off-hours activities

17. Any hobbies such as photography, woodworking, sunbathing, hiking, gardening?

18. Use of cosmetics, if any? What kind?

19. Pets? Dogs, horses, cats, etc.?

20. Personal health habits. How often wash, shower?

21. Diet—any special or unusual foods? Any fad dieting?

22. Any home preparation of foods—peeling vegetables, acid foods, fermented foods, canning foods.

23. If necessary, observe claimant's living conditions and other members of the household.

The Occurrence

1. Date and hour dermatitis first noticed?
2. Symptoms.
3. Describe the skin appearance in detail. Parts of body affected?
4. Describe the skin feeling, itching, burning, soreness?
5. Constant or intermittent? When most annoying?
6. Trace the chronology of development of the skin condition from time first noticed to present condition.
7. Any others at work with same condition?
8. Any marital problems? Financial worries? Outside tensions of any kind?
9. Any lost time? Give dates.
10. If losing time, when can return to work?

Witnesses

1. When reported to your supervisor? Plant nurse?
2. When did you first mention or show skin condition to fellow workers or anyone? Names?
3. Repeat conversations about it as well as you can remember.

Present Medical

1. When to doctor and who engaged doctor?
2. Names of all doctors who examined or treated for this skin condition.
3. History given to doctor and doctor's statement to claimant regarding condition and its cause?
4. Any patch or other lab tests made? Results?
5. Has doctor told you that you had too much acid in your system?
6. Has doctor told you when you can return to same type of work?

Past Medical

1. Previous health record.
2. Any previous similar condition?
3. Any previous dermatitis condition of any kind? Get details about onset, time loss, medical treatment, when discharged; condition of skin since discharge, any symptoms free periods, get dates; any recurrences, get dates; condition of skin prior to this flare-up?
4. Any previous patch or allergy tests? Results? When and where taken? By whom?
5. Family doctor's name and address?
6. General health—any long-standing medical problems?
7. Gall bladder? Infections? Any urological problems?
8. Mental problems? Nervousness? Use of tranquilizers?
9. Previous claims
10. Kind, against whom, amount received?
11. Name of carrier.

Third Party

1. Any third party responsible? Why?
2. If material involved, get name and address of manufacturer and distributor.

Return to Work

1. Educational background?
2. Other skills or hobbies?
3. Will employer take claimant back? If so, what kind of work is available? Be specific as to job requirements, particularly as regards the removal of the claimant from the allergen in question.

Remarks

1. Anything claimant wishes to add?

Questionnaire for Hernia Claims

The Claimant

1. Name, address, telephone, social security number?
2. How long at present address?
3. Age, date and place of birth, height and weight?
4. Wage, number of hours worked per week?
5. Dependency—marital status

6. Total—describe in detail
7. Partial
8. Previous industrial history.
9. Employers past ten years.
10. Type of work done with each—duties on prior jobs?
11. Was work light or heavy?
12. If heavy—conditions or intermittent?
13. Employment record with insured
14. How long employed with insured?
15. What work done for insured? Job title?
16. Does claimant consider work light or heavy? Why?
17. What percent is heavy—how many minutes of each hour?
18. Size of weights lifted? Dimensions of weight?

The Occurrence

1. Present injury:
2. What doing when first symptoms noticed? Complete description of process.
3. Anything in hands at time of symptom onset?
4. Was process complete before the pain left?
5. Exact mechanism of accident—slip-fall-lift-blow?
6. Description of pain:
7. What was noticed? Kind of pain or distress sharp—dull?
8. Disability—immediate or when (hour)?
9. Sweat, nausea, vomiting or faint?
10. Any outcry? Immediate rest needed? Touch point of distress?
11. Self-examination:
12. When and where?
13. What seen and found? By whom?
14. Size of protrusion? Location? Reducible by self or on reclining?
15. Complete day's work? Last day worked?
16. Modes of travel to doctor or home following accident?
17. Meals

18. Appetite following herniation. Next meal when?
19. If loss of appetite, why?

Witnesses

1. Name. Where can be located?
2. Conversation:
3. Exactly what said to fellow workers?
4. What did they say?
5. When reported to insured? Foreman? Leadman?
6. Fellow workman?
7. What reported to insured?

Present Medical

1. When to doctor? Who engaged doctor?
2. Name of all doctors who saw claimant for this disability.
3. History to doctor and doctor's statement to claimant about cause. Any VD?
4. Is he wearing a truss? If yes, since when?

Past Medical

1. Previous health record:
2. Injuries and operations—previous health?
3. Previous physical examination.
4. General health—coughs, colds, constipation.
5. Health just prior to onset of pain. Hernias in family?
6. Athletic activity—type and extent?
7. Family doctor's name and address—date of last examination by him.
8. Previous claims?
9. Kind, against whom, amount received?
10. Name of carrier.

Third Party

1. Any other person responsible for injury? How so?
2. Name of responsible party? How can be located?

3. Did claimant have any conversation with responsible party? What was said?

4. If injury ensued after an argument, what caused the argument? Related to work?

Remarks

1. Anything claimant wishes to add?

2. Why does claimant attribute hernia to work?

Questionnaire for Post Traumatic Stress Syndrome

The Claimant

1. Name, address, telephone, social security number? How long at present address?

2. Age, date and place of birth, height and weight?

3. Wage, number of hours worked per week?

4. Dependency—marital status

5. Total—describe in detail

6. Partial

7. Previous industrial history.

8. Employers past ten years?

9. Type of work done with each—duties on prior jobs.

10. Was work strenuous or did it cause tension or worry?

11. If heavy—was it continuous or intermittent? Describe factors making the work strenuous or worrisome.

12. Responsibilities.

13. Employment record with insured.

14. How long employed?

15. Job title—what work done for insured?

16. Does claimant consider work strenuous or worrisome?

17. Give factors, which cause strain or tension or worry?

18. Off-hours activities

19. Home-life happy? Any problems—financial, marital, children?

20. Any sports or recreational activities which might cause worry or excitement?

21. Is there a second job—"moonlighting," home jobs or responsibilities?

The Occurrence

1. Date and hour of incident?

2. What doing when symptoms first noticed? Complete description of process.

3. Exact mechanism of incident—slip, fall, lift or blow?

4. Describe position of body and analysis of force applied.

5. Description of pain.

6. What was noticed?

7. What kind of pain? Sharp? Dull? Severe? Describe.

8. Describe exact site of pain? Any other parts of body involved or hurt in any way? Rule out other parts of body. Pinpoint trauma and limit it.

9. Have you ever had similar pain or feeling previously?

10. Describe.

11. Description of activities after incident.

12. Immediately—did he quit at once or finish the day?

13. Activities since day of incident?

14. Any lost time—give dates.

15. If losing time—when can you return to work?

Witnesses

1. Name, where can be located?

2. The conversation:

3. Exactly what was said to fellow workers?

4. What did they say?

5. When reported to the insured? Foreman or supervisor or nurse?

6. What reported to the insured?

Present Medical

1. When to doctor and who engaged doctor?

2. Names of all doctors who examined or treated for this injury?

3. History given Dr. and Dr.'s statement to claimant regarding condition. When did doctor say claimant could return to work?

4. Were x-rays or lab test made? Where? What were the results?

5. Describe present symptoms? Any sweating, tremors, dizziness, blackouts, nightmares, insomnia, irritability, headaches? Describe exact feelings in detail. How does he relate these to the incident?

Past Medical

1. Previous health record

2. Previous injuries and operations.

3. Previous physical examinations, by who and results?

4. Any previous back x-rays or lab tests?

5. Family doctor's name and address? When did he last see him? Why?

6. General health—cough, colds, flu, rheumatic fever, stiffness, pain in joints, swelling of joints, weight loss, fatigue, gout? Any history of cancer? Any urological or gynecological diseases or symptoms? Focal infections such as abscessed teeth, sinusitis, or prostatitis?

7. If in Veteran's Hospitals, obtain medical release.

8. Any previous mental problems?

9. Any criminal record of any kind? Get details.

10. Previous claims

11. Kind, against whom, and amount received.

12. Name of carrier.

Third Party

1. Was any third party responsible for the incident, and if so, why?

2. If third party possibility, cover thoroughly.

Remarks

1. Anything claimant wishes to add?

2. Why does claimant attribute his condition to his work?

Questionnaire for Heart Claims

The Claimant

1. Name, address, telephone, social security number? How long at present address?

2. Age, date and place of birth, height and weight?

3. Wage, number of hours worked per week?

4. Dependency—marital status

5. Total—describe in detail

6. Partial

7. Previous industrial history.

8. Employers past ten years?

9. Type of work done with each—duties on prior jobs.

10. Was work light or heavy—describe factors making it light or heavy?

11. If heavy—was it continuous or intermittent?

12. Employment record with insured.

13. How long employed with insured?

14. Job title—what work done for insured?

15. Does claimant consider work light or heavy; if so, why?

16. Give factors, which cause strain or tension or worry?

17. Size of weights lifted, and/or dimensions of weight?

18. Off-hours history

19. What did claimant do off work in the two or three days preceding heart incident? Sport activities?

20. Heavy work at home or elsewhere?

21. Any emotional family problems? Sickness of relatives? Financial problems? Marital problems?

22. Trace off-duty time by hour up to time of heart incident?

The Occurrence

1. If specific incident, give date and hour. Location?

2. What doing when first symptoms noticed—complete description of the process.

3. Anything in hands at time symptom onset?

4. Exact mechanism of accident—slip, fall, lift or a blow?

5. Description of pain:

6. What was noticed?

7. What kind of pain—steady, intermittent?

8. Activity causes it to reappear? Symptom-free period—get details about severity, frequency and site(s).

9. Disability immediate or when (hour)?

10. Faint or nausea?

11. Immediate rest needed?

12. Was there any excessive physical exertion?

13. On day of occurrence or prior to day of occurrence trace employee's activities by hours from time he left home the morning of attack to hour of attack.

14. Give details about exact work he did accounting for all time up to hour of attack. Compare activity that day with other days.

15. Is this your usual work?

16. Any excessive mental strain?

17. On the day of the occurrence or prior?

18. Was there any rush work causing both physical and mental strain? Pressure to meet a deadline or too much work?

Witnesses

1. Name, where can be located?

2. The conversation

3. Exactly what was said to fellow workers?

4. What did they say?

5. When reported to the insured—foreman, leadman or fellow workmen?

6. What reported to the insured?

7. Verify exact work activities on hour by hour basis as described by employee with supervisor, leadman, co-workers or other observers.

Present Medical

1. When to doctor and who engaged doctor? Any first aid such as plant M.D., or nurse?

2. Names of all doctors who saw the claimant for this disability.

3. History to doctor and doctor's statement to claimant regarding condition.

4. If an electrocardiogram and x-rays were taken, where?

5. What were the results?

Past Medical

1. Previous health record

2. Prior injuries and operation?

3. Previous physical examination, by whom, and results?

4. Any prior EKGs, when, by whom and results?

5. Family doctor's name and address? When did he last see him?

6. General health—cough, colds, indigestion, heartburn, and prior pain in rib cage area.

7. Health just prior to onset of pain.

8. Athletic activity, the type and extent.

9. Previous claims

10. Kind, against whom, and amount received.

11. Name of carrier.

12. Previous family history

13. Has any member in family bloodline, such as father, mother, grandparents or siblings, had heart attacks or heart problems of any kind?

14. Get name of doctor who treated these relatives.

15. Seen any other doctors in past ten years?

Third Party

1. Was any other person responsible for this disability, and if so, why?

2. If third-party possibility, cover thoroughly.

Return To Work

1. Educational background?

2. Other skills or hobbies?

3. Will employer take claimant back? If so, what kind of favored work is available? Be specific as to job requirements.

Remarks

1. Anything claimant wishes to add?
2. Why does claimant attribute his condition to work?

Questionnaire for Mental Stress Claims

The Claimant

1. Name, address, telephone, social security number? How long at present address?
2. Age, date and place of birth, height and weight?
3. Wage, number of hours worked per week?
4. Dependency—marital status
5. Total—describe in detail
6. Partial
7. Previous industrial history.
8. Employers past ten years?
9. Job titles, with a full description of all work performed.
10. Comment on whether the work was strenuous and whether it caused tension or worry.
11. Employment record with policyholder.
12. How long employed with insured?
13. Job title?
14. What work done for insured? Trace each job and its duties including responsibilities. If the claimant was a supervisor, discuss fully the processes and number of people supervised. Comment on changes of processes and staffing. Hours and pressures of work, if any?
15. Disagreements with supervisors, co-workers or subordinates? Union grievances filed and results of same? Ratings of employee's job performance?
16. Specifically identify stresses, strains and tensions of the job.

The Occurrence

1. What doing when symptoms first noticed? Date and hour?
2. What were symptoms? Describe in detail.
3. When did disability begin—loss of time or transfer to other work?
4. Have claimant describe in detail the pressures and/or harassments, which he alleges, caused his mental problems.

Witnesses

1. Name, where can be located?
2. Conversations—what was said to fellow employees and their replies?
3. When reported to the insured—to what individual?
4. What was reported to the insured?

Present Medical

1. When to current treating doctor and who engaged this doctor?
2. Names and addresses of all doctors who saw claimant for this condition?
3. History claimant gave doctor and doctor's statements to claimant regarding the condition?
4. Any hospitalization or confinement? Where?

Past Problems

1. Past record—any symptoms or problems during elementary school, high school, college or other advanced education?
2. Service record—medical discharge?
3. Previous exams or consultations with psychiatrists or psychologists? Names and addresses?
4. Mental problems of any kind as a child or while living at home?
5. Previous physical exams, by whom and results.
6. Family doctor's name and address? When did claimant last see him? What for?

Current Problems

1. Any divorces or separations in present marriage?
2. Consideration of same? What about past marriages?
3. Seeing a marriage counselor or lawyer? Who?

4. Any problems with children? Delinquency or marriage?

5. Any financial problems? Debits or mortgages coming due?

6. Working more than one job? If so, get details.

7. Any criminal charges—past or present?

Previous Claims

1. Kind, against whom, and amount received?

2. Name of the carrier.

3. This includes allegations of physical injury, mental injury, harassment, discrimination or violation of civil rights.

Return to Work

1. Educational background?

2. Other skills or hobbies?

3. Will insured take claimant back? If so, what kind of favored work is available? Be specific as to job requirements.

4. What other kind of work can you do?

Remarks

1. Anything claimant wishes to add?

Questionnaire for Head Injury Claims

The Claimant

1. Name, address, telephone, how long at present address?

2. Social security number?

3. Age, date and place of birth, height and weight?

4. Wage, number of hours worked per week?

5. Dependency—marital status

6. Total—describe in detail

7. Partial

8. Previous industrial history.

9. Employers past ten years?

10. Job titles—duties on prior jobs?

11. Employment with policyholder.

12. How long employed with insured?

13. Job title?

14. What work done for insured—describe duties?

15. Does he have to work climbing ladders, scaffolds; or does he work on the ground?

The Occurrence

1. Date and hour of injury?

2. What doing when injury occurred—describe?

3. If injury caused by fall:

4. From where and what distance did he fall?

5. Did he strike anything on the way down?

6. What did he land on? Describe the surface in detail.

7. Specifically what part of his body struck first?

8. Exactly what caused the fall? Be certain to clarify whether the fall was caused by a slip, or by the claimant just getting dizzy and/or blacking out.

9. If injury caused by falling object:

10. From where and what distance did it fall?

11. How heavy was the object?

12. Describe object as to shape and bulk.

13. Specifically what part of his head did it strike, or did the object strike another part of his body and the force of the impact then knock his head into some other object or surface?

14. Was he unconscious? If so, for how long?

15. Did he raise himself from the fall without assistance?

16. Did he bleed from his mouth, nose or ear?

17. Were there marks on his face or head?

18. Scratches? Bruises? Describe.

19. Did he speak coherently following the accident?

20. Was he able to walk unaided?

21. Last day worked? Last day paid?

22. When can he return to work? Has he discussed with the insured?

Witnesses

1. Name, address, including not only actual witnesses but also positional witnesses.
2. Conversations
3. Exactly what was said to fellow workers—identify.
4. When and what reported to insured, and to whom reported?

Present Medical

1. Went to doctor and who engaged doctor?
2. Names and addresses of all doctors who examined or treated for this injury?
3. History given to doctor and doctor's statement to claimant regarding condition, and when he can return to work?
4. If lab test or x-rays were taken, when? What were the results?
5. Where?
6. If in hospital, name and address? How long in hospital?

Past Medical

1. Previous health record
2. Previous injuries, operations, blackouts, instances of dizziness, and physical exams?
3. Was the claimant taking medication at the time of the accident? Get specifics on drug(s), dosage, reason for same, and determine who prescribed same.
4. Family doctor's name and address. When did he last see him?
5. Was there a pre-employment examination?
6. Previous claims
7. Kind, against whom, and amount received.
8. Name of carrier.
9. Any prior permanent disability ratings?
10. Any injury or illness in armed forces?

Third Party

1. Did someone else cause the injury—drop the object that fell or caused him to fall?
2. Get name of employer or third party. Investigate all possibilities fully, especially other contractors on the same job.

Return to Work

1. Educational background?
2. Other skills or hobbies?
3. Will insured take claimant back? If so, what kind of favored work is available? Be specific as to job requirements.
4. What other kind of work can you do?

Remarks

1. Anything claimant wishes to add?

Questionnaire for Eye Injuries

The Claimant

1. Name, address, telephone, social security number? How long at present address?
2. Age, date and place of birth, height and weight?
3. Wage, number of hours worked per week?
4. Dependency—marital status
5. Total—describe in detail
6. Partial
7. Previous industrial history.
8. Employers past ten years?
9. Type of work done with each—duties of prior jobs.
10. Employment record with insured:
11. How long employed with insured?
12. What work done for insured? Job title?

The Occurrence

1. Date and hour of incident?
2. Exact description of what was being done when alleged injury occurred?
3. When did disability start?
4. Did anything strike the eyeball? What?
5. Did anyone examine the eyeball? Who? When?
6. What observations were made?

7. Was a foreign body removed? If so, was it removed?

8. Describe foreign body removed.

9. If detached retina, develop the following:

10. Exact time (day and hour) when visual loss was discovered.

11. How was it discovered? What doing when it became evident?

12. To whom did he report it and what did he tell that person?

13. If the visual loss is attributed to a lift, jar, bump or blow secure the details about the exact time of that event, the mechanism involved, and spell out the severity of it.

14. Also identify the symptom, if any, observed at the time of the event up to the time of the first recognition of visual loss.

15. If there was a symptom-free period give the exact dates.

16. Cover outside activities prior to the work-connected incident alleged to the time that visual loss was observed.

17. What outside activities embraced lifting, bumps, blows or jars?

18. Was process complete before pain or irritation felt?

19. What were first symptoms noticed? When? Describe.

20. Complete day's work?

Witnesses

1. Name, address (residence and/or business address) where witness may be contacted.

2. Conversation:

3. Exactly what was said to fellow workers?

4. What did they say?

5. When reported to insured? Foreman or lead man or fellow workmen or both.

6. What was the conversation when reported to insured?

Present Medical

1. When to doctor? Who engaged doctor?

2. Name of all doctors who saw claimant for this disability.

3. Hospitalized? If so, by whom?

4. Describe present symptoms in detail?

5. History given to doctor, and doctor's statement to employee about condition.

Past Medical

1. Previous health record:

2. Any trouble with eyes in past? If so, where and when?

3. Ever draw compensation for a previous eye injury?

4. If so, when.

5. Any other previous claims?

6. Any prior eye examinations? Any pre-employment eye exam?

7. Do you now wear glasses?

8. How long have you worn glasses?

9. Name any doctor, or doctors, who have examined eyes.

10. When?

11. Name of doctor who filled prescriptions for glasses? When?

12. Any prior or present history of diabetes, kidney, heart or circulatory disease? (If so, details with names of doctors, etc.)

Third Party

1. Any other person responsible for injury? How so?

2. Name of responsible party? Where can responsible party be located?

3. Did claimant have any conversation with responsible party? What was said?

4. If injury ensued after an argument, what caused the argument? Related to work?

5. If machine involved, describe.

Remarks

1. Anything claimant wishes to add?

2. Was claimant furnished with goggles and instructions for their use?

3. Why does claimant attribute eye condition to work?

Questionnaire for Hearing Loss Due to Industrial Noise

The Claimant

1. Name, address, telephone, social security number? How long at present address?
2. Age, date and place of birth, height and weight?
3. Wage, number of hours worked per week?
4. Dependency—marital status
5. Total—describe in detail
6. Partial
7. Previous industrial history.
8. Employers for entire work history?
9. Type of work done with each—duties on prior jobs.
10. Amount of noise in each as compared to present job?
11. Any pre-employment examinations including audiograms?
12. Employment record with insured.
13. How long employed with the policyholder? Give dates.
14. Job title—what work done for insured?
15. Describe the noisiness of each area, and how much time per day he spends in such area.
16. Types of machines operated for the insured and their relative noisiness. Distance he worked from those machines.

The Occurrence

1. Describe work place—area—size—any protective devices or equipment? Any instruction in their use?
2. When first noticed any loss of hearing?
3. Whom did he tell about it?
4. When first believed it was connected with the job? Why?
5. Any others working there who have same condition?
6. Any trouble hearing TV or radio?
7. Any trouble hearing bosses' orders or conversation with fellow workmen?
8. Any other symptoms besides loss of hearing— tinnitus—dizziness—headaches?
9. Any exposure to noise outside of work—other employment, family recreational activities?

Witnesses

1. When first reported to insured? Plant Nurse?
2. What history given insured or nurse?
3. When first told fellow workers? What told them?

Present Medical

1. When to doctor and who engaged doctor?
2. Names of all doctors who examined or treated for this ear condition?
3. History given to doctor and doctor's statement to claimant regarding condition?
4. What did doctor say caused condition?
5. Were audiograms or other lab test made? Where? What were the results?

Past Medical

1. Previous health record.
2. Any injuries or operations?
3. Have you ever had any similar trouble in the past? Where? When?
4. Have you ever been subjected to:
5. Pressure work
6. Explosion
7. Blasting
8. Any war experience near gunfire?
9. Have you ever had any hearing tests? Where and when?
10. Mother or father deaf? Any other deaf relatives?
11. Any deaf mute schooling?
12. Prior physical exams? When? Where?
13. Family doctor?
14. Have you ever had a physical injury to your head? If so, when and to what part of your head?
15. Ever have a ruptured eardrum?
16. Ever have physical exams at school? What school?

17. Ever have scarlet fever, Lues, Alcoholism, or infection of the ear?

18. General health—taking any medicines? Ever have streptomycin treatment for TB? Ever have any other infections?

19. Previous claims

20. Kind, against whom, and amount received.

21. Name of carrier.

Third Party

1. Any other person responsible for disability?

2. Any machinery of any kind responsible?

Remarks

1. Anything claimant wishes to add?

2. Why does claimant attribute his condition to work?

Questionnaire for Cancer Claims

The Claimant

1. Name, address, telephone, social security number? How long at present address?

2. Age, date and place of birth, height and weight?

3. Wage, number of hours worked per week?

4. Dependency—marital status

5. Total—describe in detail

6. Partial

7. Previous industrial history.

8. Employers past ten years?

9. Type of work done with each—duties on prior jobs.

10. Employment record with insured.

11. How long employed with insured?

12. Job title—what work done for insured?

13. Does claimant consider work light or heavy—why?

14. Off-hours activities

15. What did claimant do the two or three days preceding work incident? Heavy work at home?

16. Any sports or recreational activities?

17. Any hobbies such as photography, sunbathing, hiking, chemistry, woodworking?

18. Use of tobacco? Alcohol? Describe.

19. Any activity involving repetitive use, pressure or blows to the involved part? If so, describe activity in detail, and establish time and severity, and frequency of it.

The Occurrence

1. Date and hour of incident?

2. What doing when symptoms first noticed? Complete description of process.

3. Exact mechanism of incident—slip, fall, lift or blow?

4. Describe position of body and analysis of force applied.

5. Description of pain.

6. What was noticed?

7. What kind of pain? Sharp? Dull? Severe? Describe.

8. Describe exact site of pain? Any other parts of body involved or hurt in any way? Rule out other parts of body. Pinpoint trauma and limit it.

9. Ever had similar pain or feeling previously?

10. Description of activities after incident.

11. Immediately—did he quit at once or finish the day?

12. Activities since day of incident?

13. Any lost time—give dates.

14. If losing time—when can you return to work?

Witnesses

1. Name, where can be located?

2. The conversation

3. Exactly what was said to fellow workers?

4. What did they say?

5. When reported to the insured? Foreman or supervisor or nurse?

6. What reported to the insured?

Present Medical

1. When to doctor and who engaged doctor?
2. Names of all doctors who examined or treated for this injury?
3. History given to doctor and doctor's statement to claimant regarding condition. When did doctor say claimant could return to work?
4. Were x-rays or lab tests made? Where? What were the results?
5. When did you first notice symptoms of cancer? Lump? Soreness?
6. How long after the trauma? Describe its appearance and development.

Past Medical

1. Previous health record
2. Previous injuries and operations.
3. Previous physical examinations, by whom and results?
4. Any previous back x-rays or lab tests?
5. Family doctor's name and address? When did he last see him? Why?
6. General health—cough, colds, flu, stiffness, pain in joints, swelling of joints, weight loss, fatigue.
7. Any history of cancer? Any urological or gynecological diseases or symptoms? Any focal infections such as abscessed teeth, sinusitis, or prostatitis?
8. In armed forces? Veteran's hospital? Get records from VA
9. Family history of cancer?
10. Ever had any similar pain, soreness, swelling, lump or discoloration previously? Secure the details about type, when, site.
11. Previous claims
12. Kind, against whom, and amount received?
13. Name of carrier.

Third Party

1. Was any third party responsible for the incident, and if so, why?
2. If third party possibility, cover thoroughly?

Remarks

1. Anything claimant wishes to add?
2. Why does claimant attribute his condition to his work?

Questionnaire for Major Amputations

The Claimant

1. Name, address, telephone, social security number? How long at present address?
2. Age, date and place of birth, height and weight?
3. Wage, number of hours worked per week?
4. Dependency—marital status
5. Total—describe in detail
6. Partial
7. Previous industrial history.
8. Employers past ten years?
9. Type of work done with each—duties on prior jobs?
10. Employment record with insured.
11. How long employed with insured?
12. Job title?
13. What work done for insured? Describe.

The Occurrence

1. Present injury.
2. Date and hour of injury?
3. What doing when injury occurred? Describe.
4. Exact mechanism of injury?
5. If any pain at site of amputation, describe.
6. What is noticed?
7. Steady or intermittent? Symptom free—get details of severity, frequency and site or sites?
8. Disability—immediate? When?
9. Last day worked? Last date paid? Return to work?

Witnesses

1. Name, where can be located, address?
2. Who was in vicinity at time of occurrence?
3. Conversation?
4. Exactly what was said to fellow workers—identify.
5. When reported to insured—foreman, supervisor, nurse, etc.?
6. What reported?

Present Medical

1. When to doctor and who engaged doctor?
2. Names and addresses of all doctors who treated or examined for this injury?
3. History given to doctor and doctor's statement to claimant regarding condition and when he can return to work? This should include any recommendations by the doctor for light duties or modified work.
4. If lab tests or x-rays were taken, when? What were the results? Where?
5. If in hospital, get name and address?
6. How long in hospital?
7. Prosthesis needed? What arrangement for any instruction in use?

Past Medical

1. Previous health record.
2. Previous injuries and operations? Additionally, comment upon whether there were residuals from these previous injuries and operations, which would have comprised a partial disability at the time of our accident, and also whether the insured was aware of this partial disability prior to our accident. How about prior to the date that the claimant was hired?
3. Previous amputations?
4. Previous physical examinations. By whom and results?
5. Family doctor's name and address? When did he last see him?
6. Was there a pre-employment examination?

7. Previous claims.
8. Kind, against whom, and amount received?
9. Name and carrier.
10. Any prior permanent disability rating? Any prior injuries to amputated limb?
11. Any injury or illness while in armed forces?

Third Party

1. Machinery.
2. Who instructed you in use of machine and how much instruction given you?
3. How long have you been operating machine?
4. Was there a safety device on machine? Was it functioning properly?
5. Who owned the machine? What make is it? Serial and/or model number?
6. How old is it?
7. Who manufactured and installed machine? Any alterations on it?
8. Who performed maintenance? Obtain copy of maintenance log.
9. Did some malfunction of machine cause the injury?
10. Photograph and diagram of machine.
11. Third person
12. Did someone else cause the injury?
13. Were you working with someone else on the machine? Who? Was he a fellow employer or employed by someone else?

Return to Work

1. Educational background?
2. Other skills or hobbies?
3. Will insured take claimant back? If so, what kind of favored work is available? Be specific as to job requirements.
4. What other kind of work can you do?

Remarks

1. Anything claimant wishes to add?

Questionnaire for Dependency Claims

1. Name, permanent address, telephone, age, date of birth, where born.
2. Where and when married to the deceased—adjuster should view marriage certificate or obtain copy.
3. Any divorce proceedings or separation in present marital setup?
4. Any prior marriages of claimant?
5. Date and place (city and county)?
6. Children by that marriage, age of children, married, address, adoption?
7. Obtain copies of birth certificates.
8. Divorced—when and where (city and county)?
9. Any prior marriages of deceased?
10. Date and place (city and county)?
11. Children by that marriage, age of children, married, address, adoption? Obtain copies of birth certificates.
12. Divorced—when and where (city and county)? Any alimony or support payments of any kind?
13. Names, addresses, ages of any children born out of wedlock?
14. Obtain copies of birth certificates.
15. Names, address, ages of any dependents who are dependents, because of a disability, either mental or physical—describe.
16. Common law marriages
17. Where is the relationship alleged to have been entered into?
18. All jurisdictions in which the couple lived together and dates they lived there.
19. Why no ceremony performed? If one was performed later, give circumstances.
20. Did couple hold themselves out as husband and wife?
21. Did others in the locality recognize them as husband and wife? Get names and addresses of neighbors so believing.
22. Did they ever intend to have a genuine ceremonial wedding?
23. When did they intend or agree to be husband and wife?
24. Other dependents
25. Exact relationship to deceased.
26. Amount of payments and method of payments?
27. Get breakdown of household expenses?
28. Regularity of contributions?
29. Any written record or cancelled checks?
30. Who else contributes and how much to this person's support?
31. What assets does dependent have? Bank account real estate personal property stock and bonds, pension funds, social security?
32. How much is funeral bill? Has it been paid?
33. Any outstanding medical bills? Paid?

Remarks

1. Anything claimant wishes to add?

We hope this discussion assists you. It is intended to present you with information about case law and other authority applicable to the interpretation of the relevant insurance policy provisions. Every effort has been made to ensure that the information provided is accurate. However, the opinions expressed here are for internal use only. They do not constitute a substitute for legal advice as to the law of a particular jurisdiction as applied in the full factual context of a particular claim.

The opinions expressed in this discussion are those of the staff of the Property Loss Research Bureau/Liability Insurance Research Bureau and do not necessarily represent the opinions of the membership. The opinions of the staff of the Bureau do not represent an indication or prediction of any future action or position of any member insurer. You should consult with your company's management to determine your company's positions on the issues discussed.

Confidentiality Notice

Property Loss Research Bureau/Liability Insurance Research Bureau members may reproduce this material or any portion of it for the exclusive use of their employees. Any other reproduction or distribution of this material or any portion of it without the express written consent of the Bureau is strictly prohibited.

Members shall hold all information including publications, educational materials, and opinions received from the Bureau, in strict confidence. Every communication from the Bureau is confidential unless it is specifically stated therein that it is not.

Members shall not divulge any information furnished to them by the Bureau to any person who is not an officer or employee of the member without specific written permission of the Bureau. No member may furnish information originally received from the Bureau to any organization affiliated with the member, unless the member possesses a letter from the Bureau Chair, written on authority of resolution of the Bureau's Board of Directors, specifically authorizing the member to furnish information to such organization.

Key Words and Phrases

Define or describe each of the words and phrases listed below.

Legal liability (p. 3.4)

Constitutional law (p. 3.4)

Statutory law (p. 3.4)

Common law, or case law (p. 3.5)

Tort (p. 3.6)

Tortfeasor (p. 3.6)

Negligence (p. 3.6)

Vicarious liability (p. 3.7)

Contributory negligence (p. 3.7)

Comparative negligence (p. 3.8)

Strict liability (p. 3.8)

Intentional tort (p. 3.8)

Contractual liability (p. 3.9)

Statutory liability (p. 3.9)

Coinsurance (p. 3.16)

Catastrophe serial number (p. 3.17)

Sworn statement (p. 3.23)

Direct question (p. 3.30)

Open-ended question (p. 3.32)

Leading question (p. 3.33)

Scope (p. 3.49)

Replacement cost (p. 3.50)

Actual cash value (ACV) (p. 3.50)

Fair market value (p. 3.52)

Advance payment (p. 3.53)

Review Questions

1. How is legal liability different from criminal liability? (pp. 3.3–3.4)

2. What are the three sources of law in the United States? (p. 3.4)

3. Identify the elements of negligence, and illustrate each element in the context of a single example. (pp. 3.6–3.7)

4. Identify the two types of contractual obligations that may give rise to liability claims covered by insurance. (p. 3.9)

5. Give two examples of statutory liability and explain why the statutes may have been enacted. (pp. 3.9–3.10)

6. What specific claim information can be found on a loss notice form? (pp. 3.11–3.21)

7. What information can a claim representative obtain from a preliminary review of the policy? (p. 3.22)

8. Why would a claim representative take a statement from an insured, claimant, or witness during a claim investigation? (p. 3.23)

9. Describe the four qualities of an effective statement. (p. 3.23)

10. What are the advantages and disadvantages of the following forms
    of statements? (pp. 3.25–3.29)

    a. Recorded statements

    b. Written statements

11. Describe the content of a statement using the seven-part method.
    (pp. 3.29–3.30)

12. Give two examples of situations requiring special considerations
    when taking a statement and, for each, describe the steps the
    claim representative should take to ensure the statement is valid.
    (pp. 3.34–3.35)

13. Explain why diagrams, photos, and videos are important tools for
    a claim representative in claim handling. (pp. 3.35–3.36)

14. Describe three expectations a claim representative may have of an expert hired to assist with a claim. (pp. 3.37–3.38)

15. Identify two experts who might be hired for each of the following types of claims and explain why they might be retained. (pp. 3.38–3.41)

    a. A clothing store suffers a serious fire loss.

    b. A claimant is seriously injured in an auto accident.

16. What types of records and reports are found in bodily injury claims? (pp. 3.41–3.42)

17. How are the following used to detect fraud? (pp. 3.42–3.44)

    a. Industry databases

b. Internet

c. Other investigative tools

18. What investigation should a claim representative perform to
    determine the cause of loss in an auto physical damage claim?
    (p. 3.45)

19. Why is it important to verify the Vehicle Identification Number
    (VIN)? (pp. 3.45–3.46)

20. In general, what documentation should a claim representative
    include in an auto physical damage claim file? (pp. 3.46–3.47)

21. How does the investigation of the cause of loss differ between a property damage claim other than auto and an auto physical damage claim? (p. 3.49)

22. Why would a claim representative be concerned about determining liability in a first-party claim? (p. 3.50)

23. Explain the difference between replacement cost and actual cash value in relation to determining the amount of damage in a property damage claim. (p. 3.50)

24. What statements and documentation would a claim representative use in determining the cause of loss of a bodily injury claim? (p. 3.54)

25. How does a claim representative determine liability for a bodily injury claim? (pp. 3.54–3.55)

26. What must a claim representative do to verify special damages?
    (p. 3.55)

27. What types of damages are considered future damages? (p. 3.56)

28. What are the three elements used when valuing pain and
    suffering? (p. 3.57)

29. What questions must a claim representative answer to determine
    whether a claim is compensable under a workers' compensation
    statute? (p. 3.60)

30. What documentation would a claim representative obtain in a
    workers' compensation claim? (p. 3.60)

31. What benefits are payable under a workers' compensation statute? (p. 3.61)

Application Questions

1. While driving his delivery truck, Tom fails to see a stop sign and hits Pete's car broadside. The police arrive at the scene and determine that Tom does not have a valid driver's license. It has been suspended for a drunk driving conviction. They also charge him with driving under the influence of alcohol (DUI). While attempting to remove the vehicles from the intersection, the tow truck operator is overcome by fumes escaping from the back of Tom's delivery truck. The fumes were caused by the escape of a hazardous chemical that Tom was transporting to a customer. The tow truck operator has to be hospitalized as a result of inhaling the fumes. Tom and Pete are also taken to the hospital, each complaining of neck and back pain.

   Because of the accident, Tom fails to deliver the chemical to the buyer by 10 AM, as per the contract of sale. The buyer notifies Tom's employer that they have obtained the chemical from another source at a higher price because of the need for expedited delivery, and they expect to be reimbursed for this expense.

   Identify the bases for legal liability found in this case. Support your answer with facts from the case.

2. Belinda is a claim representative for XYZ Insurance Company. She receives a claim assignment from her supervisor. The claim is a bodily injury claim that resulted from a slip and fall in a supermarket. Using this information, explain what investigative tools Belinda might use to determine the following information:

   • Insured contact information

   • Claimant contact information

- General description of the accident
- Covered loss location
- Policy limits for this loss location
- Store manager's account of what happened
- Depiction of the loss location
- Maintenance record for the loss location
- Medical necessity of treatment
- Nature and extent of any preexisting medical condition
- Extent of rehabilitation necessary
- Claimant's prior injuries and/or prior claims

3. Jim is a claim representative trainee with ABC Insurance Company. As part of the training program, Jim will be asked to handle different types of claims. Jim has already received some training in the general investigative tools available to a claim representative but is confused about are the similarities and differences among the different claims.

a. Describe the similarities and differences in the investigation of cause of loss, liability, and amount of damage for an auto physical damage claim and a property damage claim other than auto.

b. Describe the similarities and differences in the investigation of cause of loss, liability, and amount of damages for a bodily injury liability claim and a workers' compensation claim.

Answers to Assignment 3 Questions

NOTE: These answers are provided to give students a basic understanding of acceptable types of responses. They often are not the only valid answers and are not intended to provide an exhaustive response to the questions.

Review Questions

1. Criminal liability or responsibility arises from laws that apply to wrongful acts that society deems so harmful to the public welfare that the government takes responsibility for prosecuting and punishing the wrongdoers. In contrast, legal liability arises from civil law, which is based on the rights and responsibilities of citizens with respect to one another and applies to legal matters not governed by criminal law. Civil law governs liability for civil wrongs against people, entities, or property, which include negligent acts, intentional acts, and strict liability. Civil law also governs liability for breach of contract.

2. The three sources of law in the United States are the following:

   (1) The Constitution, which is the source of constitutional law

   (2) Legislative bodies, which are the source of statutory law

   (3) Court decisions, which are the source of common law

3. The elements of negligence are (1) duty of care owed, (2) breach of the duty of care, (3) proximate cause, and (4) actual injury or damage.

   The following example illustrates each element: A pedestrian is injured when he falls into a hole in the sidewalk. The concrete contractor performing repairs to the sidewalk owed a duty to the public to warn them of this danger, including blocking off the area of sidewalk under repair. The fact that the pedestrian fell and was injured indicates that the precautions, if any, taken by the contractor were ineffective.

4. The two types of contractual obligations that may be related to insurance claims are the following:

   (1) Assumptions of liability stated in the contract: A landowner contracts with a contractor for repair work and insists that the contractor assume all liability for the work.

   (2) Warranties stated in the contract: The manufacturer of infant pajamas guarantees that the fabric will not burn.

5. Two examples of statutory liability are no-fault auto laws and workers' compensation laws. These examples of statutory liability were enacted to ensure adequate compensation for injuries without disputes over who is at fault. They help reduce the number of lawsuits filed.

6. All loss notice forms contain information about the producer, the insured, and the policy as well as a description of the loss. Depending on the type of loss form, it may contain information on injured parties or damaged property.

7. From a preliminary review of the policy, the claim representative can learn the following:
   • Who is covered
   • What is covered
   • When coverage is in effect
   • What causes of loss are covered
   • What is excluded

8. The claim representative would take a statement to gather information for claim decision making and to memorialize the facts and loss circumstances as remembered by the interviewee. If necessary, the statement can later be used to challenge the testimony of the individual who furnished a statement and then changes the account of the loss.

9. The following are the four qualities of an effective statement:

    (1) Coherent—it follows a logical sequence.

    (2) Complete—it is thorough for the circumstances.

    (3) Objective—it reflects events as the interviewee remembers them.

    (4) Factual—it does not contain immaterial opinions.

10. a. Advantages of recorded statements are as follows:

    - They are less time-consuming.
    - If done in person, the interviewee can be observed.
    - Exact wording is recorded.
    - Illegible handwriting is not an issue.
    - Telephone interviews save time.
    - Can be transcribed if needed.

    Disadvantages of recorded statements are as follows:

    - The equipment may fail.
    - Tapes must be stored.
    - Transcription adds cost.
    - Transcript must be reviewed for accuracy.

    b. Advantages of written statements are as follows:

    - Interviewees may be less anxious.
    - Claim representative has more control of situation.
    - Transcription is not required.
    - Interviewees may be more willing to sign the statement because they can see it.
    - Claim representative has the opportunity to evaluate the interviewee as a witness.

    Disadvantages of written statements are as follows:

    - Handwriting may be illegible.
    - It takes more time.
    - Interviewees may claim they were misquoted.
    - Paraphrasing may lead to challenges of inaccuracy.

11. The following are the seven parts of a statement's content are:

    (1) Permission and introduction—the date, time, and location of the interview; names of the parties involved in the interview; and an affirmation from the interviewee that the interview is given with permission

    (2) Identification—identifying information about the person being interviewed, such as name, address, phone number, Social Security number, and driver's license number

    (3) Setting—answers to questions such as who was involved in the loss, what was involved in the loss when the loss occurred, where the loss occurred, and why the loss occurred

    (4) Incident—a step-by-step description of how the loss occurred

(5) Post incident injuries/damages—a description of the property damage and bodily injury to individuals

(6) Miscellaneous—any information the interviewee may want to add

(7) Conclusion—a reaffirmation that the statement was taken with permission

12. Any of the following are acceptable answers related to special considerations when taking a statement:

- Hospitalized interviewee. Claim representatives must be familiar with state laws about taking statements from hospitalized people. Many jurisdictions prohibit or restrict taking statements from those hospitalized because these people may be taking medication, may be in pain, or suffering from stress. Claim representatives should also respect the wishes of the family of a hospitalized person when scheduling and taking the statement.

- Illiterate interviewee. If a person cannot read or write, the claim representative should consider a recorded statement. If a recorded statement is not feasible, the claim representative can write out a statement for the interviewee, taken in the presence of a disinterested third party. The disinterested party can read the statement to the interviewee and attest that it accurately reflects the interviewee's words. A special notation replaces the signature of an illiterate person. The disinterested party also provides a statement verifying that the party has read the written statement to the interviewee and that the interviewee acknowledges that the statement is true by making a special notation.

- Minor interviewee. Claim representatives must know whether state law allows minors to give a statement. Most states require the claim representative to obtain permission from the minor's parent or guardian before interviewing the minor. Some states require the parent or guardian be present during the interview of a minor under a certain age.

- Foreign language interviewee. When taking a statement from someone who speaks only a foreign language or who has limited understanding of the claim representative's language, the claim representative must arrange for an interpreter to assist with the statement. The claim representative should obtain the interpreter's contact information should he or she be needed to testify in court. The claim representative should give the interpreter instructions as to how the interview will be conducted. At the conclusion, the interpreter should read the entire statement to the interviewee to confirm that it is correct. Then both the interviewee and the interpreter should sign it.

13. Diagrams, photos, and videos are used to illustrate what a loss scene looks like, how an accident happened, and the extent of property damage and bodily injury. They can be used to document ownership of an item that is missing. They can provide evidence of insurance fraud.

14. A claim representation may expect an expert to do the following (any of the following are acceptable answers):

- Document the investigation

- Reconstruct the event or product that caused the loss

- Eliminate other potential causes of loss

- Demonstrate the link between the cause and the resulting damage or injury

- Prepare a report of the investigation

- Preserve the evidence

15. a. For the fire loss, a claim representative might hire any of the following:

- Origin and cause expert—to determine whether a fire started accidentally or was deliberately set

- Accountant—to determine lost revenue for the business, verify extent of stock loss, or determine the financial stability of the business
- Restoration specialist—to help clean and preserve undamaged property
- Salvor—to separate damaged and undamaged inventory and business property, prepare inventories, establish values for property, and arrange to sell the salvage
- Construction expert—to estimate the cost to repair or rebuild the building

b. For the bodily injury claim, a claim representative might hire any of the following:

- Accident reconstruction specialist—to help assess negligence
- Private investigator—to conduct surveillance if the claim representative suspects the claimant is feigning or exaggerating injuries
- Accountants or other financial analysts—to determine the value of a claimant's pre-accident ability to earn a living over the course of a lifetime and to place a value on the loss of such earnings capacity
- Medical consultants—to help the claim representative assess the medical requirements, determine whether the treatment being provided follows the doctor's treatment instructions, assess the need for rehabilitation, and determine the medical necessity of treatments

16. In a bodily injury claim, one might find any of the following records and reports:

- Police report
- Fire report
- Medical records
- Medical reports
- Employment records
- Death certificate
- Autopsy report
- Birth certificate
- Marriage certificate

17. a. To detect fraud, industry databases can be used to find a pattern of claims, preexisting conditions, unrepaired damage previously claimed, duplicate claims, or undisclosed duplicate insurance.

b. The Internet gives a claim representative access to state vital statistics, checklists for evaluating damages, product recall notices, and medical information. All of these may be used in detecting fraud.

c. Other investigative tools, such as an insurer's decision-making process or business rule engines can use insurer-specific criteria to flag claims that are suspected of being fraudulent.

18. To determine the cause of loss in an auto physical damage claim, the claim representative should request a written or recorded statement from the insured or insured driver. The claim representative should obtain a copy of the police report and any witness statements. The claim representative would also obtain an estimate of damages. Some claims may require more in-depth investigation, such as scene photos or accident reconstruction.

19. The vehicle identification number (VIN) identifies the vehicle and the registered owner, as well as specific parts to be used in repair of the vehicle. It is useful in detecting vehicles that are fraudulently reported as stolen.

20. In general, an auto physical damage claim file should contain statements from the insured, driver, and witnesses. It should contain photos of the damaged vehicle, police report, fire marshal report (if applicable), damage estimates, and any reports by experts (if applicable).

21. In a property damage claim other than auto, the claim representative will either inspect the damage or arrange for someone else to inspect it. Photos, video, or diagrams of the damage are created. A scope of loss is prepared showing the areas damaged, type of damage, a description of the proposed action, and the damaged area's measurements.

22. While the claim representative does not need to determine liability to pay the insured's claim, the claim representative should determine if a third party is responsible for the damage to the insured's property. Once the insured is paid, the claim representative can attempt to recover the amount paid from the responsible third party through subrogation.

23. Replacement cost is the cost to repair or replace the property using new materials of like kind and quality with no deduction for depreciation. Actual cash value subtracts depreciation from the replacement cost.

24. To determine the cause of loss of a bodily injury claim, the claim representative may take statements from the insured, the injured party, and any witnesses. The claim representative would also obtain a police report, any photos or diagrams of the accident location, and medical reports to compare with the description of the accident or injury.

25. For a bodily injury claim, a claim representative determines liability based on experience, case law, and the claim's facts. Ultimately, the final apportionment of liability is negotiated by the parties involved.

26. The claim representative should verify the amount of damages claimed and verify that the damages claimed are related to the accident.

27. Future damages are damages that continue past the time of settlement, such as cost of future medical treatment or amount of future wage loss.

28. The three elements used when valuing pain and suffering are:
    (1) Physical pain
    (2) Mental suffering
    (3) Mental anguish

29. To determine whether a claim is compensable under a workers' compensation statute, the claim representative should answer the following:
    • Is the injured party an employee under the workers' compensation statute?
    • Is the injury covered under the workers' compensation statute?
    • Did the injury arise out of and in the course of employment?

30. In a workers' compensation claim, the claim representative would obtain payroll records to determine employment status and wage loss. The claim representative may also obtain pre-employment physical reports, safety training reports, and other records from the human resources department, and medical reports from all who treated the injured party.

31. The benefits payable under a workers' compensation statute are:
    • Medical benefits
    • Wage loss benefits
    • Rehabilitation benefits
    • Death benefits

Application Questions

1. The following are bases for legal liability:

   - Negligence. Tom's failure to see the stop sign, causing the accident, is negligence.

   - Vicarious liability. Tom's employer may be vicariously liable for Tom's negligence because the employer should have known his license was suspended for a DUI conviction.

   - Strict liability. Tom's employer may be held strictly liable for the tow truck driver's injuries because Tom was delivering a hazardous chemical.

   - Contractual liability. Tom's employer may be liable to the chemical buyer for the extra costs incurred to obtain a replacement chemical because of the terms of the sale.

   - Statutory liability. Tom's employer may be liable for Tom's injuries under a workers' compensation statute.

2. Belinda would review the loss notice form to find both the insured's and the claimant's contact information. She might also find the insured's contact information in the actual policy. A general description of the accident can be found on the loss notice form.

   Belinda would review the policy to determine if the loss location is covered by the policy and what the policy limits are.

   Belinda may take a written or recorded statement from the store manager to obtain an account of the accident. She might visit the store to take photos of the loss location. She might ask if the store has a security video tape that would show the accident scene.

   Belinda would request copies of the maintenance log from the store manager to see whether anyone had notice of a condition or defect that may have caused the claimant's fall.

   Belinda would get a medical authorization from the claimant to request medical treatment records. She would have these records reviewed by a medical expert to obtain an opinion as to the medical necessity of treatment. She would use the medical authorization to request records of the claimant's medical history to see if there is a preexisting condition. She would use a rehabilitation expert to determine the extent of rehabilitation that might be necessary.

   Belinda would request a report from an industry database to see if the claimant had prior injuries or prior claims for similar injuries.

3. a. Determining cause of loss is similar for auto physical damage and other types of property damage. Generally, the claim representative will take statements from the insured and witnesses and make an inspection and an estimate or appraisal of the damage. File documentation is similar because both types of claims can include photos or diagrams, police reports, and fire reports.

   Determining liability is similar, as well. Generally, in a first-party property claim, the claim representative does not need to make a liability determination to pay the insured's claim. However, during the investigation of both an auto physical damage claim and other types of property damage claims, the claim representative may determine that a third party is responsible for the loss to the insured's property. The clam representative would attempt to recover the payments made to the insured by subrogating against the third party.

   Determining the amount of damage has both similarities and differences. Both auto physical damage and other property damage are valued either at replacement cost or actual cash value. How the claim representative arrives at the value for each type of claim is different. In an auto physical damage claim, the claim representative will use a reference manual to determine the cost to repair the vehicle or the actual cash value of the entire vehicle at the time of the loss. The claim representative will settle the claim with or without a deduction for salvage.

In other property damage claims, the claim representative will have to rely on experts, such as engineers, building contractors, and accountants, to help place a value on the loss.

b.   While both bodily injury claims and workers' compensation claims involve injuries, handling their claims has few similarities. Usually, they both require statements from the injured party and witnesses, photos or diagrams of how the loss occurred, medical records, wage loss information, and medical experts. Both types of claims can involve subrogation investigation. But then the similarity ends.

In a bodily injury claim, the claim representative determines liability using experience and case law applied to the claim's facts. A workers' compensation claim representative would not be concerned with liability in order to pay the injured party. Instead, the workers' compensation claim representative is concerned with compensability—whether the injured party is an employee under the workers' compensation statute, whether the injury is covered under the statute, and whether the injury arose out of and in the course of employment.

Determining damages is also very different. In a bodily injury claim, the claim representative must determine the amount of special damages (out-of-pocket expenses) and general damages (pain and suffering, inconvenience, disfigurement, and other intangibles). In a workers' compensation claim, the claim representative determines what benefits will be paid, such as medical benefits, wage loss benefits, rehabilitation benefits, and death benefits. The amounts of these benefits are generally specified by the workers' compensation statute.

Don't spend time on material you have already mastered. The SMART Review Notes are organized by the Educational Objectives found in each course guide assignment and help you track your study.

Insurance Fraud

Direct Your Learning

Educational Objectives

After learning the content of this assignment, you should be able to:

1. Explain why insurance fraud is a threat to the financial stability of the insurance industry.

2. Given a claim, identify the possible types of fraud involved.

3. Describe the motives for insurance fraud.

4. Given a claim, identify any fraud indicators present in the claim.

5. Describe the anti-fraud efforts made by the following:

    - Insurers

    - Government

    - Industry organizations

6. Define or describe each of the Key Words and Phrases for this assignment.

Study Materials

Required Reading:

- Claim Handling Principles and Practices
    - Chapter 4

Study Aids:

- SMART Practice Exam CD-ROM
- SMART Study Aids Review Notes and Flash Cards— Assignment 4

Outline

- **Importance of Insurance Fraud Detection**

- **Types of Insurance Fraud**
  - A. Hard Fraud
    1. False Claims
    2. Intentional Losses
  - B. Soft Fraud

- **Motives for Insurance Fraud**

- **Factors That Influence Fraud**

- **Fraud Indicators**
  - A. Behavioral Fraud Indicators
  - B. Medical Fraud Indicators
  - C. Lost Earnings Fraud Indicators
  - D. Fire Fraud Indicators
  - E. Auto Fraud Indicators
  - F. Burglary and Theft Fraud Indicators
  - G. Maintaining a Balanced Investigation

- **Anti-Fraud Efforts**
  - A. Insurers
  - B. Government
    1. Pre-Inspection
    2. Mandatory Reporting
    3. Immunity Statutes
    4. Civil or Criminal Penalties
    5. Fraud Prevention Bureaus
    6. Fraud Plans
  - C. Industry Organizations

- **Summary**

Key Words and Phrases

Define or describe each of the words and phrases listed below.

Insurance fraud (p. 4.3)

Hard fraud (p. 4.5)

Soft fraud, or opportunity fraud (p. 4.5)

Material fact (p. 4.5)

Misrepresentation (p. 4.5)

Concealment (p. 4.5)

Staged accident (p. 4.6)

Immunity statute (p. 4.25)

Review Questions

1. Why is the description of insurance fraud as a "victimless, white-collar crime" inaccurate? (p. 4.3)

2. What percentage of all claim dollars is estimated to be attributable to fraudulent claims? (p. 4.3)

3. What are the two most costly economic crimes in the United States? (p. 4.3)

4. What are the elements necessary to prove fraud? (p. 4.4)

5. Give an example of misrepresentation that can occur during the underwriting process. (p. 4.5)

6. Give an example of each of the following types of fraud:
   (pp. 4.5–4.7)

   a. False claims

   b. Intentional losses

   c. Exaggerated or padded claims

7. What is the primary motive for insurance claim fraud? (p. 4.7)

8. What other motives are often found in insurance claim fraud?
   (p. 4.7)

9. What reasons do people use to rationalize their sense of entitlement in relation to insurance claim fraud? (p. 4.8)

10. What factors may create an opportunity for fraud? (pp. 4.9–4.10)

11. Give three examples of behavioral fraud indicators. (pp. 4.10–4.12)

12. Give three examples of medical fraud indicators. (pp. 4.12–4.13)

13. Give three examples of lost earnings fraud indicators. (pp. 4.13–4.14)

14. Give three examples of fire fraud indicators. (pp. 4.14–4.15)

15. Give three examples of auto fraud indicators. (pp. 4.15–4.16)

16. Give three examples of burglary and theft fraud indicators. (pp. 4.16–4.17)

17. What resources do insurers have to combat insurance claim fraud? (pp. 4.21–4.22)

18. What resources do state governments have to fight insurance fraud? (pp. 4.23–4.28)

19. What resources does the insurance industry have to fight insurance fraud? (p. 4.28)

Application Questions

1. Tom has been asked to give a lunchtime presentation to his office about insurance fraud. Tom wants to begin his talk by providing the audience with the reasons that fraud is such a big concern for the insurance industry. What points should Tom make to convey these reasons to his audience?

The Supermarket Fraud Case. Bill goes to a supermarket about ten miles from his home, on a rainy afternoon. Once inside, he goes up and down each aisle until he gets to the frozen food cases. When there is no one else in the aisle, he quickly takes a ziplock bag filled with water from his coat pocket and pours the water near the base of the freezer case so it looks as if the freezer is leaking. He then positions himself to make it appear that he has slipped on the puddle. When another shopper enters the aisle, he asks the shopper to get the store manager.

When the manager arrives, Bill explains that he slipped and fell on the puddle coming from the freezer. Bill manages to stand up with the assistance of the manager. They go to the manager's office to fill out an accident report. The manager calls someone to mop up the floor. Bill tells the manager his neck and lower back are sore, as are his hands and wrists, which he put out to break his fall. Bill tells the manager he is lucky not to have hit his head in the fall. The manager tells Bill that he should see his doctor to have his condition checked. The manager also tells Bill he will report the matter to the supermarket's insurance company. Bill then hobbles out to his car and heads to the office of Dr. Bob.

Bill and Dr. Bob are old friends. Bill tells Dr. Bob what injuries he has allegedly sustained, and Dr. Bob creates a medical chart for Bill. Dr. Bob prescribes physical therapy three times a week for thirty days. The next day, Bill visits Dr. Bob for physical therapy. He signs in and gives Dr. Bob the name of the claim representative who has contacted him and the claim number assigned. Bill then leaves without receiving any treatment. Dr. Bob copies Bill's signature into the sign-in book for all the remaining treatment days. At the end of the thirty days, Dr. Bob submits his bill to the claim representative assigned to the claim.

Steve is assigned to investigate Bill's claim. Steve takes a statement from Bill and learns that Bill went to this particular supermarket because his local market does not carry a specific brand of salad dressing that he likes. Bill also states that he has never had a similar claim or similar injury. Steve checks with Bill's local market and learns that it does carry the brand of salad dressing Bill likes. Steve also runs an index bureau check and learns that Bill has had four other slip-and-fall claims in supermarkets and that he saw Dr. Bob for treatment for each claim.

  2. *Supermarket Fraud.* Identify the types of fraud presented in this claim scenario.

  3. *Supermarket Fraud.* What possible motives might Bill and Dr. Bob have for committing insurance claim fraud?

  4. *Supermarket Fraud.* What fraud indicators might Steve have picked up on in this claim scenario?

5. *Supermarket Fraud.* Bill and Dr. Bob have committed insurance fraud in a state that has a mandatory reporting statute, an immunity statute, and civil and criminal penalties for conviction of insurance fraud. What does all this mean to Steve when investigating the claim and referring the claim to a Special Investigation Unit (SIU)?

Answers to Assignment 4 Questions

NOTE: These answers are provided to give students a basic understanding of acceptable types of responses. They often are not the only valid answers and are not intended to provide an exhaustive response to the questions.

Review Questions

1. The description of insurance fraud as a "victimless, white-collar crime" is inaccurate because the losses and adjusting expenses caused by fraudulent claims are eventually paid by policyholders through increased premiums.

2. Some studies show that fraudulent claims account for 10 percent of all claim dollars. Other studies suggest a higher percentage.

3. The two most costly economic crimes in the U.S. are income tax evasion and insurance fraud.

4. The elements necessary to prove fraud are:
   - An individual or an organization intentionally makes an untrue representation.
   - The untrue representation concerns an important or material fact or event.
   - The untrue representation is knowingly made.
   - The untrue representation is intended to deceive.
   - The victim relies on and acts on the untrue representation.
   - The victim suffers some detriment, such as loss of money and/or property, as a result of relying on and acting on the untrue representation.

5. The following are some examples of misrepresentation that can occur during the underwriting process:
   - An applicant for workers' compensation insurance may deliberately under-report the amount of payroll to the insurance agent, broker, or underwriter. The applicant's misrepresentation causes the underwriter to charge a workers' compensation premium less than the premium appropriate for the risk, and the insurer thereby suffers a loss of premium income.
   - An agent, in collusion with an applicant, may over-report the square footage of a commercial building, permitting the applicant to purchase higher insurance limits with the intent of burning the building, collecting the insurance money, and splitting the proceeds with the agent.
   - An underwriter might provide an agent with a low premium quote in exchange for a payoff.

6. a. Some examples of false claims are:
      - A homeowner reporting the theft of jewelry when no theft has occurred
      - An employee reporting a fake back injury
      - A store patron intentionally pulling a display on himself and then filing a bodily injury claim
      - A patron claiming false injury or illness as a result of improperly prepared restaurant food
      - An auto body shop preparing an estimate for damage to a vehicle that does not exist
   b. Some examples of intentional losses are as follows:
      - Arson committed by the insured or at the insured's direction
      - A staged accident that results in a bodily injury

    c.   Some examples of exaggerated claims are as follows:
- Over-treatment of a legitimate injury
- Overstatement of the value of property stolen
- Overstatement of the severity of injuries
- Unnecessary treatment for injuries

7.   The primary motive for insurance claim fraud is individual profit or gain.

8.   Other motives often found in insurance claim fraud include a sense of entitlement and participation in organized crime.

9.   Reasons people use to rationalize their sense of entitlement in relation to insurance claim fraud include the following:
- Some individuals believe that if something bad happens, someone should pay for it. They use that reasoning to justify exaggerating or padding a claim to cover their insurance deductible or to recover some of the premium.
- Some individuals consider their premium payments a sort of "fund" from which they can be repaid in the event of a claim.
- Some individuals justify their sense of entitlement with the opinion that insurers are large, impersonal, wealthy institutions that will not miss a few extra dollars added to an auto claim or a workers' compensation claim.

For these individuals, committing fraud is a means to collect what they believe is rightfully theirs.

10.   The factors that may create an opportunity for fraud are an insurer's underwriting and claim practices, managed care practices, and public distrust of insurers.

11.   Examples of behavioral fraud indicators are as follows:
- The insured is excessively eager to accept blame for an accident or is overly insistent in demanding a quick settlement.
- The insured or claimant is unusually familiar with insurance, medical, or vehicle-repair terminology, and claim procedures.
- The insured or claimant is willing to accept a small settlement rather than provide documentation.
- The insured or claimant conducts transactions in person and avoids using the mail.
- The insured or claimant is recently separated or divorced.
- The insured's business was unsolicited, new, or walk-in business not referred by a current policyholder.
- The insured arrived at the producer's office at noon or at the end of the day when staff are rushed.
- The insured neither works nor lives near the agency.
- The insured's stated address is inconsistent with employment or income.
- The insured cannot provide a driver's license or other identification or has a temporary, recently issued, or out-of-state driver's license.
- The insured paid the minimum required premium.

12.   Examples of medical fraud indicators are as follows:
- Claims are exaggerated and claims are submitted for services that were never rendered.
- The diagnosis is not consistent with the treatment.

- The healthcare provider has a reputation for questionable claims.
- Medical bills are summaries rather than itemized statements.
- Medical bills are photocopies rather than originals.
- Bills indicate that treatment was given on holidays or weekends.
- All the claimants involved in one accident submit bills from the same healthcare provider.
- The extent of medical treatment is not consistent with the damage to the automobile.

13. Examples of lost earnings fraud indicators are as follows:
- The lost earnings statements is handwritten or typed on blank paper, not on business letterhead.
- The business telephone number given to verify the claimant's lost wages reaches an answering machine or answering service during regular business hours.
- The business phone number is unlisted or the business has only a post office box for an address. The business may be fictitious, or the claimant may have provided false documentation.

14. Examples of fire fraud indicators are as follows:
- The insured removes valuable inventory before a fire occurs, then claims damage to a large amount of old or out-of-season inventory.
- The building or contents were offered for sale for a long period before the loss.
- The family pet was not on the property at the time of the fire.
- There are multiple mortgages on the property.
- Contents with sentimental value were not damaged.

15. Examples of auto fraud indicators are as follows:
- For a serious accident, no police report is submitted or a police report is completed at the police station rather than at the accident location.
- No towing charge has been claimed, although repair estimates suggest that the vehicle could not have been driven from the scene of the accident.
- The vehicle that is subject to the claim is reported to be an expensive, late-model automobile recently purchased with cash.
- The accident occurred shortly after the vehicle was purchased or insured or after physical damage coverage was added to the policy.
- All the vehicles in a multi-vehicle accident are taken to the same repair facility.
- An appraiser has difficulty locating the vehicle for an inspection.

16. Examples of burglary and theft fraud indicators are as follows:
- Losses are incompatible with the insured's residence, occupation, or income.
- Losses include appraised items or scheduled property, making proof of value readily available.
- Losses include many new items or gifts for which no receipts are available.
- Loss inventory does not differ significantly from the original police report.
- The insured does not remember when or where new items were purchased.
- Receipts have incorrect sales tax figures or no store logo, are numbered in sequence, or have the same handwriting.
- The loss involves a stolen auto.

17. To combat insurance claim fraud, insurers have resources such as claim representatives trained in detecting fraud, special investigation units to investigate suspicious claims, and databases that accumulate information on insurance fraud. They also educate the consumer as to the costs of insurance fraud.

18. To fight insurance fraud, states have resources such as anti-fraud legislation that expands the definition of insurance fraud to include reckless conduct. Many state laws have increased the civil and criminal penalties for committing fraud, require insurers to cooperate with law enforcement authorities, and grant immunity from civil lawsuits to insurers that do cooperate. Many states also require the formation of SIUs, the development of anti-fraud plans, and the placement of fraud warnings on all applications and claim forms. Some states require insurers to physically inspect vehicles before a policy goes into effect. Some states have created fraud prevention bureaus.

19. To fight insurance fraud, the insurance industry has resources such as the National Insurance Crime Bureau (NICB) and the Coalition Against Insurance Fraud (CAIF), which are industry organizations dedicated to the detection and prosecution of fraud. Other industry organizations, such as the Insurance Information Institute (III) and the Insurance Research Council (IRC), compile statistical information on insurance fraud.

Application Questions

1. To convey to his audience the reasons why fraud is such a big concern for the insurance industry, Tom should make the following points:
   - Fraud can occur during the process of buying, selling, or underwriting insurance or making or paying a claim.
   - The losses and adjusting expenses caused by fraudulent claims are eventually paid by policyholders through increased premiums.
   - Studies show that fraudulent claims account for 10 percent of all claim dollars.
   - The Coalition Against Insurance Fraud estimates that insurance fraud is the second most costly economic crime in the U.S. after income tax evasion.
   - Some estimates suggest that property-casualty insurance fraud costs each household in the U.S. an extra $200–$300 per year in insurance premiums.

2. Following are the types of fraud presented:
   - Bill has filed a false claim with the supermarket's insurer, since he suffered no injuries.
   - Bill has staged an accident and feigned injury to defraud an insurer.
   - Dr. Bob is providing fictitious treatment for a nonexistent injury with the intent of defrauding the insurer.
   - Dr. Bob and Bill are submitting false medical claims to the supermarket's insurer.

3. Bill and Dr. Bob's possible motives for committing insurance claim fraud might include individual gain or profit, sense of entitlement, or participation in organized crime.

4. Steve might have picked up on the following fraud indicators:
   - Bill goes to a supermarket ten miles from home to shop.
   - Bill lied in his statement as to why he went to this particular supermarket.
   - There were no witnesses to Bill's accident.
   - Bill lied about having not had similar claims or injuries.
   - Dr. Bob has always treated Bill for these claims.

5. Steve should know that state law requires him to report this claim to law enforcement or other authorities, such as the FBI, district attorney's office, state fraud bureau, state insurance department, or the NICB. Steve should also know that he and his employer are protected from lawsuits for defamation, harassment, malicious prosecution, bad faith, or breach of privacy if they report a suspicious claim.

    Steve would also know that his employer could sue Bill and Dr. Bob for fines and damages, and the state could prosecute them for a criminal act.

 **Reduce the number of Key Words and Phrases that you must review. SMART Flash Cards contain the Key Words and Phrases and their definitions, allowing you to set aside those cards that you have mastered.**

Segment

B

Assignments

Segment B is the second of two segments in the AIC 33 course.
These segments are designed to help structure your study.

Good-Faith Claim Handling

Direct Your Learning

Educational Objectives

After learning the content of this assignment, you should be able to:

1. Explain how the law of bad faith relates to an insurer's duty of good faith and fair dealing and how the legal environment affects the law of bad faith.

2. Describe the parties to a bad-faith claim.

3. Describe the bases of bad-faith claims.

4. Describe the damages that can be awarded for bad faith or extracontractual liability.

5. Summarize the defenses available to an insurer in a bad-faith claim.

6. Describe the elements of good-faith claim handling.

7. Define or describe each of the Key Words and Phrases for this assignment.

Study Materials

Required Reading:

■ Claim Handling Principles and Practices
  • Chapter 5

Study Aids:

■ SMART Practice Exam CD-ROM

■ SMART Study Aids Review Notes and Flash Cards—Assignment 5

Outline

■ **Law of Bad Faith**

    A. Duty of Good Faith and Fair Dealing

        1. Public Interest

        2. Higher Standard of Conduct

    B. Legal Environment of Bad Faith

■ **Parties to a Bad-Faith Claim**

    A. Policyholders

    B. Claimants

    C. Excess Insurers

■ **Bases of Bad-Faith Claims**

    A. Claim Denial

    B. Excess Liability Claims

        1. Failure to Settle Within Policy Limits

        2. Refusal to Settle

        3. Strict Liability

    C. Statutory Bad Faith

    D. Unfair Claims Settlement Practices Acts

        1. Provisions of the NAIC Model Act

        2. Enforcement

        3. State Provisions

        4. Bad-Faith Lawsuits Under the Model Act

        5. Other Bases for Bad Faith

■ **Damages Resulting From Bad Faith or Extracontractual Liability**

    A. Compensatory Damages

    B. Punitive Damages

    C. Lawyers' Fees and Court Costs

    D. Interest

■ **Defenses to Bad-Faith Claims**

    A. Statutes of Limitations

    B. Lack of Right to Sue

    C. Reliance on Lawyers' Advice

    D. Insured's Collusion With the Claimant

    E. Debatable Reasonable Basis

    F. Statutory Defenses

    G. Fair Dealing and Good Documentation

    H. Comparative Bad Faith

    I. Contributory Negligence

    J. Availability of Higher Limits

■ **Elements of Good-Faith Claim Handling**

    A. Thorough, Timely, and Unbiased Investigation

        1. Health Insurance Portability and Accountability Act of 1996

        2. Gramm-Leach-Bliley Act

        3. Sarbanes-Oxley Act

        4. Fair Credit Reporting Act

    B. Complete and Accurate Documentation

    C. Fair Evaluation

    D. Good-Faith Negotiation

    E. Regular and Prompt Communication

    F. Competent Legal Advice

    G. Effective Claim Management

        1. Consistent Supervision

        2. Thorough Training

        3. Manageable Caseloads

■ **Summary**

Consult the registration booklet that accompanied this course guide for complete information regarding exam dates and fees. Plan to register with the Institutes well in advance of your exam. If you have any questions, or need updated registration information, contact the Institutes (see page iv).

Key Words and Phrases

Define or describe each of the words and phrases listed below.

Good faith (p. 5.3)

Breach of contract (p. 5.4)

Defendant (p. 5.8)

Plaintiff (p. 5.8)

Contractual damages (p. 5.17)

Consequential damages (p. 5.17)

Statute of limitations (p. 5.20)

Summary judgment (p. 5.22)

Review Questions

1. Why did the law of bad faith develop? (p. 5.4)

2. What two attributes of the insurance contract contributed to the development of bad-faith claims? Explain your answer. (p. 5.5)

3. Why must claim representatives stay informed about the bases of bad-faith claims in the states in which they handle claims? (p. 5.7)

4. Why do most bad-faith lawsuits name the insurer rather than the claim representative as defendant? (p. 5.8)

5. Identify the two types of bad-faith lawsuits. (p. 5.8)

6. Give an example of the circumstances in which each of the
   following can bring a bad-faith lawsuit against an insurer.
   (pp. 5.8–5.11)

   a. Policyholder

   b. Claimant

   c. Excess insurer

7. What are the four bases of bad-faith claims? (p. 5.11)

8. What should a claim representative do when denying coverage to
   prepare for a possible bad-faith lawsuit? (pp. 5.11–5.12)

9. What two situations generally give rise to excess liability claims? (pp. 5.12–5.13)

10. What is meant by the phrase "statutory bad faith"? (pp. 5.13–5.14)

11. What is the stated purpose of the NAIC Model Unfair Claims Settlement Practices Act? (p. 5.14)

12. What are the goals for state unfair claims settlement practices acts? (p. 5.15)

13. What other bases for bad faith can insureds use? (p. 5.16)

14. What types of damages can an insurer be required to pay a plaintiff if found liable for bad faith? (p. 5.17)

15. What can be included in compensatory damages? (p. 5.17)

16. What is the general standard of proof for awarding punitive damages? (p. 5.17)

17. List three defenses that, if proven, result in dismissal of a bad-faith lawsuit and three defenses that may reduce damages in a bad-faith lawsuit. (p. 5.19)

18. What is a common issue involving the statute of limitations defense? (p. 5.20)

19. What two things should a claim representative check to determine if a claimant has the right to sue the insurer for bad faith? (p. 5.20)

20. What proof is required for an insurer to use lawyers' advice as part of the defense to a bad-faith lawsuit? (pp. 5.20–5.21)

21. Describe the three situations in which collusion between the claimant and the insured is most likely to occur. (p. 5.21)

22. Describe when the debatable reasonable basis defense is available to an insurer. (p. 5.22)

23. Give an example of another statutory defense an insurer can use to seek dismissal of a bad-faith lawsuit. (p. 5.22)

24. Give four examples of claim practices that exhibit fair dealing and good documentation. (p. 5.23)

25. What are the elements of good-faith claim handling?
    (p. 5.25)

26. What standards should a claim representative use to determine
    whether an investigation is each of the following. (pp. 5.25–5.26)

    a. Thorough

    b. Timely

    c. Unbiased

27. What federal statutes designed to ensure privacy of confidential
    information should a claim representative be aware of, and why?
    (pp. 5.26–5.28)

28. Why is it important for a claim file to provide a complete and
    accurate account of all the activities and actions taken by the
    claim representative? (pp. 5.28–5.29)

29. What sources can claim representatives use to assist them in making a knowledgeable claim evaluation? (pp. 5.29–5.30)

30. Contrast the standards for claim representatives and lawyers in good-faith negotiations. (p. 5.30)

31. What important results are achieved through regular and prompt communication with the insured? (p. 5.31)

32. What is the basis for selection of defense counsel? (p. 5.32)

33. What are three crucial elements of effective claim management? (p. 5.33)

Application Questions

The Colossal Insurer Case. Before trial of a lawsuit against Fred, its insured, Colossal Insurer had offered Dave, the plaintiff, $100,000 to settle a claim for a serious and disabling injury arising out of an auto accident in which Fred was clearly liable. Tom, the claim representative handling the claim, thought that he could save Colossal some money by taking advantage of Dave's inexperienced lawyer. Dave's demand was $500,000 when the case was tried. Fred's policy limits were $500,000. At trial, it became known for the first time that Fred was intoxicated at the time of the accident. The jury awarded Dave $750,000. Fred was upset by the verdict, especially when he learned after the trial that the case could have been settled for $500,000. Fred threatens a bad-faith lawsuit against Colossal for the amount of the excess verdict.

1. *Colossal.* What factors could contribute to a finding of bad faith against Colossal?

2. *Colossal.* Colossal receives notice of a lawsuit alleging bad faith as a result of the $750,000 judgment in Dave's favor. The lawsuit reads as follows:

   Dave v. Colossal Insurance and Tom

   Explain whether the parties named in the lawsuit are proper parties.

3. Review Section 4 of the NAIC Model Unfair Claims Settlement Practices Act. Give a real-life claim example for any four of the acts defined in Section 4.

4. What is the rationale for the awarding of each of the following types of damages in a bad-faith case:

a. Contractual

b. Consequential

c. Punitive

d. Lawyers' fees and court costs

e. Interest

5. Dick and Jane stage an auto accident to fraudulently collect damages from Formal Insurance Company, Jane's auto insurer. Dick fabricates extensive injuries and makes a policy limit demand to Formal. Formal, suspecting fraud and collusion, consults with an attorney and then denies the claim. Formal reports Jane to the State Insurance Department Fraud Bureau. Dick sues Jane for his "injuries" and Formal refuses to defend Jane because of the suspected fraud. Dick gets a default judgment against Jane and she assigns her rights to sue Formal for bad faith over to Dick. Jane also sues Formal for falsely reporting her to the Fraud Bureau.

   What defenses are available to Formal in the lawsuits brought by Dick and Jane? Explain your answers.

6. Imagine a bad-faith lawsuit is filed on a claim you are currently handling. What evidence could you provide from your claim file that you have exhibited elements of good-faith claim handling?

Answers to Assignment 5 Questions

NOTE: These answers are provided to give students a basic understanding of acceptable types of responses. They often are not the only valid answers and are not intended to provide an exhaustive response to the questions.

Review Questions

1. The law of bad faith developed in response to the perception that insurers were placing their own interests ahead of their insureds' interests. In some cases, insureds became personally liable for losses they believed were covered by their insurance and they sued their insurers for breach of contract. However, in some cases, the breach of contract remedies were perceived to be inadequate. Eventually, courts decided that insurers have an implied duty of good faith and fair dealing when settling claims. An insurer's failure to comply with this duty can result in a bad-faith claim.

2. The two attributes are that insurance contracts involve the public interest, and they require a higher standard of conduct because of the unequal bargaining power of parties. State insurance regulators and courts wish to protect the public interest against illegal business practices and ensure that insurers pay claims that they owe. Because insurers control how claims are resolved, courts have held insurers to a higher standard of conduct to discourage insurers from abusing their position of power.

3. Claim representatives must stay informed because the bases on which bad-faith claims can be brought are constantly changing. Court decisions and legislative changes occur frequently. If claim representatives do not stay informed, they put their employer at increased risk of bad-faith claims.

4. Most states do not allow bad-faith claims against claim representatives because they are not parties to the insurance contract. However, in some states, claim representatives can be held personally liable for fraud, conspiracy, or other torts.

5. The following are the are two types of bad-faith lawsuits:

   (1) First-party bad-faith lawsuit, in which the policyholder sues its own insurer for bad faith in the handling of a first-party claim.

   (2) Third-party bad-faith lawsuit, in which the policyholder sues its own insurer for bad faith in the handling of a third-party claim.

6. Answers may vary.

   a. A policyholder can sue the insurer for bad faith when the insurer wrongfully denies a first-party claim or provides an inadequate defense of the insured in a third-party lawsuit.

   b. A claimant can sue an insurer when the insured has assigned its rights against the insurer to the claimant. In some states, a claimant who has obtained a judgment against an insured has a right of direct action against an insurer. Some states have unfair claim settlement practices acts that allow claimants to sue insurers.

   c. An excess insurer can pursue a bad-faith claim against a primary insurer through equitable subrogation or through a direct action.

7. The four bases of bad-faith claims are as follows:

   (1) Claim denial

   (2) Excess liability claim

   (3) Statutory bad faith

   (4) Violations of unfair claim settlement practices acts

8.   A claim representative should fully document the reason for the decision to fully or partially deny a claim.

9.   The two situations that generally give rise to excess liability claims are when the insurer refuses the opportunity to settle within policy limits and when the insurer refuses to settle at all.

10. Statutory bad faith is used to describe bad-faith state statutes that specifically define what constitutes insurers' bad faith and that allow a bad-faith cause of action.

11. The Model Act serves as a guide to illustrate the activities that are considered unfair claim settlement practices. The stated purpose is not to punish insurers and claim representatives but to elevate the standard of conduct for claim handling by all insurers for the benefit of all involved and to avoid bad-faith claims.

12. The goals for state unfair claim settlement practices acts are promptness, honesty, responsiveness, fair-mindedness, and evenhandedness.

13. Insureds may use violations of other statutes or regulations as evidence of bad faith. These claims are sometimes based on fraud, deceit, conspiracy, defamation, libel, and slander.

14. If found liable for bad faith, an insurer would pay the plaintiff compensatory damages, punitive damages, lawyers' fees, court costs, and prejudgment interest.

15. Compensatory damages can include contractual damages, consequential damages, and/or emotional distress damages.

16. Generally, the standard of proof for awarding punitive damages is proof of insurer behavior that is worse than ordinary wrongdoing, such as malicious, fraudulent, or oppressive behavior. Some states require proof that the insurer's conduct was intentional, reckless, gross, wanton, or recklessly indifferent.

17. Defenses that, if proven, result in dismissal of a bad-faith lawsuit are as follows:
     - Lack of right to sue
     - Reliance on lawyers' advice
     - Insured's collusion with the claimant
     - Debatable reasonable basis
     - Statutory defenses
     - Fair dealing and good documentation

     Defenses that may reduce damages in a bad-faith lawsuit are as follows:
     - Comparative bad faith
     - Contributory negligence
     - Availability of higher limits

18. A common issue involving the statute of limitations defense is the starting date of the statutory period. Some courts have held that the starting date begins when the insurer denies the claim or otherwise wrongfully withholds benefits. Other courts have held that the time does not begin to run until the damages are ascertainable.

19. To determine if a claimant has the right to sue the insurer for bad faith, the claim representative should check state statutes and check to see if the claimant has been given a valid assignment of rights by the policyholder.

20. The following proofs are required for an insurer to use lawyers' advice as part of the defense to a bad-faith lawsuit:
    - The insurer acted on the lawyer's advice.
    - The insurer disclosed all the facts to the lawyer.
    - The insurer relied on the lawyer's advice in good faith.

21. The following are the three situations in which collusion between the claimant and the insured is most likely to occur:
    (1) The insured and the claimant have an ongoing business relationship.
    (2) The insured and the claimant are related or close friends.
    (3) The insured will benefit indirectly from the claimant's recovery.

22. The debatable reasonable basis defense is available when an insurer has a reasonable basis on which to debate whether or not a claim is covered.

23. An insurer can use an immunity statute to dismiss a bad-faith lawsuit based on the insurer's reporting of a suspected fraud to the appropriate state agency.

24. Answers may vary.

    Examples of claim practices that exhibit fair dealing and good documentation include the following:
    - Request and obtain all necessary information or documentation before deciding to accept or deny a claim.
    - Include in the files detailed analyses of the coverage(s), liability issues, defenses, percentages of liability for all parties, and damages issues.
    - Support analyses with facts and documents in the files, not rumors or innuendos.
    - Avoid making derogatory or malicious comments about the insured, counsel, or witnesses.
    - Avoid exploiting or making comments about exploiting the claimant's or insured's financial hardship.
    - Avoid delays in handling a claim.
    - Avoid substantial variances between reserves and payments or offers made.
    - Avoid attempts to persuade public authorities to bring criminal charges against any person, but supply requested information about possible criminal activity as permitted by the applicable state.
    - Avoid attempting to coerce experts to change their testimony.

25. Good-faith claim handling involves thorough and timely investigation, documentation, evaluation, negotiation, and communication. It also involves seeking legal advice when appropriate.

26. A claim representative should use the following standards to determine whether an investigation is:
    a. Thorough—an investigation should be thorough enough to satisfy a judge and jury that the claim representative followed good-faith claim-handling procedures. Evidence of compliance with company procedures or best practices used in investigation are also convincing.
    b. Timely—the representative should adhere to company guidelines for contact with the insured and claimant and/or compliance with provisions of the NAIC Model Act.
    c. Unbiased—claim representatives should pursue all relevant evidence, especially evidence that establishes a claim's legitimacy.

27. A claim representative should be aware of the following federal statutes designed to ensure privacy of confidential information:

   • Health Insurance Portability and Accountability Act of 1996 (HIPAA). Claim representatives must understand that they may need authorizations to obtain and share HIPAA-protected information.

   • Gramm-Leach-Bliley Act (GLB). Claim representatives must be aware that GLB may restrict their access to financial information obtained by their company for a purpose other than a claim.

   • Sarbanes-Oxley Act. This act requires more extensive reporting of claim information, greater accuracy in setting reserves, and more extensive audits of claim files.

   • Fair Credit Reporting Act. Claim representatives should check with supervisors and managers to determine what procedures are in place to protect the confidentiality of personal information, when this information can be shared, and with whom.

28. It is important for a claim file to provide a complete and accurate account of all the activities and actions taken by the claim representative because the claim file may be read by many different people, each with a different purpose. Regardless of who reads the file, no reader should be left wondering why something did or did not happen or how a conclusion was reached.

29. In addition to their own experience, claim representatives can consult with sources inside and outside the insurance company, including:

   • Coworkers
   • Supervisors and managers
   • Defense lawyers involved in the case
   • Other lawyers not involved in the case
   • People who represent a typical jury
   • Computer-generated damage or injury evaluations
   • Jury verdict research companies

30. Claim representatives must make realistic offers and carefully consider all demands. Lawyers, in the interest of their clients, can make exaggerated demands.

31. Regular and prompt communication with the insured achieves several important results, including the following:

   • The insured feels a part of the defense and can offer assistance.

   • The insured can participate in discussions about the possibility of settlement and the handling of the claim.

   • The correspondence with the insured documents the insurer's good-faith claim handling and the basis for its judgment about settlement.

   • The correspondence establishes that the insured gave the insurer informed consent to take on the defense of the case and to decide how to defend it.

32. Defense counsel should be selected based on their experience, knowledge of the law, and success in the courtroom.

33. Three crucial elements of effective claim management are as follows:

   (1) Consistent supervision
   (2) Thorough training
   (3) Manageable caseloads

Application Questions

1. Colossal could be found to be in bad faith because the claim representative failed to put Fred's interests above that of Colossal, thereby exposing Fred to the $250,000 over his policy limit. The claim representative's failure to properly investigate the claim and find out that Fred was intoxicated at the time of the accident can also be a basis for bad faith. This failure could be construed as negligence or gross misconduct on the part of Colossal. Colossal's failure to inform Fred about the $500,000 demand could also be construed as negligence or intentional misconduct.

2. Dave may or may not be a proper plaintiff. Generally, a claimant cannot sue an insurer for bad faith because claimants are not a party to the insurance contract. However, if Fred has assigned his rights against Colossal to Dave, then Dave assumes Fred's rights to sue Colossal.

   Colossal is a proper defendant because it is Fred's insurer.

   Generally, Tom would not be a proper defendant because he is only an employee of Colossal and not a party to the insurance contract. However, if the lawsuit alleges fraud or conspiracy or some other tort on Tom's part, he may be a proper defendant.

3. The answer to this question will vary depending on which acts are chosen and your own claim-handling experience and training. The purpose of this question is to teach you to recognize acts that can lead to bad faith so you can avoid them in the future.

4. The rationales for awarding each of the following types of damages in a bad-faith case are as follows:

   a. Contractual—these damages are payable under the terms of the contract.

   b. Consequential—although these damages arise from the breach of contract, they are not specified in the contract. They are out-of-pocket expenses that can be quantified to demonstrate an actual financial loss suffered by the plaintiff.

   c. Punitive—these are damages imposed in order to punish the wrongdoer.

   d. Lawyers' fees and court costs—courts allow this type of damages because the plaintiff had to hire a lawyer and go to court to obtain the benefits the insurer wrongfully refused to provide.

   e. Interest—some courts award interest on the claimed damages because the insured was deprived of the money while the insurer had the money to earn interest.

5. The following defenses are available to Formal:

   • Lack of right to sue—Dick does not have a valid assignment of rights from Jane because of the collusion and intent to defraud.

   • Reliance on lawyer's advice—Formal can show it acted on a lawyer's advice after disclosing all the facts of the claim to the lawyer. Formal can also show it relied on the lawyer's advice in good faith.

   • Insured's collusion with claimant—Formal will have to prove that Dick and Jane conspired to defraud Formal.

   • Debatable reasonable basis—Formal can show it has evidence of Dick and Jane's attempt at fraud.

   • Statutory defenses—Formal can assert an immunity statute to defend against Jane's lawsuit.

6. Answers will vary but your answer should include evidence of a thorough, timely, and unbiased investigation; complete and accurate documentation; fair evaluation; good-faith negotiation; regular and prompt communication; competent legal advice; and effective claim management.

Ethics and Professionalism

Educational Objectives

After learning the content of this assignment, you should be able to:

1. Explain why ethics and professionalism are important to a claim representative.

2. Describe the ethical and professional dilemmas claim representatives can face.

3. Explain how codes of ethics and quality claim practices can promote high ethical and professional standards.

4. Given a claim, explain why a situation presents an ethical or a professional dilemma.

5. Define or describe each of the Key Words and Phrases for this assignment.

Study Materials

Required Reading:

■ Claim Handling Principles and Practices
  • Chapter 6

■ "Ethics and Professionalism Case Study," Course Guide Reading 6-1

Study Aids:

■ SMART Practice Exam CD-ROM

■ SMART Study Aids Review Notes and Flash Cards— Assignment 6

Outline

- **Importance of Ethics and Professionalism**
- **Ethical and Professional Dilemmas**
    - A. Conflicts of Interest
        1. Salvage
        2. Vendor Incentives
        3. Overlapping Coverages or Insureds
    - B. Claim Handling Competency
    - C. Continuing Education
    - D. Licensing
    - E. Customer Service
    - F. *Ex Parte* Contacts
    - G. Billing Practices
        1. Time and Expense
        2. Allocation
    - H. Privacy
    - I. Fraud Detection
- **Ethical and Professional Standards**
    - A. Codes of Ethics
        1. RPA and CPCU Codes of Ethics
    - B. Quality Claim Practices
        1. Customer Expectations
        2. Process Improvement Plan
- **Summary**
- **Appendix A**
- **Appendix B**
- **Ethics and Professionalism Case Study
  (Course Guide Reading 6-1)**

Actively capture information by using the open space in the SMART Review Notes to write out key concepts. Putting information into your own words is an effective way to push that information into your memory.

Reading 6-1

Ethics and Professionalism Case Study

In the "real world" of everyday insurance operation, claim representatives are often faced with ethical dilemmas. This assignment includes a case study to sharpen your ability to recognize these dilemmas and encourage you to think about how they can be resolved or avoided.

Questions pertaining to this case study appear in the Application Questions.

Ellen has worked for Radley Insurance as a claim representative for ten years. She began her employment as soon as she finished college, where she majored in business administration. When she started her employment with Radley, she attended a six-week intensive training course to learn insurance coverages, laws that affect claim handling, Radley's claim procedures, and interpersonal and work skills that would help her become a successful claim representative. Since that time, Ellen has attended three or four local claim association meetings and reads about a dozen articles from a claim magazine per year. Ellen has asked to attend many claims seminars over the past ten years but her supervisor, Grace, has never approved the requests. Ellen believes Grace has not approved the requests as a means of keeping Ellen from leaving the unit. Ellen is afraid to voice her concerns to the claim manager.

Ellen's claim-handling territory currently includes two regions without adjuster licensing laws and two regions that recently began to require adjuster licensing. The new licensing law provides that any claim representative holding the Associate in Claims (AIC) designation from the Insurance Institute of America is "grandfathered" and does not need to complete a prescribed educational course before being licensed. Ellen completes the paperwork necessary to get her license and gives it to Grace for filing with the states. She continues to handle claims in the states requiring licenses. Grace does not file the licensing application because Ellen's assigned territory has changed five times in her ten years with Radley. Grace thinks that it might change again in a few months, so she does not want to spend company funds to get Ellen's license.

Over the last four years, Ellen has worked closely with a building repair contractor in more than a dozen serious fire and wind losses and many more minor losses. Ellen refers insureds to the contractor whenever she can because she knows the contractor provides all the paperwork she needs to document her claim files. The contractor appreciates Ellen's referrals and frequently sends her expensive chocolates. Lately he has been sending her flowers. Ellen has decided that she would like to get to know the contractor on a personal basis outside work and has decided to invite him to dinner some evening next week.

Radley Insurance has a Code of Business Conduct that prohibits accepting anything of value—gifts, gratuities, incentives, or other benefits—from vendors. However, the claim department routinely ignores this prohibition, especially around the holidays when many vendors send candy and fruit baskets to the department. The underwriting and accounting departments receive similar gifts; only the accounting department returns them to the vendors.

In a recent claim, Ellen found herself in an awkward situation with two insureds and their agents. Both insureds were involved in a multi-vehicle accident and Ellen believes that neither was at fault. Both had collision coverage with $1,000 deductibles. Ellen discovered in the claim investigation that the responsible driver had minimum property damage liability limits that had already been exhausted by other claims. She was successful in recovering thirty percent of the damages that Radley paid to the two insureds directly from the at-fault driver. Radley's procedures state that any recovery should be credited to the insured's deductible first; after the insured's deductible has been returned, any excess recovery credits Radley's loss payments. However, the agents for these two insureds were good friends of Ellen's and she knew that these losses would reduce their loss contingent commissions. She therefore decided to credit the recoveries to Radley's loss payments since the insureds were not expecting any recovery anyway.

Key Word or Phrase

Define or describe the phrase listed below.

Ex parte contacts (p. 6.13)

Review Questions

1. What are the three reasons that ethics and professionalism are important for insurers and claim representatives? (pp. 6.3–6.4)

2. How does fulfilling the promises insurers make in their policies cause ethical dilemmas for claim representatives? (p. 6.4)

3. What is the benefit of ethical and professional behavior for the claim representative, insurer, and consumer? (pp. 6.4–6.5)

4. Explain the difference between a moral dilemma and an ethical dilemma. (p. 6.5)

5. What questions can claim representatives ask themselves to reach a solution to an ethical dilemma? (pp. 6.5–6.6)

6. Describe the following effects that can be used to resolve ethical dilemmas. (p. 6.6)

   a. Maximizing effect

   b. Normalizing effect

   c. Empathizing effect

7. Give three examples of how a conflict of interest can arise during claim handling. (pp. 6.7–6.8)

8. Lack of competency can cause a claim representative to commit ethical improprieties. What five factors can affect claim handling competency? (pp. 6.8–6.10)

9. How can claim representatives avoid possible *ex parte* contacts with claimants? (p. 6.13)

10. What information security practices should claim representatives employ to ensure the privacy of confidential information? (pp. 6.14–6.15)

11. What are two standards claim representatives can use to seek uniformity in ethical behavior? (p. 6.17)

12. In addition to the enforcement of a strict written policy or code of ethics, describe other methods insurers can use to promote high ethical and professional standards. (p. 6.17)

13. How do insurers identify quality claim practices? (p. 6.18)

14. How do insurers attempt to measure customer satisfaction? (p. 6.19)

15. What method have insurers relied on as a failure analysis tool? (p. 6.22)

Application Questions

1. Most insurers, producers, third-party administrators, and independent adjusters have a conflict of interest form that claim
   representatives must read and sign on a yearly basis. Review the
   conflict of interest statement required by your employer and
   answer the following questions:

   a. What benefits do the insurer and the consumer derive from
       your compliance with this conflict of interest statement?

   b. What activities or behaviors are prohibited by the conflict of
       interest statement?

   c. What are the penalties for failure to comply with the conflict
       of interest statement?

2. Using the Ethics and Professionalism Case Study in Reading 6-1, answer the following questions:

   a. Identify the ethical dilemmas Ellen faces. (Your answers should be in the form of x versus y.)

   b. What actions could Ellen take to avoid the ethical dilemmas presented in the case study?

3. Describe the process for handling customer complaints in your office.

4. Using either the process improvement plan or the Ishikawa diagram, identify an area for improvement in your office.

Answers to Assignment 6 Questions

NOTE: These answers are provided to give students a basic understanding of acceptable types of responses. They often are not the only valid answers and are not intended to provide an exhaustive response to the questions.

Review Questions

1. The following are three reasons ethics and professionalism are important for insurers and claim representatives:

    (1) Insurers and claim representatives are bound by the insurance contract to act in good faith, and, to do so, they must act ethically and professionally.

    (2) Claim representatives' behavior can affect public trust in and credibility of insurers.

    (3) Consumer regulations create legal duties for insurers, and claim representatives have an ethical and professional responsibility to comply with these regulations.

2. Fulfilling the promises made by insurers in their policies requires claim representatives to satisfy the needs of a variety of parties. When these needs conflict, claim representatives may face ethical dilemmas.

3. For the claim representative, ethical and professional conduct can be the foundation of a successful, satisfying career. For the insurer, ethical and professional conduct can help retain customers and attract investors. For the consumer, insurers' ethical and professional behavior encourages fair treatment and prompt payment, allowing the consumer to reap the benefits of insurance—peace of mind, support for credit, efficient use of resources, and reduction of social burdens.

4. The difference between a moral dilemma and an ethical dilemma is that a moral dilemma is characterized as right versus wrong, while an ethical dilemma is characterized as right versus right.

5. Claim representatives can ask themselves the following questions to resolve an ethical dilemma:

    *   Who are the stakeholders, and what are their rights?
    *   Is the information about the dilemma reliable and accurate?
    *   Who should be involved in making the decision?
    *   Who might be harmed by each option and how?
    *   What are the long-term results of each option?
    *   What would be the consequences if the decision were made public?
    *   How would I feel if my mother (or children) knew of my decision?
    *   What would a person whom I respect do in this situation?
    *   Am I using this decision for my own personal gain?
    *   Does anything about the decision not "feel right"?

6. With the maximizing effect, the claim representative focuses on the extent of the decision's effect. A decision that provides the greatest benefit to the greatest number of people would have a maximizing effect. With the normalizing effect, the claim representative focuses on determining the most common, acceptable standard of behavior. A decision to implement a legally acceptable business practice would have a normalizing effect. With the empathizing effect, the claim representative follows the golden rule. A decision that treats someone the way in which the claim representative would want to be treated in the same situation would have an empathizing effect.

7. Answers may vary.

    Examples of how a conflict of interest can arise during claim handling include the following:
    *   When claim representatives are given the opportunity to purchase salvage
    *   When vendors offer claim representatives incentives for referring business to them
    *   When the insurer provides coverage for one or more insureds involved in the same claim

8. The following five factors can affect claim handling competency:
    (1) Changes in the claim environment
    (2) Changes in job responsibilities
    (3) Normal loss of knowledge over time
    (4) Lack of time or money
    (5) Inequitable rewards and promotions

9. To avoid *ex parte* contacts with claimants, claim representatives should routinely ask claimants if they have retained legal counsel and should review all claim file correspondence for any notification of legal representation.

10. To ensure the privacy of confidential information, claim representatives should ensure the following:
    *   The information is acquired only when necessary.
    *   The information is accurate.
    *   Access to the information is strictly limited.
    *   The information is not communicated to others unnecessarily.

11. Two standards claim representatives can use to seek uniformity in ethical behavior are a code of ethics and quality claim practices.

12. An insurer can use the following to promote high ethical and professional standards:
    *   Define ethical practices in all business areas, communicate them to all employees, and require adherence to them
    *   Conduct independent reinspections of physical damage claims and perform file reviews of all types of claims at random intervals to detect and address any unethical behavior
    *   Encourage employees to consult with their supervisors and managers about ethical dilemmas and to report ethical dilemmas involving others, such as service providers
    *   Dismiss unethical employees

13. Insurers identify quality claim practices by identifying customer needs and expectations.

14. Insurers attempt to measure customer satisfaction in the following ways:
    *   Analyzing complaints
    *   Obtaining customer feedback on individual claims through a closed claim follow-up
    *   Exploring customer attitudes about service through focus groups and surveys

15. Insurers have relied on auditing as a failure analysis tool.

Application Questions

1. a., b., and c. The answers to these questions will vary depending on the contents of your employer's conflict of interest statement.

2. a.   Answers may vary.

Ellen faces the following ethical dilemmas:

- Need for education versus fear of supervisor
- Need for adjusting license versus belief that she has her license
- Acceptance of gifts from vendor versus need to maintain good relationship with vendor
- Desire for friendship with vendor versus possible undue influence by vendor
- Violation of Code of Business Conduct versus doing what is generally accepted as a business practice
- Showing preference to agents versus returning deductible to insured

    b.   Answers may vary.

Ellen could take the following actions to avoid the ethical dilemmas presented:

- Use personal time and money for continuing education
- Follow up to ensure that her license is in effect
- Maintain a professional relationship with the vendor rather than try to develop a personal one
- Ask the vendor to stop sending her gifts
- Abide by the business code even if the rest of the department does not
- Put the interests of Radley's insureds ahead of her own

3. Answers may vary. The process for handling customer complaints in your office should include such things as a complaint tracking system, timely investigation, and a well-reasoned, objective response.

4. Answers will vary but should be based on the Ishikawa Diagram in Exhibit 6.2 of *Claim Handling Principles and Practices*. The methodology used to identify an area for improvement in your office should include the following:

Process Improvement Plan

- Determining how things work and who makes them work
- Developing and testing ideas for improvement
- Implementing improvements
- Setting and comparing performance standards
- Monitoring results

Negotiation

Direct Your Learning

Educational Objectives

After learning the content of this assignment, you should be able to:

1. Describe the four different styles of negotiation and which style is generally best suited for use by claim representatives.

2. Describe the steps in the claim negotiation process.

3. Explain how claimant negotiation variables and claim representative negotiation variables affect claim negotiations.

4. Describe the claim negotiation techniques that are the following:

    • Common to all parties

    • For use with unrepresented parties

    • For use with represented parties

    • Used by represented parties

5. Describe the negotiation techniques claim representatives should avoid and the reasons those techniques should be avoided.

6. Given a claim, identify the common pitfalls in claim negotiation and how to avoid them.

Study Materials

Required Reading:

■ Claim Handling Principles and Practices
  • Chapter 7

Study Aids:

■ SMART Practice Exam CD-ROM
■ SMART Study Aids Review Notes and Flash Cards—Assignment 7

Outline

■ **Negotiation Styles**

A. Win-Win

B. Win-Lose

C. Lose-Win

D. Lose-Lose

■ **Claim Negotiation Process**

■ **Claim Negotiation Variables**

A. Claimant's Negotiation Variables

1. Claimant's Negotiation Phase

2. How Badly the Claimant Needs Money

3. Time Pressures That the Claimant May Face

4. Claimant's Emotional Reaction to the Loss

5. Claimant's Experience With or Knowledge of Insurance Claims

6. Claimant's Personality

B. Claim Representative's Negotiation Variables

1. Claim Representative's Knowledge of the Claim

2. Claim Representative's Authority Level

3. Number of Alternatives Available for a Satisfactory Claim Settlement

4. Claim Representative's Time Factors

5. Claim Negotiation Settings

6. Claim Representative's Personality

■ **Claim Negotiation Techniques**

A. Negotiation Techniques for Use by All Parties

1. Principle of Yes

2. Choicing

B. Negotiation Techniques for Use With Unrepresented Claimants

1. Collecting and Using Extraneous Information

2. Using Sales Techniques in Negotiation

3. Using Needs Analysis to Effect a Settlement

4. Making the First Offer

C. Negotiation Techniques for Use With Claimants' Representatives

1. Using Information Obtained From the Evaluation

2. Establishing Strengths and Weaknesses

3. Using Timing in Negotiations

4. Making the First Offer

5. Making Concessions

D. Negotiation Techniques Used by Claimants' Representatives

1. Limited Authority Negotiations

2. Timing in Negotiations

■ **Negotiation Techniques to Avoid**

A. Using a First and Final Offer—Boulwarism

B. Using Decreasing or Limited Offers

■ **Common Pitfalls in Claim Negotiations**

A. Allowing Personalities to Influence the Settlement

B. Trading Dollars

C. Bidding Against Oneself

D. Conceding as Deadlines Approach

■ **Summary**

Key Words and Phrases

There are no key words or phrases for this assignment.

Review Questions

1. Claim representatives engage in activities and exhibit traits that demonstrate concern for obtaining the best outcome and achieving rapport. Identify qualities important to claim representatives who seek each of the following. (pp. 7.4–7.5)

    a. Obtaining the best outcome

    b. Achieving rapport

2. Identify and briefly describe the four negotiation styles. (pp. 7.6–7.10)

3. Which negotiating style is generally best suited for use by claim representatives? Explain why. (pp. 7.6–7.8)

4. Identify the steps in the claim negotiation process. (p. 7.10)

5. What types of information might the claim representative assemble regarding the claimant during the first step in the negotiation process? (p. 7.11)

6. How can a claim representative use a best alternative to a negotiated agreement (BATNA) in the second step of the negotiation process? (pp. 7.11–7.12)

7. What general categories of needs must the claim representative identify in the third stage of the negotiation process? (p. 7.12)

8. How can parties use concessions in the final stage of the negotiation process? (pp. 7.12–7.13)

9. What are the most significant negotiation variables that can affect the claimant? (pp. 7.13–7.14)

10. How can the claimant's need for money and time pressures affect the negotiation process from the claim representative's perspective? (p. 7.16)

11. What are the most significant negotiation variables that can affect claim representatives? (p. 7.18)

12. Explain why the claim representative's knowledge of the claim and authority level are crucial negotiating variables. (p. 7.18)

13. Explain how the various claim negotiation settings can affect the outcome of the negotiation. (pp. 7.20–7.22)

14. Explain how a claim representative might use (a) the principle of yes and (b) choicing to negotiate a claim resolution. (pp. 7.24–7.26)

15. Briefly explain how a claim representative might use each of the following negotiation techniques when negotiating with unrepresented claimants. (pp. 7.27–7.30)

    a. Collecting and using extraneous information

    b. Using sales techniques in negotiation

c. Using needs analysis to effect a settlement

d. Making the first offer

16. How can a claim representative use each of the following negotiation techniques with claimant's representatives? (pp. 7.31–7.34)

    a. Using information obtained from the claim evaluation

    b. Establishing strengths and weaknesses

c. Using timing

d. Making the first offer

e. Making concessions

17. Explain how a claimant's representative might use the following negotiation techniques. (pp. 7.34–7.35)

a. Limited authority negotiations

b. Timing in negotiations

18. Identify two negotiation techniques that claim representatives should avoid using. (p. 7.35)

19. What problems could occur if a claim representative used Boulwarism in negotiations? (p. 7.36)

20. Why should claim representatives not make decreasing or limited offers when negotiating claims? (p. 7.36)

21. Identify some common negotiation pitfalls that parties sometimes make. (pp. 7.36–7.38)

22. How can a claim representative avoid allowing personalities to influence the settlement? (pp. 7.36–7.37)

23. Why are trading dollars and bidding against oneself considered negotiation pitfalls? (p. 7.37)

24. How should a claim representative avoid conceding in a claim negotiation as a deadline approaches? (pp. 7.37–7.38)

Application Questions

1. Read each of the following business case descriptions and identify the negotiation style used by the claim representative.

   a. Marv, a claim representative, was assigned an auto liability claim involving six injured claimants. Marv had to select an attorney to represent the interests of the insured in these bodily injury claims. Marv negotiated a contract with attorney Josh Brown. When visiting with Josh about the case, Marv was impressed that Josh was highly knowledgeable about such injury cases and that Marv and Josh seemed to communicate well with each other and even to anticipate what the other was thinking. The final contract that Marv agreed to with Josh was for a greater amount than XYZ usually contracts with attorneys, but Marv was glad that he had established good rapport with Josh, so he decided the cost was acceptable.

b. A claim representative for XYZ, Joyce, was assigned a theft claim. Claimant Delilah Grant explained to Joyce that she had been photographing flowers in her garden when the phone rang. She laid her 5 mega pixel digital camera on a stump and rushed inside to answer the phone. When she returned, the camera was gone. Delilah had paid $500 for the camera when it was new, five years earlier. She had insured the camera for that amount and had a receipt to show the purchase price. The policy required that Delilah pay the first $100 of any personal property loss (a $100 deductible). In the past year, the cost of such cameras has come down considerably and the exact model of camera that was stolen is no longer available. XYZ has a relationship with an electronics vendor that sells it products at a lower markup. Joyce suggested that XYZ would purchase a new 7 mega pixel camera by the same manufacturer for Joyce and would waive the deductible. XYZ purchased the 7 mega pixel camera from its vendor at the reduced cost of $350 to give to Delilah as settlement for her camera theft claim.

2. Select a closed claim with which you are familiar. Review the claim representative's documentation and identify portions that relate to each of the four steps in the claim negotiation process.

3. John, an employee of Parne Manufacturing, has suffered two previous injuries on the job for which Granton Insurance has paid workers' compensation claims. John is an easy-going fellow and takes work injuries in stride with the knowledge that manufacturing carries many occupational hazards. John's most recent injury occurred when he accidentally sawed off the tip of his left index finger. John's wife, Claire, is pregnant and expects to deliver their third child in the next month. She has been ordered to bed rest by her physician and has been unable to work at her part-time job for the past month, so they have temporarily lost that source of income. John will be unable to return to work for six weeks. Ross, a twenty-year claim representative of Grafton Insurance has been assigned to handle John's claim. Ross has thoroughly reviewed all aspects of John's claim and has investigated the Parne factory where the injury occurred. As a senior claim representative, Ross is highly esteemed in his office, and his authority level is one million dollars. Ross is very comfortable handling delicate claim situations. Parne Manufacturing is five miles from the Grafton Claim office in which Ross works.

What significant (a) claimant and (b) claim representative negotiation variables are likely to affect this claim negotiation?

4. Recommend one or more negotiation techniques a claim representative could use in each of the following claims.

   a. Royce is CEO of a successful IT service provider. While he and his family were on their annual European vacation, his home security system was breached, his home was broken into, and several expensive items were stolen. Items taken include a home theater system, five personal computers, a stereo system, a PS2 game system, and three small plasma screen TVs. Royce is not represented by an attorney.

b. Nineteen-year-old April was injured in an automobile accident when her friend, who was driving, was stopped for a red traffic light and the car was hit from behind by a sixteen-year-old motorist who had been drinking and failed to stop for the light. April's friend's car was pushed into the lane of traffic where it was struck by another vehicle. April sustained lacerations to her face and neck and suffered a broken collar bone, but she recovered from her injuries. Nine months after the accident, it appeared that April would have significant scarring on her face and neck. April is not represented by an attorney but is thinking of hiring one.

c. Millwright Manufacturing, Inc., suffered partial loss of a building and manufacturing equipment at one of its seven plants after an employee/custodian left oily rags that ignited in a closet near a water heater. A worker in a neighboring business noticed smoke coming from a window of the factory and called for emergency services; therefore, the fire was contained to one area of the plant. This plant is one of the oldest that Millwright owns, and some of the equipment that was damaged was scheduled for replacement the following year. Millwright's attorney, Cecil Clay, will negotiate the claim.

5. Janine, a newer claim representative for XYZ Insurance, negotiated her first total loss auto property claim with an unrepresented claimant, Nadine. Janine told Nadine that if she did not call to accept her offer by the following Wednesday at 4 PM, XYZ would reduce the amount of the offer by $500, because the prospective salvage buyer would refuse the salvage after that time.

Is there a problem with Janine's offer? Explain your answer.

6. Larry, a new claim representative for XYZ Insurance, was assigned to handle a partial homeowners fire loss claim. The claimant, Tom, was very headstrong and tended to drag out the claim process. Larry and Tom met on two occasions to attempt to negotiate a claim settlement on the loss, but on both occasions, Tom got angry and accused Larry of belittling his claim. Tom then vowed that he would get another estimate to justify his demands. Before the third meeting with Tom, Larry's supervisor told him that he really needs to get this claim settled at this meeting or they would need to submit the claim to arbitration. Larry's incorrect perception was that, if the claim was submitted to arbitration, it would indicate that Larry had failed to negotiate properly and that it would reflect poorly on his performance as a claim representative. In the third negotiation, Tom became angry again and called Larry derogatory names. This time, Larry gave in to Tom's demanded settlement, even though it exceeded Larry's settlement range by $2,000 and Tom failed to provide any new evidence to support the higher settlement amount.

What two negotiation pitfalls occurred in this case and how should Larry have avoided them?

Answers to Assignment 7 Questions

NOTE: These answers are provided to give students a basic understanding of acceptable types of responses. They often are not the only valid answers and are not intended to provide an exhaustive response to the questions.

Review Questions

1. a. Qualities important to claim representatives who seek to obtain the best outcome include thorough knowledge of the claim file; persistence; firmness coupled with fairness; and thorough evaluation of the claim.

    b. Qualities important to claim representatives who seek to achieve rapport include good listening skills, humor, empathy, and friendliness.

2. The following are the four negotiation styles:

    *   Win-win—a negotiator using this style seeks to obtain the best outcome and to achieve rapport with the other party, resulting in a settlement that is satisfying to all parties. This style of negotiator is simultaneously assertive and cooperative and approaches disagreements as tools to better understand other parties' wants and needs.

    *   Win-lose—a negotiator using this style sees negotiation as a contest between two opposing parties, each seeking to defeat the other. The parties' greatest concern is obtaining the best outcome for their side, and they have little interest in achieving rapport with the other party.

    *   Lose-win—a negotiator using this style is primarily concerned with achieving rapport with the other party; obtaining the best outcome is a low priority.

    *   Lose-lose—a negotiator using this style has little concern either for obtaining the best outcome or for achieving rapport. The negotiator may focus on a fast resolution without considering the other party's specific wants or needs.

3. The win-win style of negotiations is generally best suited for use by claim representatives because it demonstrates an interest in resolving the claim to the claimant's satisfaction and may help build rapport as negotiations continue.

4. Steps in the negotiation process are the following:

    (1) Prepare

    (2) Develop and evaluate alternative outcomes

    (3) Identify and evaluate each party's interests

    (4) Make concessions and create appropriate resolutions

5. During the first step, preparation, the claim representative assembles information on the claimant's lifestyle, expectations, preferences, and likely behavior; any previous claims handled by the current insurer or other insurers and their outcomes; and any information about the claimant's history that might be beneficial in the negotiation. For a commercial insured, the claim representative may assemble information about the claimant's business or employment policies, its supply contracts, and even its competitors.

6. In the second step of the negotiation process, the claim representative can develop a BATNA to help avoid accepting unfavorable terms and rejecting favorable terms. The claim representative determines the costs of the BATNA and the likely outcome and then compares any offer against the cost of the BATNA. If the offer is less costly than the BATNA, then the claim representative should seriously consider it. If the offer is greater than the BATNA, then the claim representative should reject it.

7. In the third step of the negotiation process, the claim representative should consider the claimant's essential needs, socialization needs, personal needs, and/or organizational needs.

8. In the final stage of the negotiation process, parties can use concessions, or trade-offs, to create appropriate resolutions. Negotiators can assess prospective concessions by considering the best and worst possible claim resolutions for each party and examining the effect a concession would have on the claim resolution. Because the parties' perceived value of the concession can vary, the concessions can lead to a win-win resolution.

9. Significant negotiation variables that affect the claimant include the following:
    - Which phase of negotiation the claimant is in
    - Claimant's financial needs
    - Time pressures the claimant may face
    - Claimant's emotional reaction to the loss
    - Claimant's experience with or knowledge of insurance claims
    - Claimant's personality.

10. The claimant's need for money and any time pressures determine how the claim representative should approach negotiations. The claim representative can use the claimant's financial need to effect an early and reasonable settlement. When the claimant faces some time pressure, the claim representative can combine a reasonable offer with a promise of prompt payment to encourage the claimant to negotiate a claim settlement.

11. Significant negotiation variables that affect claim representatives include the following:
    - Claim representative's knowledge of the claim
    - Claim representative's authority level
    - Number of alternatives available for a satisfactory claim settlement
    - Claim representative's time factors
    - Negotiation settings
    - Claim representative's personality

12. The claim representative's knowledge of the claim and authority level are crucial. The more the claim representative knows about the loss details, the parties, and the results of the investigation, the better prepared he or she is to negotiate a satisfactory claim settlement based on the merits of the claim. The claim representative should be given sufficient authority to settle the claim up to its estimated maximum value before the negotiation begins, or a claimant would be justified in seeking to negotiate with someone who has more authority. Assigning adequate negotiating authority demonstrates the insurer's good faith.

13. Claim negotiation settings can affect the outcome of a negotiation as follows:
    - In-person negotiation enables people to communicate more effectively using three channels of communication: words, tone, and body language, and can allow group dynamics to assist with settlement. Personal appearance offers information about the claimant's economic status, education, and personal life and helps the claim representative assess the claimant's potential credibility at trial. Sometimes a claimant's reaction to physical evidence can be informative.
    - Telephone negotiations during which the parties listen actively are generally quicker and more convenient than in-person negotiations. The conversations are usually shorter because the parties get to the point more quickly and avoid casual conversation.

- Internet negotiations using some form of blind bidding process can deliver an equitable settlement, based on the positions of the parties in dispute. A live facilitator can help the parties through the process and summarize the shared information. This process removes the personalities from the negotiation process and, for certain types of claims, it can result in a faster claim resolution with significantly lower legal costs.

14. a. To use the principle of "yes," a claim representative could begin negotiations with questions that will generate "yes" answers by asking question concerning points on which the parties agree. According to the principle, if the party answers "yes" enough times, he or she is likely to answer "yes" to subsequent questions.

   b. To use choicing, the claim representative could first present a choice that the other party will find least desirable and then a more attractive second choice. Based on comparison, the second choice will seem more attractive. Established rapport with the other party first helps the claim representative predict what choices will be less appealing and more appealing to that party.

15. a. Claim representatives look for clues in extraneous information that claimants provide about themselves and then use this information to development a settlement that meets the claimant's needs. Conversations with claimants can provide information about the claimant's education level and understanding of the claim processes. If the claim representative can arrange the meeting in the claimant's home, the claim representative can make observations about the claimant's lifestyle, hobbies, and other interests and may discover arbitrary or genuine deadlines for resolving the claim. All these details can be used to create claim resolutions that uniquely meet the claimant's needs.

   b. Claim representatives can use sales techniques in negotiations by using understanding of the claimant's wants and needs as the basis of the negotiation and by mirroring the behavior of the claimant to develop greater rapport. These approaches help the claim representative develop a better relationship in which to "sell" the claim settlement.

   c. When using needs analysis, claim representatives should be aware of the possibility that a claimant may be operating at a level at which money is not the most important need. In smaller losses, an insured who has esteem needs may be more concerned that the claim representative will take advantage of him or her and may be less motivated to settle the claim. Needs analysis may also help in negotiating claims involving total losses, such as in a house fire, because the claimant may have returned to the physiological level of safety and security level needs.

   d. Claim representatives might want to make the initial offer in negotiations with unrepresented claimants because those claimants may not know the value of their claim and may suggest inflated settlement amounts on the assumption that they will be negotiated down. Making the first offer enables the claim representative to set a reasonable expectation for the claim settlement.

16. a. Thorough knowledge of the claim gained from the investigation will help the claim representative develop initial offers or counteroffers and explain their rationale based on the facts of the case.

   b. The claim representative should establish the strengths and weaknesses (negotiation chips) of the claim, and then use the least significant chip first to seek a concession because it will be the easiest concession to obtain. Chips can be replayed and combined to create a stronger argument. The claim representative should save the most powerful chip for last to preserve the value of the other negotiating chips.

    c. The claim representative can use timing in negotiations with a claimant's attorney because the best time to settle is just before the claim becomes a lawsuit. At that point, the attorney has usually spent only a couple of hours working on the claim. Once a suit entails, the attorney's per-hour earnings on the claim declines as the time increases.

    d. Claim representatives can entice a reasonable demand on a claim when they begin the negotiation by asking the claimant's representative what fair settlement value would settle the case that day. Then the claim representative can use that figure to make an initial settlement offer that is more enticing to the claimant.

    e. Claim representatives should make concessions only when the facts of the claim justify a reevaluation of the claim. For example, when there is a compelling reason to settle the claim immediately, the claim representative may make concessions to accomplish that settlement. If the other party demands a specific settlement amount that is within the pre-negotiation settlement range, the claim representative may concede and accept the demand to avoid prolonging the negotiation.

17. a. Attorneys, public adjusters, and other claimants' representatives may use the limited authority negotiation technique because they cannot legally or ethically settle a claim without first speaking to their client, who is not present in most cases. The need to contact the claimant gives the claimant's representative the opportunity to leave the claim representative waiting, which may entice the claim representative to offer more money to settle the claim.

    b. Insurers benefit from settling claims before litigation begins by avoiding additional court and legal costs. A claimant's attorney may use this timing technique in negotiations to encourage a claim representative to accept a higher demand and avoid the additional costs just before the case goes to trial.

18. Claim representative should avoid using a first and final offer (Boulwarism) and decreasing or limited offers as negotiation techniques.

19. If a claim representative uses Boulwarism in negotiations, the claimant may refuse the offer, ending the negotiations and possibly resulting in a more costly resolution for the insurer. Boulwarism invites conflict and prevents collaboration.

20. Claim representatives should not use decreasing or limited offers because they invite conflict by placing unreasonable constraints on the other party. Once a claim representative makes an offer in a negotiation, it should stand unless the facts of the claim warrant a change.

21. Negotiation pitfalls include the following:
   - Allowing personalities to influence the settlement
   - Trading dollars
   - Bidding against oneself
   - Conceding as deadlines approach

22. Claim representatives should avoid allowing personalities to influence claim settlement by maintaining their focus on resolving the claim. They should object to any form of abuse, but good-faith claim handling precludes retaliation to personal attacks. In response to personal attacks, the claim representative should inform the other party that, if the offensive behavior continues, the negotiation will cease until the party is prepared to negotiate in a civil manner.

23. Trading dollars and bidding against oneself are pitfalls because claim negotiations should focus on the facts of the claim. Trading dollars focuses instead on the offers and demands. The settlement amount should be a byproduct of the negotiation. Bidding against oneself could signal that the claim representative lacks confidence in the claim evaluation or is overly eager to settle the claim. Concessions should be made only if the facts of the claim change.

24. As deadlines approach, claim representatives should use the knowledge of those deadlines as inducement to work more quickly to settle claims sooner and should avoid accepting excessive settlements to meet any deadlines.

Application Questions

1. a. Marv's negotiation style in this claim was lose-win because the contract was for a greater amount than XYZ usually contracts with attorneys.

   b. Joyce's negotiation style in this claim was win-win because both parties benefited from this arrangement.

2. Answers will vary, but the answer should reflect elements of all four steps of the claim process: prepare, develop and evaluate alternative outcomes, identify and evaluate each party's interests, and make concessions and create appropriate resolutions.

3. Answers may vary.

   a. Claimant negotiation variables evident in this case may include how badly the claimant needs money, experience with insurance claims, and claimant's personality.

   b. Claim representative's negotiation variables evident in this case may include claim representative's knowledge of the claim, authority level in negotiation, the setting because an in-person settling could be arranged easily, and the claim representative's personality.

4. Answers may vary.

   a. The claim representative might use a needs analysis technique when negotiating this claim to discover a settlement that would satisfy Royce's high-level needs such as belongingness and love, esteem, or self-actualization.

   b. The claim representative might use collecting and using extraneous information as a negotiation technique to find some way to meet April's needs because the scarring cannot be prevented and could affect April's future employment possibilities and social aspects of her life.

   c. The claim representative might use techniques such as establishing the strengths and weaknesses, making the first offer, and using timing (if the attorney delays the settlement).

5. There is a problem with Janine's offer; making decreasing offers is a technique claim representatives should avoid because it invites conflict. Janine should not reduce her offer unless the facts of the claim change and merit such a decrease.

6. Two negotiation pitfalls that occurred in this case are that (1) Larry allowed personalities to influence the settlement and (2) he conceded as a deadline approached, even though the facts of the case did not warrant any concessions. When Tom became angry, Larry should have told him that they would end the negotiation and reschedule it when they could continue in a civil manner. Larry should have realized that arbitration really is not a deadline but a right guaranteed by the policy for both parties. If Larry was dealing with a genuine deadline, he should have worked more quickly earlier in the claim to avoid any looming deadlines and should not allow deadlines to influence the settlement amount.

Managing Litigation

![Direct] **Direct Your Learning**

Educational Objectives

After learning the content of this assignment, you should be able to:

1. Given a third-party lawsuit against an insured, describe the activities a claim representative would perform to manage the lawsuit.

2. Given a bad-faith lawsuit against an insurer, describe the activities a claim representative would perform to manage the lawsuit.

3. Explain how a claim representative can manage litigation expenses.

4. Define or describe each of the Key Words and Phrases for this assignment.

Study Materials

Required Reading:

■ Claim Handling Principles and Practices
  • Chapter 8

Study Aids:

■ SMART Practice Exam CD-ROM

■ SMART Study Aids Review Notes and Flash Cards—Assignment 8

Outline

- **Managing a Third-Party Lawsuit**
  - A. Receiving the Summons and Complaint
  - B. Checking the Summons and Complaint
    1. Parties
    2. Service
    3. Time to Answer
    4. Statute of Limitations
    5. Jurisdiction and Venue
    6. Allegations
    7. Damages
  - C. Referring the Lawsuit to Defense Counsel
    1. Defense Counsel Selection
    2. Transmittal Form Completion
    3. Insured Notification
  - D. Assisting Counsel
    1. Litigation Plan
    2. Complaint Answer
    3. Discovery
    4. Assisting at Trial
    5. Trial Assistance
    6. Post-Trial Activities

- **Managing a Bad-Faith Lawsuit**
  - A. Receiving the Summons and Complaint
  - B. Checking the Summons and Complaint
    1. Parties
    2. Service
    3. Time to Answer
    4. Statute of Limitations
    5. Jurisdiction and Venue
    6. Allegations
    7. Damages
  - C. Referring the Lawsuit to Defense Counsel
  - D. Assisting Counsel
    1. Litigation Plan
    2. Complaint Answer
    3. Discovery
    4. Trial Preparation
    5. Trial Assistance
    6. Post-Trial Activities

- **Managing Litigation Expenses**
  - A. Creating a Litigation Plan
  - B. Creating a Litigation Budget
  - C. Auditing Legal Bills
  - D. Evaluating the Litigation Plan and Counsel Performance

- **Summary**

Use the SMART Practice Exam CD-ROM to self-test. The CD-ROM constructs individual assignment or comprehensive sample exams, allowing you to test your recall of important information. Feedback is provided, targeting the areas requiring further review.

Key Words and Phrases

Define or describe each of the words and phrases listed below.

Complaint, or petition (p. 8.4)

Summons (p. 8.4)

Service of process (p. 8.5)

Answer (p. 8.5)

Actual service (p. 8.7)

Substituted service, or constructive service (p. 8.7)

Jurisdiction (p. 8.8)

Venue (p. 8.10)

Allegations (p. 8.11)

Counterclaim (p. 8.16)

Default judgment (p. 8.17)

Discovery (p. 8.17)

Request for production of documents (p. 8.18)

Interrogatories (p. 8.18)

Deposition (p. 8.19)

Admissions (p. 8.21)

Stare decisis (p. 8.22)

Motion to dismiss (p. 8.24)

Motion *in limine* (p. 8.24)

Motion for summary judgment (p. 8.24)

Voir dire (p. 8.27)

Burden of proof (p. 8.27)

Preponderance of evidence (p. 8.27)

Flat fee (p. 8.40)

Phased fee (p. 8.40)

Review Questions

1. What are the four steps in the process of managing the litigation of claims? (p. 8.4)

2. Explain how a complaint, a summons, and service of process are used to initiate a lawsuit. (pp. 8.4–8.5)

3. Why is time of the essence when answering a complaint?
   (p. 8.5)

4. Upon checking the summons and complaint, what decisions must
   the claim representative make? (p. 8.5)

5. A complaint usually begins by identifying the parties in the lawsuit by name and address. What should the claim representative
   do with the defendant's information? (p. 8.6)

6. Differentiate between actual service and substituted service.
   (p. 8.7)

7. How is service on a corporation accomplished? (p. 8.7)

8. Why is it important for the claim representative to determine when and how service was accomplished? (p. 8.7)

9. What three issues does a claim representative look for when reviewing the court's jurisdiction over a particular lawsuit? (pp. 8.8–8.9)

10. What courts are in the federal court system? (pp. 8.9–8.10)

11. What types of courts do most state court systems include? (p. 8.10)

12. Why is venue important to a claim representative? (pp. 8.10–8.11)

13. What are the four functions of the body of a complaint?
    (p. 8.11)

14. Why does the claim representative review the demand for
    damages in a complaint? (p. 8.12)

15. What criteria should a claim representative use to select defense
    counsel for a particular lawsuit? (p. 8.13)

16. What information does a suit transmittal form usually contain?
    (pp. 8.13–8.14)

17. Why is it useful for the claim representative and the defense
    counsel to develop a litigation plan? (pp. 8.15–8.16)

18. Generally, what three possible objectives does a litigation plan outline? (p. 8.16)

19. What does the answer to the complaint usually contain? (pp. 8.16–8.17)

20. What are the five most commonly used methods of discovery? (p. 8.18)

21. What are two purposes of depositions? (p. 8.19)

22. What is an example of each of the following? (p. 8.19)

    a. Party witness

    b. Nonparty witness

23. Identify the parts of the following case citation. (p. 8.23)

    Baker v. Abel & Associates, 511 U.S. 1995, US Supreme Court, (2001)

24. What must a court find in order to grant a summary judgment motion? (p. 8.24)

25. Differentiate between a jury trial and a nonjury trial. (p. 8.26)

26. What are three bases for an appeal of a trial court decision? (p. 8.30)

27. How does the time limit to answer a bad-faith lawsuit differ from the time limit to answer a non-bad-faith lawsuit? (p. 8.32)

28. Who is usually named as the defendant in a bad-faith lawsuit and why? (p. 8.32)

29. What is a potential problem relating to service of a bad-faith lawsuit? (p. 8.33)

30. Why is providing the content of the answer to a bad-faith complaint the biggest challenge in a bad-faith lawsuit? (p. 8.35)

31. What are the three areas of discovery that cause significant concern for insurers and defense counsel? (p. 8.36)

32. What litigation management tools can a claim representative use to help provide an effective defense of an insured at a reasonable cost? (p. 8.39)

33. Why does a litigation plan help reduce the insurer's defense costs? (p. 8.40)

34. What categories of activities might be included in a litigation budget? (p. 8.40)

35. What information should each task in a litigation budget contain? (p. 8.41)

36. What information in the insurer's billing guidelines for defense attorneys can the claim representative use when reviewing a legal bill? (p. 8.41)

37. What questions might a claim representative ask when evaluating the litigation plan and the attorney's performance on a case? (p. 8.43)

Application Questions

The Brown v. Thomas Case. A summons and complaint is served on
Andy Thomas on March 1, 2004. Andy sends the summons and complaint to his agent, Gene Jones. Gene receives it on March 15. Gene
reviews the summons and complaint and determines that it pertains
to an auto accident Andy had on January 5, 2004. Gene sends the
summons and complaint to XYZ Insurance Company for defense. XYZ
Insurance Company receives the summons and complaint on April 3.
The summons and complaint is matched to a claim file.

The summons and complaint identifies Ann Brown as the plaintiff
and A. Thomas & Sons as the defendant. It states that the accident
occurred on January 5, 2004, at the intersection of Broad and Main
Streets in Malvern, Pennsylvania. The lawsuit has been filed in state
court in Cherry Hill, New Jersey.

In the allegations, Ms. Brown states that Andy Thomas was ticketed
for reckless driving and driving while intoxicated. She alleges serious
bodily injury resulting from the accident and requests judgment in the
amount of $1 million.

1. *Brown v. Thomas Case.* Analyze the case scenario as if you are the
   claim representative assigned to this claim. What activities would
   you perform to manage this lawsuit?

2. *Brown v. Thomas Case.* According to the claim file, no tickets
   were issued at the scene of the accident. Neither Andy Thomas
   nor Ann Brown was taken to the hospital after the accident.
   According to Andy's statement, the accident was a minor one. He
   indicates he tapped Ms. Brown's car in the rear when she stopped
   at a stop sign, as he was blinded by the sun and didn't see her.
   Given the information, create a litigation plan for this lawsuit.

3. *Brown v. Thomas Case*. Ultimately, the case of *Brown v. A. Thomas & Sons* is tried before a jury. During the trial, Andy's defense counsel makes several objections to the admission of evidence proffered by Ann's attorney. The judge overrules each of defense counsel's objections. At the end of the trial, the jury returns a verdict of $750,000.

   What recourse does the claim representative and defense counsel have if they disagree with the verdict?

4. Compare and contrast the management of a bad-faith lawsuit with that of a non-bad-faith lawsuit.

5. Claim representative Jane has been asked to review legal bills submitted by defense counsel handling a litigated claim. Identify some of the items Jane should look for when reviewing the bills.

Answers to Assignment 8 Questions

NOTE: These answers are provided to give students a basic understanding of acceptable types of responses. They often are not the only valid answers and are not intended to provide an exhaustive response to the questions.

Review Questions

1. The four steps in the process of managing the litigation of claims are as follows:

    (1) Receiving the summons and complaint

    (2) Checking the summons and complaint to identify the parties, the applicable statute of limitations, the jurisdiction and venue, and the allegations

    (3) Referring the lawsuit to counsel, which involves selecting an attorney to represent the insured, preparing a suit transmittal letter, and notifying the insured of the selection

    (4) Assisting counsel in creating a litigation plan, answering the complaint, preparing evidence, preparing for trial, and managing pre-trial and post-trial activities

2. A lawsuit is initiated by the filing of a complaint or petition, which specifies the grounds or allegations on which relief can be granted. The complaint is attached to a summons and delivered to the defendant. The summons specifies the amount of time to answer the complaint. A sheriff or another court-designated officer makes the delivery. The delivery of the summons and complaint is called service of process.

3. Time is of the essence in answering a summons and complaint because the summons contains a deadline by which the answer must be filed.

4. After receiving the summons and complaint, the claim representative must identify the parties in the complaint, determine the applicable statute of limitations and whether it has expired, and verify that the jurisdiction and venue are correct. The claim representative must also determine whether the insurance policy provides a defense against the allegations and coverage for any possible damages that may result from the allegations. Claim representatives cannot assume that all claims contained in lawsuits they receive are covered by the policy and are therefore eligible to be defended.

5. Using the complaint, the claim representative must verify that the defendant is an insured under the applicable policy. When a commercial insured is involved, the claim representative may have to investigate the entities listed in the complaint to determine whether the defendant is an insured. If the claim representative fails to verify the defendant is an insured on the policy, the insurer may erroneously provide a defense to an uninsured party.

6. Actual service is in-hand delivery of the summons and complaint to the defendant. Substituted service is any method of notifying the defendant other than personal delivery of the summons and complaint.

7. In the case of a corporation, the articles of incorporation designate the person authorized to accept service on behalf of the corporation, and that designation is filed with the secretary of state in the state of incorporation.

8. It is important for the claim representative to determine when and how service was accomplished because the deadline to answer the summons and complaint is based on the date of service.

9. When reviewing the court's jurisdiction over a lawsuit, the claim representative must verify that the court has jurisdiction over the parties to the suit, the subject matter of the suit, and the dollar amount at issue in the suit.

10. The courts in the federal court system are the following:
     - U.S. Supreme Court
     - U.S. Circuit Courts of Appeal
     - U.S. district courts
     - Special federal courts such as the Court of International Trade

11. Generally, state court systems have the following courts:
     - Lowest court, such as small claims courts
     - Courts of limited jurisdiction, such as probate court
     - Trial courts
     - Intermediate appellate courts
     - Highest appellate court

12. Venue is important to the claim representative because when several different courts meet the requirements of jurisdiction and venue, the plaintiff chooses the court that is most likely to favor the plaintiff's lawsuit. This is an accepted practice; however, some plaintiffs may engage in a more questionable practice called forum shopping—manipulating the facts of a lawsuit to take advantage of a favorable venue, or forum. The claim representative should review the summons and complaint to determine whether the venue is questionable, and, if so, alert defense counsel.

13. The body of the complaint serves the following four functions:
     (1) Gives notice
     (2) Reveals facts
     (3) Formulates legal causes of action
     (4) States the damages sought

14. The claim representative should review the demand for damages section carefully to determine whether the damages sought exceed policy limits. If so, the claim representative should advise the insured that the policy may not cover the total potential damages in the case. This information is usually contained in what is called an excess letter.

15. When selecting defense counsel, claim representatives should try to match the attorney's experience level to the subject matter and complexity of the lawsuit. Claim representatives should also select defense counsel who will meet the service needs of the insured and the insurer. Defense counsel should be willing to work as a team with the claim representative in defending the insured.

16. The suit transmittal form usually contains a summary of the lawsuit and the claim investigation to date and includes the claim representative's opinions and expectations about the lawsuit's outcome. If the lawsuit is the first notice of the claim, the lawsuit transmittal letter informs defense counsel of how the claim representative intends to investigate the allegations.

17. It is useful for the claim representative and the defense counsel to develop a litigation plan because this process can lay the foundation for effective communication between the claim representative and counsel throughout the trial, and the litigation plan itself can reduce the possibility of misunderstandings and disagreements with counsel. By agreeing on a goal at the outset, the claim representative and counsel can more easily work as a team to achieve the desired result. A litigation plan should also clarify the roles and expectations of the parties.

18. The following are the three possible objectives of a litigation plan:

    (1) Defend the lawsuit

    (2) Settle the lawsuit

    (3) Obtain more information to decide whether to defend or settle the lawsuit

19. The answer to the complaint contains the defendant's initial response to the complaint's allegations, presents affirmative defenses to the allegations, and provides defense counsel the opportunity to file a counterclaim if the defendant has been wronged.

20. The five most commonly used methods of discovery are the following:

    (1) Requests for production of documents

    (2) Interrogatories

    (3) Depositions

    (4) Physical or mental examinations

    (5) Admissions of facts not in dispute

21. The two purposes of depositions are: (1) They allow each party to the lawsuit to discover what the other party's witnesses know about the facts of the matter and (2) because the testimony is transcribed, it can be used to challenge any conflicting testimony given by the same witness at trial. Such a challenge can discredit the witness, and in some cases, expose the witness to a perjury charge.

22. Answers may vary.

    a. An example of a party witness is the plaintiff.

    b. An example of a nonparty witness is an expert witness.

23. *Baker v. Abel & Associates* is the case name. Baker is the plaintiff and Abel & Associates is the defendant. 511 is the volume number of the case reporter in which the case can be found. U.S. is the abbreviation for the name of the case reporter. 1995 is the page number where the case can be found. US Supreme Court is the name of the court that decided the case, and 2001 is the year the case was decided.

24. To grant a summary judgment motion, the court must find that no genuine issues of material fact are in dispute and that the moving party (the party who made the motion) is entitled to judgment as a matter of law.

25. In a jury trial, a group of people are selected to hear and consider the evidence in a case and decide what facts are true. In a jury trial, the jury decides all questions of fact and the judge decides all questions of law. In a non-jury trial, the judge decides all questions of both fact and law.

26. The following are three bases for an appeal of a trial court decision:

    (1) Trial court's ruling on the admissibility of evidence

    (2) Judge's instructions to the jury

    (3) Verdict is against the weight of the evidence

27. The time limit to answer a bad-faith lawsuit does not differ from the time limit to answer a non-bad-faith lawsuit.

28. The insurer—not the claim representative—is usually named as the defendant, because the insurer has sizable assets available to pay a judgment.

29. A potential problem in a bad-faith claim is that the service may have been accomplished at a location far from where the claim is being handled. For example, service may have been made at the insurer's corporate headquarters rather than at the local claim office.

30. The biggest challenge in a bad-faith lawsuit is providing the content of the answer to the complaint. It must be accurate and consistent with corporate policy. Formulating an answer to allegations in a bad-faith complaint can require substantial research by the claim representative.

31. The three areas of discovery that can cause significant concern for insurers and defense counsel are (1) the discovery of corporate financial information, (2) the discovery of documents believed to be privileged, and (3) the discovery of the claim file itself.

32. The claim representative can use a litigation plan, a litigation budget, legal bill audits, and an evaluation of defense counsel's performance to help provide an effective defense of an insured at a reasonable cost.

33. A litigation plan helps reduce an insurer's defense costs because it ensures that the claim representative and the defense attorney are working toward a common goal. If the claim representative and the defense attorney have different goals, they may end up working at cross purposes, resulting in duplicated effort, unmet expectations, and additional legal expense to rectify the situation.

34. The categories of activities in a litigation budget can include the following:
    - Case review, including initially reviewing material from the claim representative and interviewing the insured and other involved parties
    - Legal research
    - Initial pleadings, including drafting an answer to the complaint, and cross-claims or counterclaims
    - Discovery, including drafting interrogatories, answering the opponent's interrogatories, preparing for and attending depositions, and complying with document production requests
    - Locating and retaining experts
    - Motions
    - Negotiations and conferences
    - Trial

35. Each task in a litigation budget should include a description of the task and the name of the party assigned to perform the task. The task should show a time estimate and the cost estimate. The cost estimate may be a simple calculation of the number of hours multiplied by the hourly rate, or it may be a "not to exceed" estimate, which places a limit on the amount the attorney can spend without first discussing it with the claim representative. Outside expenses, such as travel costs, court reporters' fees, and expert witness fees, should also be budgeted.

36. The insurer's billing guidelines usually require a detailed, itemized record of work performed, which includes the task performed, how long the task took in tenth-of-an-hour increments, the name of the attorney or paralegal who performed the activity, and any expense associated with the task. The billing guidelines also specify the hourly rate to be charged by each attorney and paralegal; travel expenses allowed; and associated expenses, such as overnight mailing or photocopying charges, that can be charged to the case. The claim representative will use all this information when reviewing a legal bill.

37. A claim representative might ask the following questions when evaluating the litigation plan and the attorney's performance on a case:

    * Was the final outcome of the case satisfactory?

    * Was the case's final outcome the outcome that was specified in the plan at the beginning of the case? If not, why not?

    * Was the original plan realistic, given the facts known at the time?

    * Was the plan revised in a timely manner to reflect changes in facts as they became known?

    * Were the plan and any subsequent revisions agreed on by both the claim representative and the attorney, or were changes made unilaterally?

    * Did the attorney adhere to the plan?

    * Were any expenses incurred that were unanticipated by the plan and the budget? If so, how could this be avoided in the future?

Application Questions

1. Answers may vary in the order in which these activities may occur. To manage this lawsuit, the claim representative should confirm that A. Thomas & Sons is a policyholder and that Andy Thomas is an insured under the policy. The claim representative should determine the date the answer is due from the summons and calculate the date. If there is time to refer the file to defense counsel, the claim representative should prepare the referral. If there is insufficient time, the claim representative should obtain an extension of time to answer from Ms. Brown's attorney.

   The claim representative should find out if Andy is listed as a party who can accept service for A. Thomas & Sons. The claim representative should ask Andy how he received the summons and complaint to see if service was proper.

   The claim representative should check with defense counsel to determine whether New Jersey state court in Cherry Hill is the proper jurisdiction and venue based on the information given.

   The claim representative should determine whether the lawsuit was filed within the applicable statute of limitations.

   The claim representative should match the allegations in the summons and complaint to the facts contained in the claim file and make notes on issues that arise.

   The claim representative should send an excess letter to the insured if the amount demanded in the summons and complaint exceeds the insured's policy limits.

2. Answers can vary. However, the plan should begin with a decision as to whether to defend, settle, or obtain more information. Discovery can include a request for production of documents, interrogatories, depositions, physical examination, admission of facts not in dispute, and possible pre-trial motions.

3. If they disagree with the verdict, defense counsel and the claim representative can agree to ask the court to decrease the amount of the judgment. They can also appeal the verdict to a higher court if there are decisions of law, such as the admissibility of certain evidence, which the appellate court can review.

4. Many aspects of managing a lawsuit are the same whether the lawsuit is a bad-faith lawsuit or a non-bad-faith lawsuit. These aspects include checking the summons and complaint, rules of service, time to answer, checking for jurisdiction and venue, trial preparation, assistance at trial, and post-trial activities.

    For other aspects, including the following, management of the two types of lawsuits differs:

    - Receiving the summons and complaint—in a bad-faith lawsuit, the summons and complaint may be served on the insurer's corporate office, local office, or an insurer representative. In non-bad-faith lawsuits, the insured is served.

    - Parties—generally, bad-faith lawsuits are brought against the insurer and sometimes the individual claim representative. In a non-bad-faith lawsuit, the insured is usually the defendant.

    - Statute of limitations—for both kinds of lawsuits, the claim representative should check the applicable statutes of limitations to determine if the lawsuit has been filed within the time limit. If a bad-faith claim is included in a lawsuit for coverage, the claim representative should also determine whether the policy applicable to the underlying claim specifies a time limit for filing a lawsuit.

    - Allegations—allegations in a bad-faith lawsuit may be specific to how the underlying claim was handled, or general, alleging a pattern or practice occurring with many different claims. In contrast to the relative simplicity of investigating allegations that involve a single claim, investigation of a pattern of practice over many years can be complicated.

    - Damages—because damages in bad-faith claims may be punitive in nature, the dollar value damages sought is often extremely high.

    - Referring the lawsuit to defense counsel—for both types of lawsuit, the claim representative must assign the case to defense counsel for handling. Insurers usually draw from a different list of experienced attorneys for bad-faith lawsuits than for other lawsuits because specific expertise is needed.

    - Assisting counsel—in comparison with other lawsuits, the claim representative who handles a bad-faith lawsuit may be more actively involved in the discovery and trial preparation. In a bad-faith lawsuit, the attorney's client is the insurer, and the claim representative handling the lawsuit is the primary point of contact with the client.

    - Litigation Plan—a litigation plan is created for the defense of both kinds of cases. For bad-faith lawsuits, the claim representative and defense counsel must review all information available about handling the underlying claim to determine whether a bad-faith loss exposure exists. They must communicate openly with one another about the contents of the claim file, and they must be realistic about the potential for significant financial consequences and loss of public trust that may result from a bad-faith lawsuit.

    - Complaint answer—procedurally, preparing the answer is similar for both types of cases. However, formulating an answer to allegations in a bad-faith complaint can require substantially more research by the claim representative.

    - Discovery—discovery is procedurally the same for both kinds of cases. It is the content in a bad-faith lawsuit that can be very demanding. Claim representatives who handle bad-faith claims must be able to locate information from many sources within the insurer. Three areas of discovery can cause significant concern for insurers and defense counsel in a bad-faith discovery that do not occur in a non-bad-faith lawsuit: (1) discovery of corporate financial information, (2) discovery of documents believed to be privileged, and (3) discovery of the claim file itself.

5. Jane should look for the following items when reviewing the legal bills:

- Dates of the major activities on the bill should correspond with dates of the same activities in the claim file. For example, if the bill lists a thirty-minute phone call with the claim representative on a specific date, the claim representative should have a corresponding entry in the claim activity log.

- Only the work of parties (partner, associate, paralegal) agreed to in advance by the handling attorney and the claim representative should be included on the bill.

- Mathematical computations should be checked for accuracy. Despite law firms' use of computerized billing systems, errors do occur.

- Only authorized investigative activity should be included on the bill.

- Only authorized attorneys should have appeared at depositions, hearings, motions, or trials. Billing for any additional attorneys or legal staff should be questioned.

- Itemized incremental billing should be based on a reasonable time for the specific activity billed. Attorneys bill in tenth-of-an-hour increments, so six minutes equals 0.1 hour, twelve minutes equals 0.2 hour, eighteen minutes equals 0.3 hour, and so on. For example, unless a letter is extremely long, it usually does not take someone fifteen minutes to review it.

- Absent a compelling reason, most attorneys should not bill more than 10 hours per day.

- Administrative costs, such as general postage, local travel, word processing, and other items of overhead, should not be billed unless specifically agreed to, either in the billing guidelines or by the claim representative.

- Airfare, hotel, and meal charges should comply with the billing guidelines.

About Institute Exams

Exam questions are based on the educational objectives stated in the course guide. The exam is designed to measure whether you have met those educational objectives. The exam does not test every educational objective. Instead, it tests over a balanced sample of educational objectives.

How to Pass Institute Exams

What can you do to make sure you pass an Institute exam? Students who successfully pass Institute exams do the following:

- Use the assigned study materials. Focus your study on the educational objectives presented at the beginning of each course guide assignment. Thoroughly read the textbook and any other assigned materials, and then complete the course guide exercises. Choose a study method that best suits your needs; for example, participate in a traditional class, online class, or informal study group; or study on your own. Use the Institutes' SMART Study Aids (if available) for practice and review.

- Become familiar with the types of test questions. The practice exam in this course guide will help you understand the different types of questions you will encounter on the exam.

- Maximize test-taking time. Successful students also use the sample exam to practice pacing themselves. Learning how to manage your time during the exam ensures that you will complete all of the test questions in the time allotted.

Types of Exam Questions

The Correct-Answer Type

In this type of question, the question stem is followed by four responses, one of which is absolutely correct. Select the *correct* answer.

Which one of the following persons evaluates requests for insurance and determines which applicants are accepted and which are rejected?
a. The premium auditor
b. The loss control representative
c. The underwriter
d. The risk manager

The Best-Answer Type

In this type of question, the question stem is followed by four responses, only one of which is best, given the statement made or facts provided in the stem. Select the *best* answer.

Several people within an insurer might be involved in determining whether an applicant for insurance is accepted. Which one of the following is primarily responsible for determining whether an applicant for insurance is accepted?
a. The loss control representative
b. The customer service representative
c. The underwriter
d. The premium auditor

The Incomplete-Statement or Sentence-Completion Type

In this type of question, the last part of the question stem consists of a portion of a statement rather than a direct question. Select the phrase that *correctly* or *best* completes the sentence.

Residual market plans designed for individuals who have been unable to obtain insurance on their personal property in the voluntary market are called

a. VIN plans.

b. Self-insured retention plans.

c. Premium discount plans.

d. FAIR plans.

"All of the Above" Type

In this type of question, only one of the first three answers could be correct, or all three might be correct, in which case the best answer would be "All of the above." Read all the answers and select the *best* answer.

When a large commercial insured's policy is up for renewal, who is likely to provide input to the renewal decision process?

a. The underwriter

b. The loss control representative

c. The producer

d. All of the above

"All of the following, EXCEPT:" Type

In this type of question, responses include three correct answers and one answer that is incorrect or is clearly the least correct. Select the *incorrect* or *least correct* answer.

All of the following adjust insurance claims, EXCEPT:

a. Insurer claim representatives

b. Premium auditors

c. Producers

d. Independent adjusters

AIC 33 Sample Exam

The following sample exam consists of two sections—Part A and Part B. On the actual exam, you must answer all questions in both Part A and Part B of the exam. Each question is worth one point. Each Part A question should be answered independently of the others.

Part B questions may include or refer to specific facts, cases, or exhibits. In Part B, your answers must be based on the information provided. When several questions are based on the same set of facts during a computer-administered exam, those facts will appear in a separate window and remain in view for the duration of the questions.

Part A

1. Two elements of risk are
   a. The possibility of loss and the probability that the loss will occur.
   b. An uncertain outcome and the possibility of loss.
   c. The probability of loss and an uncertain outcome.
   d. A certain outcome and the inevitability of loss.

2. All of the following are risk control techniques, EXCEPT:
   a. Avoidance
   b. Separation
   c. Duplication
   d. Centralization

3. All of the following are indirect costs of insurance, EXCEPT:
   a. Opportunity costs
   b. Moral hazards
   c. Increased litigation
   d. Social burdens

4. Staff claim representatives are typically employed by the
   a. Insured.
   b. Third-party administrator.
   c. Claimant.
   d. Insurer.

5. Insurers use all of the following measures to determine an insurer's profitability, EXCEPT:
   a. Loss ratio
   b. Expense ratio
   c. Profit ratio
   d. Combined ratio

6. Reinsurance is a mechanism that
   a. Ensures that insurers will have sufficient funds to pay claims.
   b. Allows an insured to collect more than the policy limit on a claim.
   c. Allows an insurer to collect higher premiums.
   d. Ensures that an insurer will not write too many risks in a given location.

7. In 1945, Congress passed legislation providing that states would regulate insurance. This legislation further provided that if states failed to do so or under certain conditions, federal antitrust laws would apply. This legislation is called the
   a. McCarran-Ferguson Act.
   b. Clayton Act.
   c. Unfair Claims Settlement Practices Act.
   d. Sherman Act.

8. An organization that coordinates insurance regulation among the states, but has no direct regulatory authority is the
   a. Insurance Regulatory Information System (IRIS).
   b. National Association of Insurance Commissioners (NAIC).
   c. Insurance Services Office, Inc. (ISO).
   d. South-Eastern Underwriters Association (SEUA).

9. All of the following are purposes for exclusions in insurance policies, EXCEPT:
   a. Assist in keeping policies uniform in content
   b. Eliminate coverages the typical insured does not need
   c. Eliminate coverage for uninsurable loss exposures
   d. Reduce the likelihood of coverage duplications

10. When analyzing the policy, the claim representative should identify the coverages that
   a. Were in force throughout the current policy term.
   b. Were in force on the date of the loss.
   c. Apply in most claims.
   d. The agent or insured listed on the loss notice.

11. Which one of the following losses would best be described as an indirect loss?
   a. Loss to a satellite dish that was struck by lightning
   b. Rain damage to oak flooring after a windstorm damages the roof
   c. Hail damage to a roof
   d. Hotel expenses while fire damage to a home is repaired

12. Two general categories of damages in a liability claim are compensatory and
    a. Special.
    b. Punitive.
    c. Future.
    d. General.

13. In determining an individual case reserve, a claim representative considers all of the following, EXCEPT:
    a. Data from past claims that are similar
    b. The nature and extent of the injury
    c. Actuarial analysis
    d. Liability factors

14. A document that reserves the insurer's and policyholder's rights under the policy without the need for the insured's signature or consent is
    a. A reservation of rights letter.
    b. An estoppel agreement.
    c. A waiver.
    d. A nonwaiver agreement.

15. A claim has been open for fifty days. Which one of the following would a claim representative complete to describe the status of the claim?
    a. Initial report
    b. Interim report
    c. Actuarial report
    d. Underwriting report

16. All of the following are alternative dispute resolution techniques, EXCEPT:
    a. Mediation
    b. Arbitration
    c. Concession
    d. Appraisal

17. Liability based on negligence requires four elements—a legal duty owed, failure to meet that duty, bodily injury or property damage, and
    a. An intentional act resulting in bodily injury or property damage.
    b. Expenses incurred in treating a bodily injury or repairing damaged property.
    c. The injured party must not have contributed to the loss.
    d. Proximate cause between the failure to meet the duty and the resulting injury or property damage.

18. Failure to exercise the care of a reasonable person under the circumstances so as not to cause harm is
    a. An intentional tort.
    b. Negligence.
    c. Strict liability.
    d. Contract liability.

19. All of the following pieces of information can be found on a liability loss notice form, EXCEPT:
    a. Insured contact information
    b. Policy information
    c. Description of the loss
    d. Insured's date of birth

20. For a recorded statement, a claim representative should
    a. Answer coverage questions during the interview.
    b. Ask the interviewee to use verbal responses.
    c. Ask others present to interrupt and add details.
    d. Provide the interviewee with a lawyer.

21. Which one of the following types of questions can be used to suggest a particular answer?
    a. Direct
    b. Indirect
    c. Leading
    d. Open-ended

22. To determine the cause of loss in a property damage claim, a claim representative may retain which one of the following experts?
    a. Origin and cause
    b. Accountant
    c. Salvor
    d. Appraiser

23. When determining damages in a total auto loss, which one of the following calculations would the claim representative use if the auto retained some salvage value?
    a. Fair market value – Deductible – Salvage
    b. ACV – Salvage – Any remaining deductible
    c. Fair market value – Salvage – Any remaining deductible
    d. ACV – Deductible – Salvage

24. In most claims, the claim representative must determine the cause of the loss and the loss amount. In workers' compensation claims, the investigation differs and the claim representative instead determines the

    a. Extent of injury and the cost of the treatment.

    b. Compensability of the claim and the benefits payable to the insured.

    c. Compensability of the claim and the benefits payable to the injured worker or his or her family.

    d. Location where the injury occurred and the cost of the treatment.

25. Concealment is

    a. Failing to disclose a material fact for the purpose of misleading another party.

    b. Making a statement that is untrue, even if the person making the statement does not know it is untrue.

    c. Deliberately deceiving an insurer for the purpose of unwarranted financial gain.

    d. Asking the insurer for reimbursement of a greater sum than was actually incurred in the loss.

26. Primary motives for insurance fraud include all of the following, EXCEPT:

    a. Individual financial gain or profit

    b. Sense of entitlement

    c. To understand the mechanics of insurance

    d. Participation in organized crime

27. Which one of the following employee behaviors would be an example of lost earnings fraud?

    a. Reporting that an injury occurred at home even though it occurred at work

    b. Collecting workers' compensation benefits after having fully recovered from the injury and becoming capable of returning to work

    c. Visiting relatives out of state while receiving workers' compensation benefits for a work-related injury

    d. Stopping the workers' compensation benefits and returning to work before making a full recovery

28. The presence of one or more fraud indicators in a claim does not conclusively prove fraud. The claim may still be legitimate. What can a claim representative do to remain objective during the claim investigation?

    a. The claim representative can perform a balanced investigation into the facts of the claim.

    b. The claim representative can focus on the fraud indicators and ignore any reasonable explanation given by the insured.

    c. The claim representative can accept the explanations of the insured at face value and ignore the fraud indicators entirely.

    d. The claim representative can pay the amount claimed without any further investigation.

29. All of the following are red flags for auto fraud, EXCEPT:

    a. No police report is made after a serious accident.

    b. The police report is completed at a police station rather than at the accident location.

    c. The vehicle involved is a heavily financed luxury vehicle.

    d. No towing charge is claimed, even though the inspection suggests the vehicle could not have been driven from the accident scene.

30. All of the following are burglary and theft fraud indicators, EXCEPT:

    a. The loss is incompatible with the insured's lifestyle.

    b. All the items lost are new or gifts for which no receipts are available.

    c. The insured cannot remember where or when new items were purchased.

    d. The insured has receipts for photos of most but not all major items lost.

31. Which one of the following statements is true regarding anti-fraud efforts?

    a. Legislation that expands the definition of insurance fraud is ineffective in reducing fraud.

    b. Allowing professionals who commit insurance fraud to keep their licenses is effective in reducing fraud.

    c. Pre-inspection programs are proving to be effective in reducing theft claims for nonexistent or phantom vehicles.

    d. Mandatory reporting laws require that law enforcement agencies report suspected fraud to insurers.

32. States have adopted immunity statutes that eliminate the threat of a civil lawsuit against insurers that

    a. Form SIUs.

    b. Develop anti-fraud plans.

    c. Place fraud warnings on claim forms.

    d. Share information about fraudulent claims.

33. Good faith requires an insurer to give consideration to the insured's interests that is
    a. Less than the consideration it gives its own interests.
    b. At least equal to the consideration it gives its own interests.
    c. Greater than the consideration it gives its own interests.
    d. Not related to the consideration it gives its own interests.

34. A policyholder would sue his or her own insurer for bad faith in a
    a. Declaratory judgment action.
    b. Summary judgment action.
    c. First-party lawsuit.
    d. Third-party lawsuit.

35. All of the following are categories of goals shared by state unfair claim settlement practices acts, EXCEPT:
    a. Efficiency
    b. Promptness
    c. Honesty
    d. Fair-mindedness

36. Contractual damages in a bad-faith claim would include
    a. The amount of an excess verdict over policy limits.
    b. The full amount of coverage up to the policy limits.
    c. Interest or other statutorily prescribed damages for delay.
    d. Expenses associated with filing the lawsuit and the litigation process.

37. Which one of the following is part of a defense to bad-faith claims?
    a. Lawyer's advice
    b. Inadequate claim management
    c. Biased investigation
    d. Uninformed evaluation

38. An example of comparative bad faith is
    a. The second claim representative assigned to the claim does a worse job than the first claim representative.
    b. The insured and the claimant both feel the insurer acted in bad faith.
    c. The insured acted in bad faith while alleging bad faith on the part of the insurer.
    d. The insurer's bad faith is more severe than the insured's bad faith.

39. Good-faith claim handling involves all of the following, EXCEPT:
    a. Timely investigation
    b. Confidential communication
    c. Evaluation
    d. Negotiation

40. Effective claim management is having
    a. On-the-job training.
    b. Hands-off supervision.
    c. Manageable caseloads.
    d. Low settlement authority.

41. Ethical behavior means
    a. Doing what is legal.
    b. Doing what everyone else does.
    c. Doing what your supervisor or manager tells you, given the situation.
    d. Doing what is the better course of action given two or more legal courses of action.

42. All of the following are reasons that ethics and professionalism are of utmost importance to insurers and claim representatives, EXCEPT:
    a. Insurers and claim representatives are bound by the insurance contract to act in good faith.
    b. Insurers can use ethics and professionalism to denigrate the competition.
    c. Ethics and professionalism can affect public trust and credibility of insurers and claim representatives.
    d. Consumer regulations create legal duties for insurers, and claim representatives have an ethical and professional responsibility to comply with them.

43. Which one of the following approaches to ethical decision-making is used when the claim representative considers how he or she would want to be treated in the same situation?
    a. Maximizing effect
    b. Normalizing effect
    c. Cost/benefit effect
    d. Empathizing effect

44. Claim representatives who lack competency can commit ethical improprieties by doing all of the following, EXCEPT:
    a. Issuing a reservation of rights letter on a claim involving a coverage issue
    b. Paying claims that are not covered by the policy in the given situation
    c. Overpaying claims
    d. Denying covered claims

45. *Ex parte* contacts are
    a. Contacts in which all parties have a chance to be heard.
    b. Contacts in which only one party is heard.
    c. Contacts that are kept confidential.
    d. Contacts that are infrequent.

46. Claims in which fraud is suspected can become an ethical dilemma for the claim representative because
    a. The claim representative conducts a balanced investigation.
    b. The claim representative does not investigate as thoroughly because SIU is also investigating.
    c. The claim representative follows good-faith claim-handling practices during the investigation.
    d. The claim representative consults with his or her supervisor or manager about a course of action.

47. Codes of ethics are used to
    a. Promote disagreement about what constitutes ethical behavior.
    b. Help evaluate a claim representative's job performance.
    c. Provide detailed specifics and set out minimum standards of ethical compliance.
    d. Seek uniformity in ethical behavior, as well as to promote high ethical and professional standards.

48. All the following activities provide a foundation on which to build quality claim practices, EXCEPT:
    a. Determining customer expectations
    b. Determining employee's expectations
    c. Improving service based on customer expectations
    d. Developing claim practices to meet customer expectations

49. Which one of the following qualities is important to claim representatives seeking to obtain the best negotiated outcome?
    a. Win-lose negotiation style
    b. Desire to avoid confrontation
    c. Firmness coupled with fairness
    d. Desire to save money on the reserve

50. Which two qualities contribute to rapport in a claim negotiation?
    a. Good listening skills and empathy
    b. Single-mindedness and persistence
    c. Thoroughness and attention to detail
    d. Lack of concern and aloofness

51. One of the four steps of the claim negotiation process is
    a. Deliver an ultimatum.
    b. Set a short deadline for acceptance.
    c. Insist on the other party making the first offer or demand.
    d. Develop and evaluate alternative outcomes.

52. Claim negotiation settings include all of the following, EXCEPT:
    a. In-person negotiation
    b. Internet negotiation
    c. Telephone negotiation
    d. Third-party negotiation

53. Which one of the following is a negotiating technique that any party can use?
    a. Principle of yes
    b. Boulwarism
    c. Trading dollars
    d. Setting deadlines

54. Which one of the following negotiating techniques can help smooth negotiations with unrepresented claimants?
    a. Boulwarism
    b. Establishing strengths and weaknesses
    c. Using needs analysis to effect a settlement
    d. Trading dollars

55. Using decreasing or limited offers should be avoided because
    a. It moves the negotiation along.
    b. It places unreasonable constraints on the other party.
    c. It saves the insurer money.
    d. It establishes strengths and weaknesses.

56. Common pitfalls in claim negotiations include all of the following, EXCEPT:
    a. Establishing rapport with the claimant
    b. Trading dollars
    c. Bidding against oneself
    d. Conceding as deadlines approach

57. All of the following are steps in managing the litigation of claims, EXCEPT:
    a. Receiving the summons and complaint
    b. Verifying that the insured has the assets to pay any possible judgment
    c. Referring the lawsuit to counsel
    d. Assisting counsel in creating a litigation plan for handling the lawsuit

58. In civil cases, courts generally have jurisdiction over a party only if that party
    a. Resides in that state.
    b. Does business in that state.
    c. Resides in or does business in that state.
    d. Resides in and does business in that state.

59. The federal court system includes
    a. Probate courts.
    b. Small claims courts.
    c. Courts of limited jurisdiction.
    d. Circuit courts of appeal.

60. Which one of the following is a possible objective for a litigation plan?
    a. Ask insureds to hire their own attorney and defend themselves.
    b. Allow the lawsuit to be decided by a default judgment.
    c. Obtain more information to decide whether to defend or settle the lawsuit.
    d. Ensure that the defense attorney can bill a minimum of $25,000 on the case.

61. Which method of discovery can be described as sworn statements made about the activities or knowledge of a party or witness concerning the subject matter of a lawsuit that can be used as trial evidence if that party or witness cannot attend trial?
    a. Interrogatories
    b. Depositions
    c. Requests for admissions
    d. Pleadings

62. When might defense counsel file a motion for summary judgment?
    a. Before the answer is filed
    b. Before the jury announces its verdict
    c. At the close of discovery but before trial starts
    d. After the jury verdict is announced

63. A litigation budget should include all of the following, EXCEPT:
    a. Acceptable settlement range for the claim
    b. Description of tasks
    c. Parties who will handle various tasks
    d. Time estimate

64. When auditing or reviewing a legal bill, the claim representative checks to see whether
    a. The case was closed within thirty days.
    b. The attorney is handling other cases for the insurer during the same time period.
    c. The insured liked the attorney.
    d. Itemized incremental billing is based on a reasonable time for the activity billed.

Part B

65. Rebecca's roof and siding were damaged by a hail storm. The roof was twenty-eight years old, and the siding was wood, which was in poor condition with peeling paint. Rebecca decided to replace her composition shingles with more expensive wood shake shingles and to replace her wood siding with long-wearing vinyl siding. Rebecca's insurer paid her hail claims based on the cost to replace the shingles and siding with the same materials, less the deductible, and Rebecca had to pay the difference in the costs out of her pocket. What principle of insurance does this demonstrate?

    a.   Indemnity

    b.   The law of large numbers

    c.   Adverse selection

    d.   Insurable interest

66. ABC Insurance Company's 2006 financial records show the following information:

Incurred losses	$65 million
Loss adjustment expenses	$20 million
Earned premium	$80 million
Underwriting and related expenses	$20 million

The loss ratio for ABC in 2006 would be

    a.   101.10%.

    b.   102.33%.

    c.   106.25%.

    d.   108.75%.

67. A twenty-six-year-old man suffers a severe head injury in an auto accident. He is expected to remain comatose for the remainder of his life. He was the sole provider for his wife and three children. The reserve method that would most likely be used for this third-party injury claim is

    a.   The average value method.

    b.   Actuarial analysis.

    c.   The roundtable technique.

    d.   The formula method.

68. Jim's 2003 Corvette was damaged in a collision. Prior to the accident, Jim had been trying to sell the car for $40,000. After it has been repaired, Jim is getting offers to buy the car for only $25,000. Jim calls his claim representative and wants to know why his car is not worth as much after the accident and whether his insurance policy will cover the loss in value. What part of the policy should the claim representative direct Jim to review?

    a. Exclusions

    b. Insuring agreement

    c. Endorsements

    d. Declarations

69. Tom is handling Ellen's water damage claim. Tom tells Ellen to throw out the wet carpet and personal items because he does not need to see them. When Ellen's inventory of damaged items is received, Tom believes it is inflated. Tom denies the claim on the basis that he was not able to inspect the damaged items. Tom's denial is invalid because

    a. Ellen has not agreed to it.

    b. Tom did not issue a reservation of rights letter before evaluating the claim and therefore cannot use any policy condition to deny the claim.

    c. Tom did not have the claim investigated by SIU.

    d. Tom told Ellen to discard the damaged items; therefore, he is estopped from denying the claim on the grounds that the goods were unavailable for inspection.

70. Dave is daydreaming of his coming vacation while driving to work. He fails to see that Karen has stopped her car in front of him because a school bus dropping off passengers blocks his view. Dave brakes sharply and manages to stop the car, but not before he lightly taps Karen's rear bumper. Karen and Dave inspect both cars and can find no damage on either car. There were no injuries. What element of liability based on damages is missing from this fact pattern?

    a. Duty owed

    b. Duty breached

    c. Proximate cause

    d. Damages

71. John, a claim representative, prepared to take a recorded statement from a slip-and-fall claimant. Which one of the following would be an effective open-ended question for John to ask the claimant?

    a. Was the floor wet?

    b. Did you see water on the floor?

    c. How did the fall occur?

    d. Who called the ambulance?

72. A telephone claim representative was assigned an auto accident claim. In the course of the investigation, he found discrepancies between the accident description in the insured's statements and the accident description in the insured's comments in the police accident report. These descriptions also differed from those offered by three witnesses whom the claim representative had interviewed. An inspection of the accident scene might help clear up some of the discrepancies, along with an inspection of the damaged vehicles. Which one of the following actions should the claim representative take to best provide an adequate liability investigation in this accident?

  a. He should discuss these concerns with his supervisor or manager.

  b. He should seek assistance from a field claim representative to diagram or photograph the accident location and ask that the car be inspected.

  c. He should refer the claim to the insurer's special investigation unit personnel for a thorough investigation of the circumstances of the accident.

  d. He should consult in-house counsel about the claim and the discrepancies.

73. Insurance fraud can be classified as either "hard" or "soft" fraud. Which one of the following is an example of soft fraud?

  a. The insured states that the television that was stolen was six months old rather than its actual age of six years.

  b. The insured reports a theft of jewelry from his home when no theft has occurred.

  c. The employee fakes a back injury to get paid time off from work.

  d. The insured intentionally burns his restaurant down.

74. State government and regulators attempt to fight insurance fraud with a variety of anti-fraud legislation. Claim representatives have a role in these fraud-fighting efforts because of which two anti-fraud legislations?

  a. Pre-inspection and mandatory reporting

  b. Pre-inspection and immunity statutes

  c. Immunity statutes and civil and criminal penalties

  d. Mandatory reporting and immunity statutes

The *Bad-Faith Case*. An insurer refused to settle with the claimant for an amount that was within the insured's liability policy limits of $100,000. At trial, the claimant was awarded $125,000. The insured sued his insurer for bad faith.

75. *Bad-Faith*. Under breach of contract theories, how much of the judgment would the insurer likely pay?

  a. $0

  b. $50,000

  c. $100,000

  d. $125,000

76. *Bad Faith.* Under bad-faith theories, how much would the insurer likely pay?

  a. $0
  b. $62,500
  c. $100,000
  d. $125,000

77. *Bad Faith.* What would be the likely basis for the insured's bad-faith claim?

  a. Violation of an unfair claims settlement practices act
  b. Failure to investigate
  c. Failure to settle within policy limits
  d. Unreasonable denial

78. Peter is a claim representative for ABC Insurance Company. Peter is handling a fire claim for a leather goods store. Much of the inventory is going to be deodorized and sold at a salvage sale. Peter has his eye on a leather coat for his wife's birthday that he otherwise could not afford. What should Peter do?

  a. Ask the insured to sell it to him at a reduced cost and then have it professionally cleaned
  b. Peter should not purchase the coat from the insured or the salvor because it would be a conflict of interest
  c. Ask the salvor to tell him what the highest bid is for the coat and he will top it by $100
  d. Ask his brother to go to the salvage sale and buy it for him

79. Jay has four claims assigned to attorney Ryan. Ryan travels for two days and visits all four insureds, taking statements, answering interrogatories, and preparing them for depositions. When reviewing the legal bills, Jay notices that each of the cases has been billed the full two days of travel time. This is an example of what type of ethical dilemma?

  a. Allocation
  b. Privacy
  c. *Ex parte* contact
  d. Overlapping insureds

80. Mary reports the theft of her five-year-old laptop to her homeowner's insurer. The claim representative assigned to the claim advises Mary that the insurer can replace the laptop with a newer, more powerful model by using a replacement service. What negotiation style is exemplified by this fact pattern?

  a. Win-lose
  b. Win-win
  c. Lose-win
  d. Lose-lose

81. Jeremy is handling a claim for serious bodily injury. He is getting ready to begin settlement negotiations. As part of his preparation, Jeremy determines the minimum amount he is willing to offer and the maximum amount he is willing to offer. Jeremy is in which step of the claim negotiation process?

    a.   Make concessions

    b.   Identify each party's interests

    c.   Prepare

    d.   Develop alternative outcomes

82. Donald is negotiating a product liability claim with Mr. Brown. Mr. Brown found a foreign object in his favorite breakfast cereal and he now gets nauseated every time he looks at that brand of cereal. Donald has offered Mr. Brown a monetary settlement but Mr. Brown is insisting on a letter of apology signed by the cereal company's president. Mr. Brown is operating at what level of Maslow's hierarchy of needs?

    a.   Belongingness

    b.   Physiological

    c.   Safety and security

    d.   Esteem

83. Jill receives a summons and complaint on a claim she is handling. She notices that the summons and complaint was filed in the U.S. District Court in a neighboring state. What should Jill do with this information?

    a.   She should ignore this information.

    b.   She should ask opposing counsel for an extension of time to answer the complaint.

    c.   She should check to see that jurisdiction and venue are proper.

    d.   She should discard the summons and complaint because it was filed improperly.

84. Claim representative Dawn has received a notice of deposition for a claim that alleges that she acted in bad faith. This deposition means that

    a.   Dawn must submit to a physical and mental examination.

    b.   Dawn must submit to an oral examination of her activities or knowledge of the subject matter of the lawsuit.

    c.   Dawn must submit specific written answers to a set of questions sent to her by the other party.

    d.   Dawn must appear in court on a specified date.

85. Claim representative Wendy and attorney Linda negotiate a fee arrangement in which there is a specific fee for each phase of litigation. This type of fee arrangement is called

    a.   Flat fee.

    b.   Phased fee.

    c.   Negotiated fee.

    d.   Retainer.

Answers to AIC 33 Sample Exam

1. b	30. d	59. d
2. d	31. c	60. c
3. d	32. d	61. b
4. d	33. b	62. c
5. c	34. c	63. a
6. a	35. a	64. d
7. a	36. b	65. a
8. b	37. a	66. c
9. a	38. c	67. c
10. b	39. b	68. b
11. d	40. c	69. d
12. b	41. d	70. d
13. c	42. b	71. c
14. a	43. d	72. b
15. b	44. a	73. a
16. c	45. b	74. d
17. d	46. b	75. c
18. b	47. d	76. d
19. d	48. b	77. c
20. b	49. c	78. b
21. c	50. a	79. a
22. a	51. d	80. b
23. d	52. d	81. d
24. c	53. a	82. d
25. a	54. c	83. c
26. c	55. b	84. b
27. b	56. a	85. b
28. a	57. b	
29. c	58. c	